A Portrait of Achievement
North East England

by D. H. Williams MCIM

The KINGDOM of
NORTHUMBRIA

G R O U P

First published 2005 by AC Group, Stannington, Northumberland, NE61 6DS

ISBN-13: 978-0-9551720-0-7

ISBN-10: 0-9551720-0-4

Designed and produced by AC Group, this book has been typeset in 9/13.5 pt ITC Cheltenham. Special orders and quantities of this book are available for corporations, professional and commercial organisations. For details, telephone AC Group +44 (0)1670 789 489, fax +44 (0)1670 789 464, or e-mail info@ac-group.co.uk.

This publication has been printed and bound in Great Britain by NB Group, one of the North East's top privately owned printing companies. With a CTP litho print facility, the capability is from 1 to 10 colour, and up to B1 size and with bindery.

I wish to dedicate this book to my wife Linda, Mark, Susana, our families and dear friends.

Acknowledgements

I would particularly like to thank my wife Linda for being so supportive and understanding with me for being the cause of incessant discussions about this book, and working totally unreasonable hours. Both Linda and Anne's proof reading has been invaluable. For their individual skills, contribution, advice and assistance in the production of this book, I would like to thank (in alphabetical order), Chris, Darrell, both Daves, Graham, Kathleen, Ken, Linda, Mem, Paula and Tracey. I would specially like to thank Paula who has assisted me for over two decades, and during the last seven years with the word processing of this book.

The publisher has made every effort to contact individual copyright holders. In addition to the author's own landscape and commercial photography, and private collection of prints and postcards, the publisher is greatly indebted to the following for their permission and assistance in the reproduction of photographs and prints: Associated Sports Photography, Barratt Developments, Beamish Museum Archives, Blendex, Calder Industrial Materials, Canford Audio, Fergusons Transport, High Gosforth Park, Image Visual Communications, Lilley and Gillie, The Literary and Philosophical Society of Newcastle upon Tyne, K. Medd, Newcastle International Airport, Newcastle Chronicle and Journal, Newcastle upon Tyne City Library and Arts, One NorthEast, Port of Tyne Authority, Sir T. Cowie, Sir P. Vardy, Siemens Power Generation, Swan Hunter, Trinity House, Vickers Defence Systems, and Ward Hadaway.

Contents

A Message from Mark Knopfler O.B.E.   vii

Foreword by the Duke of Northumberland   ix

Introduction   x

CHAPTERS   **PAGE**

One   The banks of the Tyne   1
           merged by Pons Aelius

Two   Northumbria – The roots of new   23
           commercial routes

Three   North East coal fuels the   51
           industrial revolution

Four   A century of great industrial   81
           trade expansion

Five   Pioneering Electricity –   107
           new lamps for old

Six   Landmarks of change   135
           and fame in Northumbria

Seven   Ships – Empire trade   163
           origins from three rivers

Eight   A time for transformation –   187
           the twentieth century

Nine   A capital of sport, entertainment   213
           and arts

Ten   A portfolio of our greatest assets   237

A MESSAGE FROM MARK KNOPFLER O.B.E.

Most people involved with the North East, in building its future as a business and artistic community, are aware of its beginnings. You won't know where you're going if you don't know where you've been, and this profile of Northumbria past and present by Don Williams is an excellent guide, not just to individuals in the commercial sector but also those in education, local government, sport, leisure and the arts.

If you love Northumbria as I do, or if you are a potential participant in the future of the region, wherever you are, you will find this profile of much value.

I am delighted that the commercial achievements of our region so steeped in history have been brought together and recorded in the pages of this book: A Portrait of Achievement – The Kingdom of Northumbria. Over the years, Northumbria has been the heart of many traditional industries, with coal mining, ship building, engineering, agriculture and fishing. However, change is inevitable. There have always been challenges facing entrepreneurs and commercial enterprises, and now through technology, we have one certain advantage over our forefathers, better communications worldwide. It was George Stephenson who found that by establishing a railway line in 1825, this was the foundation of a rail network which was the beginning of great inland trade expansion.

Today, both locally and worldwide, there are new opportunities to be developed. Together with my family, we are proud of Northumbria's heritage and actively encourage enterprise and a spirit of success. We also have many natural assets in Northumbria, a superb coastline, beautiful countryside, and remains from early Christian, Roman and Norman times. The great architects of the industrial revolution have left their landmarks too, with lovely country estates and gardens, many of which are open for the enjoyment of the public.

With such picturesque countryside and comparatively quiet roads it is almost natural that major motor car manufacturers choose Northumberland as an ideal place to launch their new models. It has become an area for film locations including Hadrian's Wall, Belsay Hall, as well as Bamburgh, Aydon and Warkworth Castles. Alnwick Castle has also seen its share of film action with The Spaceman and King Arthur, Ivanhoe, Robin Hood – Prince of Thieves and Elizabeth I and Harry Potter. At the castle we are also pleased to encourage visitors to see the designs, furnishings and collections which significantly transformed the castle from the time of the first Duke of Northumberland.

Whatever the aspect, the outlook for Northumbria is governed by its people. Within the chapters of this book are some of those who had inspiration, some who achieved through dedication but all having a common determination to provide a better product or service than anyone else. Although times may change, I believe the ingredients for success remain constant. For the benefit of our future, I would like to wish all those who will achieve and make history, all good fortune today.

Northumberland

Duke of Northumberland DL, ARICS
Alnwick Castle Northumberland

Introduction

For thirty five years, I have lived and earned my living in Northumbria. It has been a love-hate relationship and one from which I have never wished to move, but many times over the years wished I could influence change. A fitting tribute for this book is to all those who by strength of character have shaped today's truly magnificent living and working environment. This justifiably deserves every admiration and what better tribute could I offer than to publish this account of the Kingdom of Northumbria – A Portrait of Achievement.

By describing in unity the people who live and work together in Northumbria, there are three distinctive identity flavours based on those who live and work close to one of the rivers, the Tyne, Wear or Tees. Each community proud of its place in the Kingdom of Northumbria, has given a complementary but significantly stylised stamp on their part of regional development. As a matter of respect to the folk, their trades and activities, the theme of this book is based on roots, growth and branches of achievement.

Industrial and commercial growth stemmed from Newcastle and materially developed regionally after the first quarter of the nineteenth century. As an aid to perspective in comparative terms, the population of Newcastle was approximately 19,000 in 1730 and this was equivalent to twice the combined population of Sunderland, Stockton and Darlington. Middlesbrough was a hamlet with less than a hundred inhabitants.

To develop an overall regional picture, it should be taken into consideration that Northumbria was one of two early northern Kingdoms, the Celtic Kingdom of Strathclyde (from the Clyde to the Mersey) and the Kingdom of Northumbria (from the Forth to the Humber). The nucleus of the lordship of Northumbria focused on the land between the Tyne and the Tees, and in Saxon times this was granted in a piecemeal fashion by north country kings to the guardians and magnates of the relics of St. Cuthbert (a Celtic Monk, AD 600, renowned for his work in the conversion of Saxon worshippers of Odin and Thor to Christianity).

Throughout the ages, a common history and a common way of life have given a strength of unity to the people of Northumbria. Together, influences of the sea, rivers, hills, border country and the natural resource of coal, have shaped the character of the region's folk. A first impression is that this character is warm hearted and offers fine hospitality. This is without question, but the character is also shrewd, reserved, forthright, tough in fibre, dogged in purpose, independent to the point of obstinacy and with outstanding qualities of self reliance and adaptability. These are all told traits which have been fostered through the centuries of relative isolation and by the transformation of a rough and dangerous homeland into a reservoir of skills.

Over recent years, North East has shrugged off its cloth cap and whippet image. As new enterprise has been attracted to the area, so too have an increasing number of immigrants, many who show total surprise to find such a wealth of resource. They are quick to make use of the relative ease in work related travel, uncongested country roads, beautiful coastline, inland waters, forests and hills, thriving arts, night life, shopping and sports activities. All of this is focused in an area steeped in history, having a heritage for which everyone living in Northumbria may be truly proud.

A side of life in Northumbria which I have found most difficult to conjure with is the difficulty of the changing economic times. Where traditionally, workforces would be secure, families suddenly have been thrown into an abyss of unemployment and situations where natural in built pride has had to take a severe dent. Within the final quarter of the last century, those industries which were the backbone of our regional stability, coal mining, iron and steel and shipbuilding, seemed to be cut away one by one with the news seemingly forever being doom and gloom. Once again, I take my own cloth cap off to all those people who have literally picked themselves up and adapted to change.

Throughout Northumbria ways of earning a living have not been easy for centuries. The adoption of change from tough, manual skills in disappearing traditional industries to new high tech and high spec work places has required the learning and application of different skills, and a willing aptitude to cope with immigrant cultures. The result proves that those living and working in Northumbria can shrug off the past, work well and apply themselves once again with pride, welcome the new and also extend warm-hearted traditional hospitality. This book is dedicated to the past and present, a reminder to those who knew, and an insight to those who are new; it serves to highlight the landmarks in the making of a great Kingdom of Northumbria.

D H Williams

Member Chartered Institute of Marketing

Chapter One

The banks of the Tyne – MERGED BY PONS AELIUS

The Kingdom of Northumbria with its capital Newcastle has been influenced by four key features, its proximity to the Scottish border, position as a main river crossing, accessibility to the sea and being central in the development of the coalfields. History began to make its regional mark more than eighteen hundred years ago when Britain was being brought under the rule of the Roman Empire. In 120 AD a rampart was constructed between Bowness in Cumberland through to Newcastle at Wallsend, making this the northern limit of the Roman province of Britain. As part of a strategy to assist the speed and deployment of Roman legions and to reinforce their dominance of the frontier in the face of any barbarous resistance, the Romans built a bridge across the river Tyne. Constructed with a wooden superstructure, supported by stone piers, the bridge (also maintained by a fort on the north side), was named Pons Aelius as a tribute to Emperor Publius Aelius Hadrianus. The remains of a shrine and commemorative slab which were part of the bridge may be seen today at the Black Gate Museum.

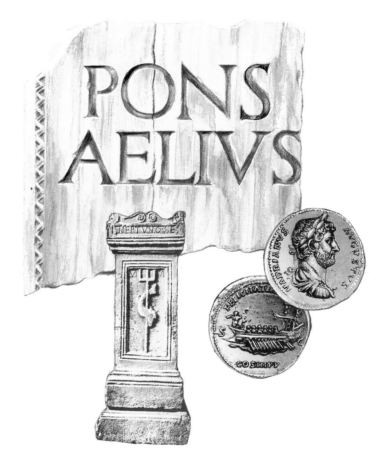

1068 – Monkcastle on Tyne destroyed by William the Conqueror

When the defence of the capital called the Roman forces home from Britain, for more than a century (AD 441–600) Newcastle continued as a principal fortress and was the centre of relentless warfare. Once Christianity was established in the north during the seventh century several monasteries were established. Newcastle was the first of these and assumed the name Monkcastle or Monkchester with its fortified position generally affording protection (except when repeatedly ravaged by the Danes) to the nuns and monks. After the union of the kingdom under Egbert, the town continued much the same until it was destroyed by William the Conqueror in 1068. Following grievances against his Norman knights, Walcher, the ruling Earl of Northumberland was murdered by an angry mob at Gateshead in May 1080. In reprisal measures, William the Conqueror ordered the building of a new castle on the site of the former Roman fortress. After Robert Curthose, his eldest son completed the construction, the church of St Nicholas, patron of merchants, was built in 1091 and trade was encouraged at the castle's gates.

Facing page:
Celtic missionaries first brought Christianity to Northumbria. St Aidan established a priory on Lindisfarne (Holy Island), in the year 635

1

When built in 1080, Novum Castellum, as the new castle was named, was the first mound-and-bailey constructed castle, with a wooden tower crowning an artificial earthen mound surrounded by a moat. There are no original remains and through the work of William Rufus (between 1172 and 1177) was replaced by a rectangular stone keep, one of the finest built in the country during King Henry II's reign. After this the Roman walls of the town were repaired and extended but it was not until 1274 in King Henry III's reign that the outer gateway known as the Black Gate was constructed. It was named Black after a seventeenth century London merchant

Above: *Newcastle with castle, walls and gates during Henry II's reign*

Right: *Black Gate, Newcastle*

Patrick Black who bought the castle after it was seized by Parliament in 1644 and then built a short street or gate of houses on the approach to the castle's entrance. The castle was later bought for £600 by Newcastle Corporation in 1809. So, today's City of Newcastle upon Tyne was borne of its name more than 900 years ago, although at that time with a peasant population of merely a few hundred souls, it was more like a village than a town. However, with the needs of an army garrison and traffic across the Tyne, here were the humble beginnings of commerce and industry.

Local government in Newcastle

From Anglo-Saxon times local government was based on units being known as the shire, the parish and an intermediate area, the ward. The Bishop of Durham as Count Palatine controlled the judicial process in the shire courts and during Norman times a system of baronial and manorial courts was instigated. The title of burgess and their rights through the laws of Newcastle were adopted by David I for his Scottish royal boroughs after his son Prince Henry took Newcastle from King Stephen in 1140. Burgesses of Newcastle were subject only to the King's reeve, entitling them to hold land, merchant goods, and have law-suits in Newcastle settled quickly. They were given a monopoly in the trade of wool, hides and cloth whilst they also had sole rights to purchase goods from ships whilst riding at anchor at the mouth of the Tyne. The King required an annual rent (known as a fee-farm) from the burgesses which in 1201 amounted to the sum of sixty pounds. In 1216 Newcastle was privileged to have a merchant guild which could elect its own mayor, known then as chief bailiff. Through time there were numerous changes in the collection of rents and tax whilst during this

North Shore, Newcastle

*The Flesh Market,
Newcastle, later known
as the Cloth Market*

houses built in the old town. During this period, the main local activity centred around market trade. In a part of the town called Pandon, at a crossing of the Pandon Burn was Stock Bridge where fishermen would trade. Other markets were held at Sandhill, in the Oat Market, the Cloth Market (originally called the Flesh Market for the sale of meat), and the Bigg Market where the trade was in barley. It was a scene where animals wandered freely in the streets except when the bellmen ordered their removal in times of pestilence. Newcastle's wealth derived from the export of grindstones, wool, coal and by the end of the thirteenth century was exporting more hides than any other part of the country. The expansion of home based cloth and leather industries caused a decline in wool exports by the end of the century. The countryside provided rough pasture for sheep and cattle whilst food was an important export. Fishing was to become a particularly important industry on the Tyne. In 1225, Prior Germanus had a portion of the marsh near the Pow Burn at North Shields. This was reclaimed and he built sheels (fishermen's huts), allowing the men the privilege of having boats of their own in return for supplying fish free of charge to the monastery. This trade, a source of revenue to the Church and of prosperity to the neighbourhood, was stopped for a time by Newcastle merchants. However, by 1433, it flourished again and there was not merely a local but also an export trade in smoked herring, cod, ling, salmon and Shields produced salt.

early period the duties of the chief bailiff can only be inferred. However, it is known that they did attend the borough court which heard pleas and was also used for the registration of title deeds. By 1223, there was a Common Seal of the Corporation of Newcastle and by 1251, a royal approval was given to the chief bailiff to be styled mayor. After 23 May 1400, Henry IV carved out a new county for Newcastle from Northumberland. After this time a sheriff would be elected annually by a committee of twenty four burgesses responsible for the selection of the mayor. The sheriff came to preside as judge over hearings in the Guildhall whilst the mayor's court dealt with cases where both parties involved freemen in Newcastle.

1294 – The first ship recorded built on the Tyne

The earliest record of a ship built on the Tyne was a galley, one of twenty ordered from different ports around the country in 1294, for Edward I. The oaks used in this probably came from the Town Moor which at that time was woodland, a source of fine oaks which made their way into ships and

1342 – Crafts guilds organised

After London, Bristol and York, Newcastle was the fourth most wealthy town in England by 1334. However, unless an

individual was religious (including being part of a guild), noble or of the military, they were considered seditious and, therefore, suitable candidates for the gallows. By 1342 there were specialised lay workers organised into craft guilds for skinners, tanners and saddlers, fullers, dyers, tailors, bakers, brewers, butchers, cordwainers and smiths. Fewer than the craftsmen but carrying more social weight were the dealers and merchants (drapers or wool merchants, boothmen or corn merchants and mercers or general dealers), who were eventually incorporated in 1547 as the Company of Merchant Adventurers. By 1515 the number of trades guilds had increased with the addition of twenty-one bye-trades. Membership of these lesser guilds amongst others included colliers, keelmen, porters and shipwrights but only gave them freedom to work in that trade. For these individuals, a general trading license was not available, nor the opportunity for them to participate in government. A year later the Royal Court of Star Chamber decreed that general trading was limited to members of the guilds of mercers, drapers, corn merchants and spicers with admittance of these lesser freemen to the guilds by an agreed payment.

Rich merchants monopolise the Tyne

Newcastle's key traders, particularly those involved in exporting and importing, had through the organisation of trades guilds, gradually gained control of all trading as well as politics. Struggles over

The Mayor's barge and keelboats on the Tyne

5

power also developed between the richer and poorer of these burgesses. A separate and more powerful group organised themselves within the body of Merchant Adventurers. There had also been perpetual struggles between the burgesses and the ecclesiastical coal mine owners, the Prior of Tynemouth and the Bishop of Durham. Newcastle's burgesses wished to secure control of coal exporting on the Tyne. Following the Reformation this issue was finally settled in favour of the burgesses. However, it was during the course of this conflict that the burgesses, trying to force the Prior and the Bishop to sell their coal only from Newcastle, began to claim the right of hosting or acting as host to merchant strangers. This meant that a burgess should be a party to every transaction with a visiting merchant. Anything traded on the Tyne from corn to coal had to be bought or sold through a burgess. It was for this reason that by Tudor times the coal merchants of Newcastle became known as hostmen. In 1600 the Company of Hostmen was incorporated through a charter granted by Elizabeth I. This assigned to them an exclusive right to trade in coal on the Tyne and sanctioned election arrangements giving them a virtual monopoly of the municipal offices. In return for their assent, there was to be a levy by the Crown of a shilling tax on every chaldron of coal shipped from the Tyne.

The keelman – a porter on water

The keelman and keel was peculiar to the Tyne and Wear rivers in the early days of the coal trade. The name keel originates from an Anglo-Saxon word *ceol*, meaning a boat. Keels differed little from those used by the early Scandinavian raiders. The keels were used to carry goods from the shore to ships lying in the middle of the river. They were mainly used for ferrying coal although they were also used for all kinds of goods for shipment.

1492 – The Society of Trinity House incorporated

With a progressive increase in shipping, improvements to the Tyne and coastal waters were necessary to provide safer passage and assistance to mariners. For this purpose and from its 13th century origins, the Brethren of Trinity House were granted permission to collect dues from ships in Newcastle by Henry VII. In 1492, the title of the fraternity was changed to the Society of Masters and Mariners, an incorporated body with additional power from Henry VII to collect royal shipping dues. At this time, the Brethren found a permanent location at Broad Chare, Quayside and in 1505 saw a resolution for the building of a chapel, hall and lodgings for the poor Brethren. Surrounding a paved courtyard the premises remain in use to the present day. In 1537, a Royal Charter granted by Henry

Trinity House, Quayside, Newcastle, 1770

VIII directed the construction of light houses at the mouth of the Tyne for which foreign ships paid four pence and English two pence on entering the river. Elizabeth I and James I each granted Royal Charters founding a new name of Master, Pilots and Seamen of the Trinity House of Newcastle upon Tyne. Their work was to maintain sole pilotage of all sea ways from Holy Island to Whitby and the Tyne's lighting. This jurisdiction lasted over 300 years when responsibility was transferred to the Tyne Improvement Commission, a body of eighteen commissioners representing the corporations, the ship owners, coal owners, traders and payers of river dues.

1640 – The Scots occupation of Newcastle

During the last years of Elizabeth's reign, following Henry VIII's legacy that broke traditional ties with Rome, power struggles developed within the Church of England between Anglicans and Puritans. In 1639, an attempt by Charles I and Archbishop Laud to force the Presbyterian Church of Scotland into an Anglican strait-jacket finally provoked northern people into rebellion. During the great civil war which ensued Newcastle and Durham were both seized by the Scots. In 1640 at the Battle of Newburn, the Scots crossed the Tyne west of Newcastle and defeated Charles' army. Although the English only had light losses, they fled leaving Newcastle's garrison deserted. Under the command of General Lesley, Newcastle was occupied for a year until August 1641 when Charles negotiated a truce and the Scots agreed to disband on receipt of £60,000.

1643 – Parliament blockades the Tyne

By 1642 the civilians brought industry and trade almost to a complete standstill and on 14 January 1643 Parliament passed an ordinance forbidding ships to sail to Newcastle for coal, salt or corn. This blockade was designed to prevent the King profiting from any exports to Holland, the source of his armaments. Exports of coal had been rising before the civil war to approximately 45,000 tons with some 3,000 ships entering the Tyne in a normal year. During the Parliamentary blockade in 1644 with a mere 200 ships only 3,000 tons of coal could be shipped. After the battle of Marston Moor (near York) on 2 July 1644, when the Parliamentarians and Scots defeated the Royalists (killing 3,000 soldiers), the Scots besieged York to eventually take it on 16 July, and then directed their forces north. On 13 August 1644 General Lesley (who had now been created Earl of Leven, as Scottish ally of the Parliamentary party), captured and occupied Stockton Castle. Newcastle was the next target. A siege lasted ten weeks before Newcastle's walls were finally penetrated by gun powder on 20 October. The castle held out for a further two days until its occupant John Marley surrendered. Tynemouth Castle also surrendered and was taken on 27 October. During the Scottish occupation, Newcastle's coal trade came to a standstill. Possession remained with the Scots until the end of the war. Charles I surrendered at Newark in 1646 and was escorted to Newcastle for imprisonment. In 1647 after receiving £200,000 from Cromwell, Charles was released and the Scots left Newcastle. However, in spite of war losses and damage, within a decade, Newcastle was on course for full recovery and evidence of this was the new Guildhall and Exchange built in Sandhill between 1655 and 1658. By

Holy Jesus Hospital, Manors, Newcastle

1665, Newcastle was the fourth most populated provincial town outside London with around 2,500 householders.

Hospitals for the under privileged

There were extremes of wealth and poverty. In acknowledgement of the plight of the poor, Newcastle's Corporation constructed the Hospital of the Holy Jesus at Manors. It was founded and endowed by the Corporation in 1681 for the support of the poor and impotent freemen or their widows and unmarried children. The inmates were allowed £4 a year which over time was increased to £6 and then to £13. Near Newcastle's Wall Knoll Tower, overlooking the suburb of Sandgate stands the Keelman's Hospital, built in 1701 by the keelmen through their own subscriptions. The Bishop of Ely is said to have remarked that he had heard of and seen many hospitals, the works of rich men but this was the first he ever saw or heard of which had been built by the poor. Originally, the hospital had sixty rooms besides offices and a club room. In the early part of its use there

The Keelmen's Hospital, City Road, Newcastle

was great friction between the keelmen and hostmen over the administration of the hospital when there was concern that hostmen wished to acquire control of the foundation.

1740 – Mob riots about food shortages

With grievances about control and corruption, action against the Corporation began in 1685 when through a mandate James II ordered the replacement of the existing common council. The objective was to bring the town administration under royal control. This would be achieved by ensuring Catholics were elected and by a subsequent charter, restricting future Corporation appointments and members of parliament to the existing mayor and officers. During Michaelmus 1688, having refused the royal nominations for mayor and sheriff, the guild electors sought legal opinion which effectively nullified James II's charters. This made way for new elections with Protestant officers and the borough's administration was soon once again in the hands of prominent merchant families. At last in 1730, freemen who were not members of the Merchant Adventurers' Company re-established their twelfth century rights against restrictive trading when the merchants unsuccessfully prosecuted a freeman baker for buying corn. However, the mayor and officers of the Corporation retained considerable power, with the mayor controlling the local militia. Use of the militia was particularly prevalent at this time due to unrest caused by press-gang activities, food shortages and rising prices. The worst of the riots occurred in 1740 after bread grain prices had become so exorbitant that a mob of pitmen, sailors and keelmen were ready to use force unless lower prices came into effect.

Having temporarily appeased the mob, the mayor Cuthbert Fenwick disbanded the militia. Two weeks later an even hungrier mob determined to use force to bring prices down. On 25 June 1740 intent on action from the mayor and merchants they marched to the Guildhall. Before the militia could be re-assembled, the marchers broke into the Guildhall, ransacked the mayor's parlour and the town's treasury (valued at £1,200) and in the process destroyed the town's archives. It took three companies of regular soldiers brought from Alnwick to suppress the rioting mob but not before they rampaged through the streets targeting food shops.

1715 – Jacobites and Geordies

During the early 1700s, there was to be further unrest, history being dominated by the Jacobite rebellions. Jacobite was a nickname given to those people with a loyalty to exiled James II. The trouble started in 1714 when Queen Anne was dying, with an unsuccessful plot to exclude George of Hanover, a German protestant from the throne in favour of James II's son and heir James Edward Stuart, (the Old Pretender). Although the country's majority was against the return of a Catholic monarchy, in 1715 a leading Jacobite rebel, Tom Forster of Bamburgh marched an army into England. Every Northumberland town supported him except Newcastle. As Newcastle folk supported King George they become known as Geordies. The Jacobites were defeated at Preston in November 1715. There was a subsequent 1745 uprising in support of the Young Pretender, Charles Edward Stuart. However, an end came with his defeat and subsequent escape to France after a battle at Culloden Moor in April 1746. This resulted in Newcastle and the town's

Geordies rejoicing with fireworks, illuminations and vast amounts of drink.

Merchants provide payments for troops

Financial institutions, the Banks of the Tyne became a reality when capital was required for new founded industrial ventures. Trades people needed wages in cash at a time when coins of the realm were scarce. Locally money had been channelled to pay George II's troops stationed in Newcastle throughout the 1745 rebellion. It was Ralph Carr who used his financial abilities to establish the first banking house. He began as a general

The Royal Mail Coach travelling through The Side, Newcastle

merchant in 1737 with dealings in coal, iron, wood fuel, corn, glass, alum, alcoholic beverages, as well as tea, butter, tobacco and snuff. He also acted as a ships' insurance broker. Government contracts for overseas traders were valuable and with assured payments this gave merchants access to large sums which could be used profitably for short term finance. Ralph Carr used this to his advantage and provided payments needed to keep local government troops.

Ralph Carr's bank was established in 1755 on Pilgrim Street. It was the first outside London to open its doors for the receipt of deposit and current accounts, discounting of bills of exchange and transfer of money by draft on London agents. He brought several partners into the business and the bank issued its own bank notes which by 1757 became acceptable tender to the Collector of Excise. Within a few years other banks opened and indeed there was an institution called the Tyne Bank founded in 1777. One of the original partners was Joseph Lamb who began

Thomas Bewick's workshop, Amen Corner, Newcastle

business as a linen draper and later had interests in soap making at the Close. By the time of his death in 1800, he had extensive business interests including a partnership in the Northumberland Glass Works at Lemington, a calico printing works in Carlisle, a copperas works at Willington, and large share holdings in collieries at Shiremoor, Heddon and Percy Main.

As more and more merchant banks were established, so was the demand for a trade in engraving printing blocks to produce bank notes. This craft of engraving was virtually monopolised in Newcastle by a gentleman named Jameson who conducted his business from premises situated at Amen Corner, adjacent to St Nicholas Cathedral. Sadly for Jameson, in 1760 he was charged with using his own engraved printing blocks to produce bank notes for his own gain. Although he could have been found guilty of a capital offence and hanged, he managed to create doubt in the court by producing a witness who it was subsequently discovered gave false evidence. Luckily for him, Jameson was found not guilty and by law could not be brought back to court for a retrial. However, with his reputation in tatters, his business was finished and so Jameson's workshop and living quarters were then taken by two brothers William and Ralph Beilby. Their family had a background in engraving and the business could be re-established under the Beilby name. It was at this same workshop seven years later on 1 October 1767 that a certain young Thomas Bewick was apprenticed to Ralph Beilby, and this was to bring Bewick's engraving expertise to world fame.

New bank for Bessie Surtees' family

By the late eighteenth century there were five banks operating in Newcastle, Ralph Carr's original bank being known as the Old Bank until his retirement in 1787 when it became Ridley and Company. Ralph Carr was considered to be a wealthy man of his time being worth over £100,000 when he died in 1807. In 1768 the Exchange Bank was founded by Aubone Surtees (father of Bessie Surtees) and Rowland Burdon. Aubone Surtees was admitted as a member of the Merchant's Company in 1737, and of the Hostmen's Company in 1757. He had a wine business in the Close and a timber business at Pandon Gate. With considerable financial skills, the family's network of industrial interests, largely orchestrated through the bank, was extensive. Two of Aubone's sons, Aubone and John were involved with lead mining concerns at Arkendale and Derwent and with the formation in 1797 of the Tyne Iron

Works at Lemington. As the region's trade developed other new banks opened their doors, one of these was established by Jonathon Backhouse in 1774. The Backhouse Bank was situated in Darlington's High Row.

The elopement of Bessie Surtees with John Scott

John Scott, a well educated son of a wealthy Newcastle merchant had met Elizabeth (Bessie) Surtees during a visit to church. Having fallen desperately in love, her father was determined to keep her from seeing John. They eloped together on 18 November 1772 when she descended by ladder from a window in the Surtees family home at Sandhill near Newcastle's quayside. Together they travelled to Scotland to be married. Later, her father relented his feelings and the families were united. John Scott began a distinguished career in the legal profession before rising through the ranks of the political arena to be Lord Chancellor, a post he held for 25

Left: *Bessie Surtees elopes with John Scott from the Surtees family home, Sandhill, Newcastle*

Below: *Thomas Bewick, the world famous woodcut and engraving artist*

*Legal tender, a
Northumberland Bank
Note printed in Newcastle*

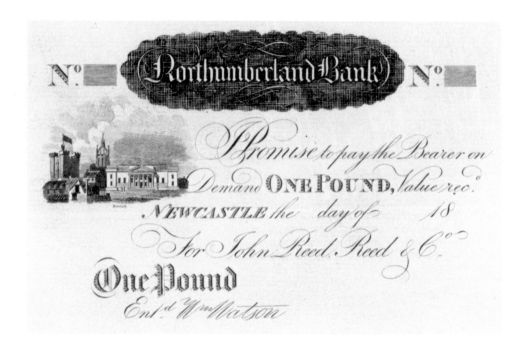

years. He was made Viscount Escombe and Earl of Eldon in 1821. He made his last speech in the House of Lords in 1834. John Scott, Lord Eldon died (1838) aged 86 years.

Thomas Bewick defies bank note forgery

The signals indicating the difficulties banks could encounter were demonstrated after the Commercial Bank with seven years of trading failed in 1793. Its demise was caused by a run on gold during a monetary panic. There were a number of these caused by the mounting anxiety of a potential invasion by the French. In particular, between 1803 and 1805 when Napolean was gathering a great naval flotilla, the general alarm provoked a financial panic. Throughout the country there was a run on the banks which caused the government to abandon the gold standard. The Exchange Bank collapsed in 1803 causing the Surtees family financial difficulties. Later in 1826 Aubone and his elder brother William took a lease on the

Benwell Colliery, and traded as William Surtees & Co., Coal Owners. Banks began to experience other problems as forgers were making their own impressions on the banking scene. In an effort to combat this, the talents of a distinguished wood engraver Thomas Bewick was commissioned to produce a printing block for bank notes which would defy forgery. Bewick was able to add difficult to match engraving detail into the wooden printing blocks.

The formation of building societies

From these early days, merchants and industrialists realised the growth of commerce and the development of wealth in the region was through the institution of banking. This single fact has been the main influence towards economic development with all of those involved in the financial sector through to the present day. By 1915 there were over thirty branches of eight main banks in Newcastle. There were also other enterprising financial organisations which quickly grew. Soon after the first Co-op Society was founded by Joseph Cowan at Blaydon in 1858, others adopted a similar co-operative scheme to finance and build homes for themselves. The arrangement was that they agreed to pool their finances being enough to build the first house and meantime accumulate sufficient savings for the construction of the next. Eventually, as many other individuals were keen to join the scheme, the concept was developed commercially and building societies were born. One of the first to be established in this way was the Universal Building Society. Some initial investors did not desire a home immediately but favoured a return on their money in the form of interest.

The first plastic money in Newcastle

Banks and building societies were not the only means to obtain finance. As long as there have been people without means, there have been small scale money lenders. Following the great wars and particularly in times when commodities were scarce, and when there was rationing, the black market, pawn brokers and money lenders flourished. There were traders or tallymen who would sell goods on tick or lend money in return for regular high interest repayments, or the never never, as those who used their services were more acquainted. The first plastic money was introduced in Newcastle a quarter of a century before credit cards were introduced into this country (1966). It followed the shortages and rationing during the Second World War in Newcastle at Byker. There, Shields Road bustled with small shops and two enterprising departmental stores, Beavans and J T Parish. At a time when many of the local

people didn't have enough money in the household to buy goods, Parish produced their own plastic coins. The concept was that shoppers would take credit in the form of these tokens to buy items from the store. This worked well but use became more widespread and Parish's plastic paid for virtually anything in the Byker community. It was quite common for £10 worth of tokens to be exchanged for £8 cash. Ironically, it

F Beavan Ltd., was a traditional department store promoted as "The store that aids economists", and today, is a catalogue shop

was the advent of the plastic credit card which opened the doors to competition for J T Parish and they eventually had to close their family run department store at the end of the 1970s. By the beginning of the new millennium almost 120 million bank and building society plastic cards were in use in the UK. Of these, one or more cards were recorded as being held by over 85% of the adult population. Cash machines (ATM's) arrived in 1967 and in just over thirty years, there were approximately 28,000 in daily use. Debit cards were first introduced in 1987. The growth in use of plastic credit cards was predicted to increase with more being purchased over the telephone and through the internet. Corresponding to the surge of credit card business, so fraud also rocketed. Banking institutions invested £300 million on smart chip cards to combat this crime, working towards greater internet security and other card-not-present transactions.

National Provincial Bank, Raby Street, Byker; opened 1905 and closed during 1990s

Banking and shopping from home

All of these developments led to further changes in our banking and spending patterns. Banks encouraged customers to use the internet for transactions and closed many of their branches. Many retailers began to have web sites for customers ordering online from their own homes. Some of the UK retail supermarkets were forerunners in these schemes, also providing banking and financial services. This quiet commercial revolution was affecting everyone's lives. More and more people were working from home. Our lives were being influenced by mobile phones. Communication was in our pockets and worldwide markets had become more accessible through the internet. The future for Northumbria seemed to be increasingly governed by service industries, something the North East rarely provided in the past. Tourism had become of prime importance bringing funds directly into the heart of Northumbria. Whereas, shopping centres would largely recirculate money within the region or withdraw it to the headquarters of national and multi-national retailers.

A new face replaces the coal face

So, this was our bridge for the twenty first century, somewhat different to that short time at the height of the industrial revolution when Northumbria was the richest part of the richest country in the world. If you wanted coal you came to the North East. If you wanted engineering goods you came, or if you wanted armaments or chemicals, iron or machinery, and, in particular, you came if you wanted ships. The common phrases 'taking coals to Newcastle', or 'the world over you'll find a rat, a flea and a Newcastle grindstone' highlighted the North East's perception of being a focal point for world markets. As service industries replaced the industries which once blackened our skies with smoke, dazed us with noise and cluttered our landscape, the face of Northumbria was emerging richer and as a delight for all to see and admire.

Brewing, milling and leather

The following three profiles describe typical businesses developed from early trading.

Brewing – A profile of a vintage business in 1892

Written in the style of the time. Arthur's Hill Brewery. Bell Street, Westgate Road, Newcastle upon Tyne.

As far as breweries go, Newcastle upon Tyne was well provided and the malt liquors produced in the capital of Northumberland, as well as in the county itself, could well compete with the famous Midland districts for their quality, wholesomeness and taste. This brewery which had long been noted for the supply of first class ales and stouts, was built in 1840 by Mr James Burdess. During this time he owned the Duke of Wellington in Barrack Road, and had also brewed in a partnership at the Newcastle Arms, Erick Street, Newcastle. In the early 1870s James Burdess sold his interest in Arthur's Hill Brewery to move and operate from the Albion Yard Brewery, New Road. The new proprietor of Arthur's Hill Brewery was Mr John Meikle. The business was reorganised raising its importance in relation to other brewery interests in the district. The brewery premises fronting Bell Street, Westgate Road, were not generally easily accessible. However, although not large, as breweries go, it was arranged and equipped in the most scientific manner.

The whole of the plant was fitted so recently as 1890, by the famous house of Hodgson & Co., Edinburgh. The brewery was equipped with every convenience and accessory for conducting its operations under up-to-date and scientific auspices.

A small, efficient brewing operation

On the first floor, the operation was divided into two. Half of this space was devoted to the brewer's office, mash tun, brewing copper, grist case and hop stoves, and the other part for the fermenting-room. The fermenting-room contained four fermenting vessels capable of holding 1,500 gallons each. The vessels were connected to a vertical copper refrigerator, over which stood a capacious cooler. On the second floor there was a malt store and grist mill. It was evident that all water used on the premises was boiled in steam jacketed

Above: *The Mashing Room, Arthur's Hill Brewery, Newcastle*

Below: *Mr John Meikle, Proprietor of Arthur's Hill Brewery*

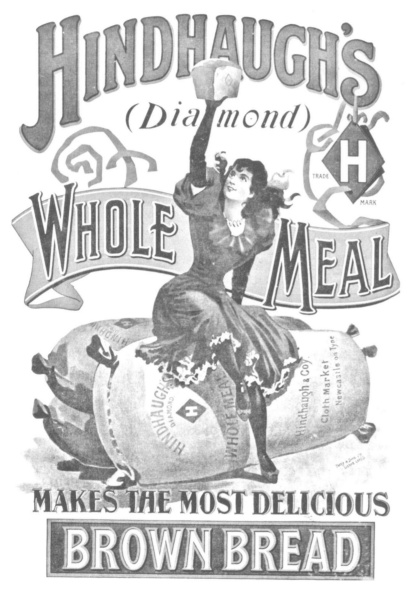

MAKES THE MOST DELICIOUS
BROWN BREAD

scrupulous cleanliness was enforced to ensure the reputation of the brewery. The deserved success could be clearly demonstrated by the extensive demand for the mild, and pale ales and stouts.

Merchanted goods like Glenlivet popular

In addition to the supply of these beverages, of which as many as 400 hogsheads would be kept continually in stock, Mr Meikle's business could be seen to have a thriving and wide reaching trade as a merchant in wines, spirits and cigars. One of his chief specialities, a noted blend of Glenlevit whisky was very popular. Due to business demands, Mr Meikle found it necessary to establish central offices at 14 Bigg Market, Newcastle with branches at Gateshead, North and South Shields, Jarrow, Howdon, Walker, Blyth and Sunderland. The Scottish brewer, Archibold Arrol bought the interests of the Arthur's Hill Brewery in 1895 and sometime later the premises became a confectionery factory.

Early agricultural offshoots – A profile of a grain and feed firm in 1892

Written in the style of the time. Messrs. John Hindhaugh & Co. Millers, Corn Merchants, Dealers in Feeding Stuffs, etc.
38 Cloth Market, Newcastle upon Tyne.

In the 1890's few trade marks were so familiar throughout the North of England as the Diamond H, which could be seen on sacks and bags at corn dealers, flour merchants, grocers and druggists almost all over the country. John Hindhaugh and Co., was equally well known, and the founder was one of the most remarkable men of his time. Latterly the firm owed its prosperity to his successors, proprietors, Mr. Jonathon Barker Ellis, and his brother, Mr. Joseph Baxter Ellis, nephews of the founder. The business consisted of a large milling

coppers before being admitted to the vessels, and that the wort copper fire, and boiler and engine were situated in a separate shed. There were no open fires in the main brewery. With a competent head brewer and carefully selected quality malt and hops it is no wonder that the output exhibited an unusual degree of excellence. Throughout every process of manufacture the most conscientious care and

business at Gallowgate, Newcastle, and an extensive dealers and manufacturers of feeding stuffs and other lines, at 38, Cloth Market. The premises at Gallowgate comprised of a great range of massive four storied buildings. There were mills, granaries, stables, and out buildings, around three sides of a capacious yard. These were enclosed on the Gallowgate side by shops, through which a spacious waggon way led to the works entrance. A large stock of raw material and finished products were kept at the mills which operation was devoted soley to milling and preparation of food products and feeding stuffs.

The milling of wheat, barley, peas, etc

In the main block of the building there were two powerful stone mills fitted with unusually large and well constructed mill stones. These mills were used for grinding wheat, barley, peas, etc., the meal falling into a trough, from which it was conveyed by a worm to the delivery vessel. Next was an ingenious contrivance for preparing and making the different feeds for cattle. The various ingredients – oats, beans and the like – after being thoroughly screened, cleansed and crushed, were conveyed into separate hoppers. From these hoppers each kind of corn was carried from a shaft with movable offshoots to an eccentric shaft which then discharged small quantities of corn from the several shoots in succession. The discharges fell into a receiving trough, where they were thoroughly mixed, and thence conveyed by a worm, and delivered into sacks in a perfectly uniform condition. In this way as many as twelve different varieties of ingredients – oats, maize, locust beans, peas, spices, etc, could be accurately and expeditiously compounded.

Trademark guarantee of purity and quality

In other departments there were a great many ingenious machines, crushing linseed, splitting beans, elevating grain in shoots or cases by automatic screws, screening and cleaning corn with sieves and sifting machines, and thoroughly purifying the grist, etc., by dust extractors

Messrs. John Hindhaugh & Co. premises, Gallowgate and the Cloth Market

fitted with revolving fans. Further operations included two pairs of very fine mill stones which produced whole meal for brown bread, for which the firm had an exceptional reputation. This was prepared with the greatest possible care, from the finest selected wheat, to form a remarkably digestible and nutritious food stuff. When finished it was made up in small cotton bags, each with the trade mark H, regarded throughout the kingdom as a guarantee of purity and quality. The business had a very extensive wholesale trade and there were generally many dozen large sacks, containing hundreds of these small bags, awaiting transit to various parts of the country. About sixty hands were employed by the firm, and, with the extensive machinery, the exceedingly large output averaged over 100 tons per day. The machinery was powered by a large double cylinder horizontal steam engine. Annexed to these works were the stables, where a large number of powerful horses were kept. Their splendid condition bore testimony to the company's special horse feed, as well as the condition of the stables, and careful grooming. Also in the out buildings there were two beautifully kept milch cows, kept to supply the families of the partners with pure milk. With their busy hands and machinery, there was no doubt that these were the largest producers of feeding meals of any mills in the north of England.

Consignment

The centrally situated premises at the Cloth Market, comprised offices, warehouses, granaries, oil and cake stores, etc., covering about 2,000 square yards, and consisted of a range of substantial four and five storied buildings. Extensive improvements had been made to the works

with the introduction of a powerful gas engine and additional crushing machinery. The 26 h.p. Crossley Otto gas engine installed for driving the crushing machinery, was fitted with a double flywheel. The department for fancy bird seeds, offered about a dozen different varieties, giving employment to fifteen young women, who were kept busy filling packets, weighing, and packing in boxes. These packets were made up in 1lb and 1/2lb sizes, and never less than ten tons was mixed and packed at one time. This was very quickly distributed to the dealers, many of whom purchased large consignments. Arrangements were made to facilitate the loading and unloading of goods; and there were steam cranes with chain lifts for holding, raising and lowering heavy parcels with one hand. The hoists were worked by a vertical steam engine, which also supplied the motive to a linseed cake crusher. This appliance consisted of a huge pan, in which two colossal edge stones revolved.

Unrivalled grain and feed supplies

There were several large stores crammed full of oats, peas, beans, linseed, rices, tapioca, oatmeal and other dry goods. The sack store was a place where the sack cloth was subject to careful scrutiny for flaws after use. Next was a large department in which poultry food was prepared and mixed by a system of hoppers and revolving shafts similar to those referred to in the Gallowgate works, nine or ten different varieties of grain being used. The newest portion of the warehouses was devoted to the storage of oil cakes, one of these stores holding up to 300 tons. Throughout a year three cargoes were received, each of about 250 tons, of oil cake from Russia alone, not to mention similar lots of English linseed

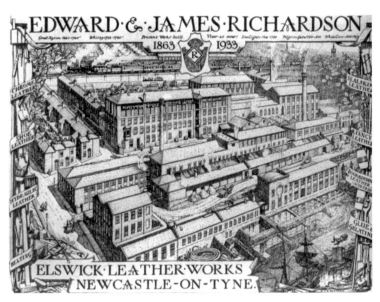

and cotton cakes, etc. They were sole agents in the north for the noted Waterloo round cakes, but, also supplied every known description of feeding stuffs. Their Diamond H products in wholemeal, ground rice and Scotch oatmeal, were their own unrivalled manufacture. Altogether sixty hands were employed on these premises, which were well secured against risks from fire, and had excellent health and safety standards. The partners were gentlemen of the highest social and commercial standing in Tyneside, and were much respected for their public spirit and for the promotion of the welfare of the working population. By none were they more respected, than their own employees. Mr. Joseph Baxter Ellis filled the office of Sheriff of Newcastle in 1888, and chief magistrate of the borough in 1889. He had the honour of entertaining the Right Hon. W. E. Gladstone when that distinguished statesman paid a memorable visit to Newcastle in October, 1891. Both the partners were among the most industrious and hard working business men in the north, personally supervising every

department, and sparing no effort to maintain the commercial status and prestige of the company.

Tanning – a profile of a trade preserved by ancient practice, as described in 1894

Written in the style of the time – Messrs. E. and J. Richardson. The Elswick Leather Works, Newcastle upon Tyne.

The ancestors of this firm had been continuously in the tanning trade for over two centuries, since the late 1600's and in 1894 Elswick Leather Works occupied a site of three acres, fronting to the river Tyne, just where it was seen to be the greatest width above the city. The works at this time had some new wiring installation and was partially electric lighted. From the upper stories of the drying lofts there was an extensive view of the Ravensworth Hills and the Teams Valley. Originally the location was selected for access to the river water but recourse was subsequently to the purer supply of the Newcastle Water Co. Then the river water which at high tide would contain nearly as much salt as the sea, would only be used for soaking, washing and cleaning.

Above: *Leather belting being made at the Elswick Leather Works, Newcastle*

Situated within the city boundaries, and dealing with animal and vegetable substances, both subject to rapid decomposition, great precautions were taken in the interests of the health and safety of its 170 employees and the environment.

Traditional processes of preservation

There were several ways practicable in which alterable vegetable substances, like tanning materials, and putrescible animal tissues, such as hide or skin tissue, could be preserved safely and innocuously, viz.: First, by being kept free from moisture; second, by being kept in a frozen state; third, by preservation in alcohol; fourth, by being saturated with common salt; fifth, by preservation in caustic lime; sixth, by the use of carbolic acid in one form or another; seventh, by the use of freshly burnt and finely powdered charcoal; and eighth, by a boiling temperature. These methods were all more or less employed as occasion and circumstances required, and such antiseptics as alum, borax, creosote, and bichloride of mercury were also used. Nothing, however, proved more useful in preventing anything objectionable or

Above left: *Hides being soaked in dye-filled vats*

Above right: *A method of scudding hides using blunt knives cleaned off any remaining hair*

annoying to the neighbourhood on the score of health, than a plentiful supply of finely powdered and freshly burnt charcoal which was obtained from the spent tanning material, and would otherwise have been a waste product. The tanneries of Tyneside were fortunate to have in the manufacture of white lead a use for spent bark, which was a material help to the leather trade, for besides its use in this way or for charcoal its disposal was difficult. Of all the preservative processes mentioned, the ancient practice of tanning could be described as most remarkable in that of all preserved and durable substances there has been nothing like leather.

A variety of manufactured skins

At the Elswick Leather Works the principle skins manufactured were those of the sheep, goat, calf, seal, colt and pig, but many others would on occasion be converted into leather. During a factory tour the firm had processed a large quantity of South African snakes, many thousand lizards, and chameleons or iguanas from South America; whilst amongst a variety of leathers the skins of alligators from Florida, and winter moles from Northumberland, dressed with the fur on, would await customers in the firm's warehouse. An instructive case of specimens illustrating this ancient trade was prepared at Elswick for the use of schools, accompanied by a printed explanation written by Prof. Henry Richardson Proctor, F.C.S., who was for a time associated with the Elswick firm as chemist, but later holding the position of Lecturer on Tanning at the Yorkshire Technical College, Leeds. There he helped to raise the manufacture of leather in all its branches from the uncertain and empiric art which for so long it was, into a scientific light of knowledge and precision. These educational cases were formerly given to teachers in schools, but as requests became too numerous a charge was made. The Elswick firm maintained a large and well appointed laboratory, where the difficulties of leather manufacture even in experienced hands were researched.

The curiosities of tanning

There were many interesting manufacturing operations. These included methods by which leather is tanned, dyed, shaved, split, levelled, polished, enamelled, grained, buffed, softened, curried and finished. The curiosities of tanning could be illustrated with the tanned section of a skin, with its fibrous structure, its porous character, its property of resisting wear, its toughness, its tensile strength, and nevertheless its liability to tear. It was surprising to find a wounded skin, healed up and afterwards tanned sometimes being processed. The section of a walrus hide was seen to be an inch thick. The tanned skin of the white whale or porpoise was demonstrated to be strong enough for an unbreakable boot lace, and yet can be torn

almost as easily as brown paper. The skin of a snake would bear an immense tensile strain although extremely thin, whilst the thick skin of the whale is so much like a loose woven blanket no use could be made of it.

Over two centuries of trade supply

The leather produced by the firm had a great variety of uses: the finest morocco leathers employed in bookbinding, purse and pocket book making, enamel leathers for carriage building and travelling cases; but the greater part was for the boot and shoe trade, as, despite many substitutes, leather remains unequalled for the protection and covering of the foot. The ancestors of this firm had been continuously in the tanning trade for over two centuries. The partners were Mr. David Richardson, Mr. Jas. Alaric Richardson, Mr. Lawrence Richardson, Mr. Frank Richardson, and Mr. Gilbert H. Richardson. Heavily stocked with leather made expressly for boots and shoes, the firm expressed their scepticism of what was termed over-production. They stated they were surrounded by poverty stricken people, whose shoes were so bad as to be a danger to their health, rather than an aid to their efficiency and comfort. They emphatically declared the opinion that if the people were shod as they ought to be, every shoe shop and every shoe factory in the country would be immediately cleared of stock. In this matter Messrs. E and J Richardson hoped for better future government policy.

The firm continued in business until 1972. It survived by concentrating on industrial applications and became part of the industrial hose and belting manufacturing company George Angus & Co.

Chapter Two

Northumbria – THE ROOTS OF NEW COMMERCIAL ROUTES

T he industrial revolution was not merely an overnight transformation of developments which brought about mass production of goods from about 1760. It was an economic process of evolution and change which spanned over several centuries, gaining an increased pace through the progression of time. Clearly, without a defined beginning and end, its roots were founded in the vast European markets created through the new shipping and commercial enterprise routes. Throughout the country many of the new processes and manufacturing innovations were already in place but with poor internal communications the revolution took about half a century before starting to become effective. In the first instance, the basic fabric of the country's infrastructure had to improve. The roads were in an appalling state and the lack of any other alternative transport other than by river or sea was a severe handicap to industrial progress.

1660s Turnpike companies take the stage

People journeyed mainly by horseback and were lucky if they achieved twenty miles per day. The roads were usually overrun with robbers and footpads, and as a result, travellers were pleased to break their journeys in the security of an inn or ale house. The ale houses hung out a garland or bush as a sign to welcome travellers. By 1577, conditions at inns improved and travellers could expect a private chamber warmed by a good fire with the comfort of a huge four poster bed and clean linen. It was not until the main road sections were improved during the 1660s by the private turnpike companies that the stage coach with its team of powerful horses came into being. Initially these coaches ran from Newcastle to York stopping on the way at Darlington and Thirsk. In 1658 there was a coach from London to Edinburgh which took thirteen days, or six from Newcastle.

1750 – Transport a shilling per ton per mile cost to London

Most roads were simply tracks of deeply rutted earth, worn through increased use of heavy horse drawn waggons. In spells of bad weather these highways were impassable quagmires so that villages and towns became isolated for weeks in bad winters. By ancient custom, each parish had the responsibility to maintain their local roads and bridges but the growth of inland trade

Opposite: *Northumbria, the platform for the railways of Britain*

Below left: *Great rivalry between coach operators*

THE
Royal William
COACH,
BETWEEN
NEWCASTLE AND
BERWICK.

The Public are respectfully informed that, on and after
MONDAY, THE 19th MARCH,
The above COACH will leave
BERWICK every Morning, (Sundays excepted,) at Six o'Clock,
Belford, at a Quarter before Eight,
And, after Breakfasting at Alnwick, will leave at 10 o'Clock.
And arrive at
MR. DODSWORTH'S,
QUEEN'S HEAD, NEWCASTLE, AT TWO O'CLOCK;
And leave the Queen's Head, Newcastle, at .past 11 o'Clock, A.M.;
AND AFTER DINING AT ALNWICK,
Will leave at Four o'Clock.
And arrive at Berwick at 8 o'Clock.
Fares from Newcastle to Berwick, 18s. Inside, 7s. Outside.
Do. to Alnwick, 7s. Do. 4s. Do.

RAPID, SAFE, AND CHEAP TRAVELLING
By the Elegant *NEW RAILWAY COACH,*

THE UNION,

Which will COMMENCE RUNNING *on the* STOCKTON *and* DARLINGTON RAILWAY, *on* MONDAY
the 16th *day of October,* 1826,
And will call at Yarm, and pass within a mile of Middleton Spa, on its way from Stockton to Darlington, and *vice versa.*
FARES.   Inside 1½d.—Outside, 1d. per Mile.   Parcels in proportion.
No gratuities expected by the Guard or Coachman.
N.B. The Proprietors will not be accountable for any Parcel of more than £5. value, unless entered and paid for accordingly.
The UNION will run from the Black Lion Hotel and New Inn, Stockton, to the New Inn, Yarm, and to the Black Swan
Inn, near the Croft Branch, Darlington ; at each of which Inns passengers and parcels are booked, and the times of starting may
be ascertained, as also at the Union Inn, Yarm, and Talbot Inn, Darlington.
On the 19th and 20th of October, the Fair Days at Yarm, the Union will leave Darlington at six in the morning for Yarm,
and will leave Yarm for Darlington again at six in the evening ; in the intermediate time, each day, it will ply constantly between Stockton and Yarm, leaving each place every half hour.

on a national scale made this completely impractical. From 1663 private turnpike companies were formed to improve main road sections, recovering costs by levying tolls on users. In 1751 a Newcastle and Carlisle turnpike road was opened. As far as Chollerford it was constructed on the foundations of the Roman wall and is still known locally as the military road. On the available roads, the cost of transport for coal and other goods was practically prohibitive with the average transport charge from the north to London being a shilling a ton per mile. In 1772 stage coach services were established from Newcastle to London, the price for each passenger was three pence per mile. (Old imperial, 240 pennies = one pound). Some better off travellers preferred to have a post-chaise (a much smaller lighter carriage) where luggage was conveyed by waggon or pack horses and cost about five shillings (old imperial, 12 pennies = one shilling) for every half pound weight carried a hundred miles.

The inland markets could scarcely obtain many commodities, especially bulky or heavy goods like coal, pottery and farm produce. In order to reach these inland markets the only means was by trains of pack horses. These original bridle paths and pony tracks are often sought today by ramblers and holiday makers on their visits to Northumbria. During this time, the spine of the northern road system was the Great Post Road from Boroughbridge through Darlington, Durham and Newcastle to Berwick. In 1786, it was along this road regular mail coach services began, one north to Edinburgh and one south to London. The coaches travelled at a speed of 7mph and a fare from Newcastle to London was four guineas (one guinea = 21 shillings, £1 = 20 shillings). In 1789, a turnpike road was established between Norton and Monkwearmouth, Sunderland. By 1796, the Union mail coach was running between Sunderland and Whitby twice a week. It was the first post coach to travel through Stockton. The network of routes gradually increased into the 1800s, and in 1806 a mail coach started to run between South Shields and York. The peak of the coaching era was in the 1820's when competition between owners was intense. John Croall's coach *Chevy Chase* ran to Edinburgh from Newcastle on the Otterburn route; James Bedford's *High Flyer* took the Wooler route and the *Union* took the Great North Road. The end of the stagecoach did not happen when the first public railway opened. The first railways were considered to be like public highways. As long as you paid a toll and obeyed the rules, normal horse drawn carriage wheels could be removed and substituted for flanged wheels. In the early days of the railways, most of the coaches were horse drawn, the great advantage was the reduced friction on rails which increased the load capacity and travelling speed. Surprisingly, it was some time before the railways took the mail completely from the coach owners. The last G.P.O. mail coach to Edinburgh ran in 1847 and by 1860 all coaching was finished. In the years to 1880 the various turnpike trusts were wound up, and the road maintenance passed to the county authorities. Although turnpikes assisted agriculture, like the railways, they also allowed goods and produce in, and sometimes competition was to the detriment of inland producers.

1781 – George Stephenson born in Wylam

Wylam village near Newcastle had a part to play in the subsequent history of the railways. It was here that the Wylam waggonway was opened in 1748 to carry coal through to Newburn and Lemington staiths. George Stephenson was born in June 1781 at a cottage called High Street House, Wylam and a waggonway was virtually on his doorstep. As Wylam took a place in history for being the birth place of the founder of the railways it is noteworthy that up to the time of writing Wylam has one of the oldest railway stations remaining in use. The scene was set for locomotives in 1782 when James Watt designed a rotary steam engine. In 1802, Cornishman Richard Trevethick invented a high pressure steam engine or puffer, making a travelling engine practical. After 1810, there were a series of developments which led to the famous locomotive designs of George Stephenson. In 1811, John Blenkinsop of Walker devised a rack-and-pinion engine with much

improved tractive power. After successful trials in June 1812, this train ran regularly on Hunslet Moor in Yorkshire and was soon adapted for the Kenton–Coxlodge waggonway to the Tyne. It was after the original wooden waggon way was replaced by a plate-railed track that William Hedley's *Puffing Billy* and *Wylam Dilly* locomotives came into service. William Hedley, manager of Christopher Blackett's Wylam colliery, designed the *Puffing Billy* engine in 1813 and this was to carry coals along the plate-railed track of the Wylam railroad to the staiths at Lemington. These trains were designed for five-foot gauge and remained in service until 1862 when the line was converted into a standard gauge railway. At this time Sir Thomas Henry Liddell, the chief lessee of Killingworth Colliery also decided to adopt steam transport and commissioned George Stephenson to design a superior locomotive to any other. Stephenson quickly achieved this objective and his first locomotive the *Blucher* was used continuously from 1814.

Malleable iron rail tracks introduced

Two years after Watt's rotary engine invention, in 1784 Henry Cort discovered a

Above: *George Stephenson, the creator of Britain's railways*

Below: *Locomotive, old "Billy", pictured in Newcastle early 1900s*

process of puddling to refine pig iron using the reverberatory furnace. With Henry Cort's invention it was also now possible to make rails of malleable iron which soon replaced wooden rails on waggonways for horse drawn trucks both above and below ground. In 1820 George Stephenson was a partner in the Bedlington Iron Company and may have supervised laying some of the first new malleable rail tracks to their works from a neighbouring colliery.

Shortcuts towards better communication links

By the beginning of the nineteenth century the Tees was already established as an important centre for agricultural shipments. One of the greatest difficulties in stimulating further commercial growth was communications. The Tees was navigable and had two ports at Stockton and Yarm. However, a change in the course of the river was also to change the course of the country's transport infrastructure. In 1808 an Act authorised the formation of the Tees Navigation Company. Through this it was empowered to cut a canal (the Mandale Cut), which effectively straightened a navigable stretch of the Tees reducing the distance from the port of Stockton to the estuary by two and a half miles. During a celebratory dinner of the opening of the Mandale Cut on 18 September 1810 and in the interest of further communication improvements, Stockton's Recorder Leonard Raisbeck successfully moved a resolution for an investigation into a canal or railway which would link the south western part of the Durham coalfield to Stockton. The benefits were clear, this coalfield was easier to mine but the reserves were almost inaccessible without incurring huge transport costs. In 1767 the

South Durham Canal Project was an attempt to provide this transport link. Following a route proposed by James Brindley and his assistant Robert Whitworth, George Dixon cut a short piece of canal across the Cockfield Fell. Then following a trial of a flat bottomed boat on the canal, Dixon believed that he could prove the practicality of the scheme to the Earl of Darlington. Unfortunately, the scheme was abandoned after the Earl refused to provide the finance. A later proposal by Ralph Todd in 1796 was also abandoned due to funding difficulties. In fact as a result of the wars with the United States and France, money was so scarce that no further action was taken until after the Treaty of Paris and Peace of Ghent in 1814. Then there was a revival of interest and great diversity of opinion, in favour of the alternatives. However, the Dixons had proved to be quite a remarkable family.

The Dixons and The Mason and Dixon's Line

From a Quaker family, the brothers George and Jeremiah Dixon were raised at Cockfield, between Barnard Castle and Bishop Auckland. Both had been given a sound education in mathematics by John Kipling of Barnard Castle. Jeremiah had invented several useful machines for colliery works but had become well known for his mathematical and surveying skills. In 1769 he had been sent to the island of St Helena by the Royal Society to observe the transit of Venus. However, before this he had been employed in the United States to survey and set the boundary between the former slave states of Maryland and Virginia, and the free state of Pennsylvania. Jeremiah and another English mathematician and surveyor, Charles Mason completed their work surveying the border (latitude 39 deg.

43 min, 26.3sec.), between November 1763 and December 1767. Some years later in 1820 during a slavery debate in Congress, John Randolf made great use and reference to the boundary as the Mason and Dixon's line. This was so widely publicised by the newspapers in America that their names then became associated as an enduring reference to this landmark. The family line of surveyors was to continue with George Dixon's grandson John, who was born at Cockfield in 1796. Although the family owned the Cockfield colliery, this was sold to Jonathon Backhouse whilst John was still a youth. John began his business career as a clerk in the bank of Backhouse and Company. Later at the insistence of Jonathon Backhouse (one of the main promoters of the Stockton and Darlington railway), he was transferred to the service of the newly established railway company. At first he was a clerk and became a surveyor assisting George Stephenson survey the Stockton and Darlington line in 1821. John Dixon worked closely with Stephenson to lay the foundations of his own profession and to apply new guidelines for civil engineering. He worked as a surveyor in the construction of the projected line between Liverpool and Manchester. John was also an engineer for several other railway lines before returning as consulting engineer to the Stockton and Darlington Railway Company in 1845.

Edward Pease invests in the Stockton and Darlington Railway

By the summer of 1818, Jeremiah Cairns of Yarm contacted his relative George Overton, a Welsh engineer, about his transport recommendations. Finally the advocates of the railway had won with Overton's findings being accepted on the

Edward Pease, promoter of the Stockton and Darlington Railway Company

basis of cost and practicalities. A prospectus was then issued for the formation of the Stockton and Darlington Railway Company. The Bill was poorly prepared, met considerable opposition and was defeated in April 1819. At a second attempt, the Bill, although better presented almost failed since it did not comply with standing orders which required that 80% of the share capital should be subscribed before going to committee. It was a Darlington Quaker, woollen merchant and banker, Edward Pease who stepped in to pay the required balance and then became the key figure of the new company. Edward Pease had so much confidence in the proposed railway that he was able to persuade fellow Quakers in Norwich and London to provide investment capital and loans. Once the railway line was given Parliament's approval in 1821, Edward Pease appointed George Stephenson to act as the company's consulting engineer. The initial proposals were for the railway line to be worked by horse drawn waggons containing coal and other raw materials. It was George Stephenson who convinced

Edward Pease and other members of the Stockton and Darlington Railway Co, about the benefits of using steam locomotives and their potential for passengers.

1825 – Stockton and Darlington Railway opened

The first rail of the public railway was laid near St John's Well, Stockton, on 22 May 1822. During the same year George Stephenson's Hetton Colliery railway construction was completed. It consisted of an eight mile stretch of railway connecting the Hetton collieries with Sunderland over Warden Law. It was the largest in the world to be worked by locomotives and served as a model for the Stockton and Darlington Railway and remained in use until 1959. Conventional locomotives were used to haul coal waggons at each end of the line but stationary engines drew the waggons to the top of a 700ft incline. From the summit the waggons continued over another four inclines by gravitation. Developments in railways had begun to gather pace and boosted by difficulties with traditional horse drawn coaches in bad weather. In February 1823 mail coaches found it impossible to

reach Durham or Newcastle for a week due to snow blocking the roads. Two years later, the famous line from Whitton Park Colliery (near Shildon) to Stockton was opened on 27 September 1825. The celebrations began with a grand cavalcade with the steam engine *Locomotion* hauling the coach *Experiment* with 18 passengers and 38 waggons carrying coal, flour and other goods. The train collected many more than the original 300 ticket holders who clambered aboard goods waggons, and more than 40,000 spectators witnessed the event. The procession took 65 minutes to cover 8.75 miles to Darlington and after stopping to take on water and more passengers, took 3 hours 7 minutes to cover the 12 miles to Stockton. On the descent into Stockton, the train was reported to reach an amazing speed of fifteen miles per hour. When it arrived at 3.45pm, *Locomotion* and its cavalcade was greeted by a cheering crowd, the national anthem and a gun salute. Once the first public railway lines were open, potential passengers were decidedly cautious. An old unsprung stagecoach mounted upon a

Stephenson's Locomotion No. 1, the first steam locomotive to run on a public railway

strong frame of railway wheels, was the only passenger accommodation. Gradually passengers overcame their fears and by 1845 there were thirteen million third-class railway fares.

1850 – Newcastle Central Railway Station opened by Queen Victoria

The same year a Newcastle to Carlisle railway was planned in place of a previously proposed canal which would facilitate the export of Tyne coal to Ireland. The main part of the railway with a terminus at Redheugh, Gateshead was opened on 11 June 1838, whilst during 1839 it was linked to Newcastle by the Scotswood railway bridge. The Newcastle to Carlisle line was the first cross country rail link to be completed. It cost an average of £20,000 per mile over a distance of 63 miles to construct. During the first years the best known engine operating between Newcastle and Carlisle was the *Comet*, a locomotive constructed by R & W Hawthorn. Following the Newcastle to Carlisle connection, the Brandling Junction Railway was formed. On the south of the Tyne, this linked the railway between Gateshead and Monkwearmouth, and had a branch to South Shields. A connecting line, from the Newcastle and Carlisle Railway Company's station at Redheugh to the terminus of the Brandling Junction Railway, on the east side of Gateshead completed the line between the east and west coasts. Then new railways soon developed with new lines and bridges being built throughout the country. Locally John Green designed great viaducts at Ouseburn and Willington Dene taking the railway through to North Shields. When opened in 1839 this line carried over 51,000 passengers in a week. Eventually, the Newcastle and Carlisle Railway Company acquired a site

suitable for a junction for the proposed London to Edinburgh trunk line. In conjunction with the York, Newcastle and Berwick Railway Company they commissioned architect John Dobson to design a railway station for Newcastle. The Central Station became one of Dobson's finest achievements, opened by Queen Victoria in 1850 and was given a gold medal for design novelty at the 1858 Paris Exhibition.

The Rocket and Locomotion No. 1 built in Newcastle

The engines which operated on the newly established railway lines had numerous design faults. Initially to improve the engines George Stephenson and his son, Robert, together with Edward Pease of Darlington and Michael Longridge of Bedlington set up workshops in Forth Street (behind Newcastle Central Station). In 1823 the Forth Banks Locomotive Works, was established, and in 1831 expanded to a site

Central Station, Newcastle designed by John Dobson

adjacent to the works of R & W Hawthorn. Hawthorn's were also synonymous with the construction of locomotives. It was at Forth Banks that Robert Stephenson & Co., built *The Rocket* and *Locomotion No. 1*, the world's first passenger steam locomotive. In 1829 George had his greatest triumph when *The Rocket*, an engine capable of reaching 36 mph stunned the world at the Rainhill Trials in Liverpool. By 1850, over a period of twenty five years, the Forth Street works had produced more than a thousand locomotives which found their way to markets throughout the world. The firm Robert Stephenson & Co., expanded its operations into bridge building and general civil engineering work. (Stephenson relocated to a much larger site at Darlington in 1901, and the Forth Street premises were bought by Hawthorn's.) After the opening of the Newcastle and Carlisle Railway in 1838, train excursions soon became regular events. The first of these was a special half fare excursion for the employees of R & W Hawthorn on 14 June 1840.

1854 – The North East Railway Co., established

By the middle of the nineteenth century Newcastle was the centre of one of the most complex railway networks in Britain operated by the North Eastern Railway Company. Some of the early branch lines had been developed through extending the use of mineral carrying trains from isolated valleys and moorland for passenger use. Throughout the 1840s, Sunderland born George Hudson, who was particularly interested in the railways of the North East, led an initiative to consolidate many of the small local lines into great trunk systems. These amalgamations were accelerated by the railway boom of 1845–47. The North Eastern Railway Company was established in July 1854 through the amalgamation of a number of operating companies, which included the York and North Midland, the Leeds Northern, the Malton and Driffield, and the York, Newcastle and Berwick. The original Newcastle and Carlisle Railway Company became part of the North Eastern Railway Company in 1862 giving it a virtual monopoly along with its counterpart, the Great Western Railway in South West England. In 1864 George Hudson, then known as the Railway King, died. He had played a key role in bringing together the lines of the northern railway network, most of which converged on York.

1841 – The start of the East Coast railway track

There was great rivalry over railway development and through the work of the Great North of England Railways, the Darlington to York line was opened in March 1841 but it took a further three years before the Newcastle to Darlington Junction Company opened a line to Gateshead. This meant there was a railway between London and Gateshead ready to be extended to Bewick when the Royal Border Bridge was built by Robert Stephenson in 1847. With a route through to the Tyne, a section across the 100 foot deep Tyne gorge was all that was needed to link Newcastle. This was achieved by Robert Stephenson, the engineer of the High Level Bridge, and it was opened by Queen Victoria on 28 September 1849. Also, to link Newcastle with Edinburgh, the North British Railway was given authorisation to complete this line in two stages with a Berwick and Edinburgh section and then a Newcastle to Berwick section, both engineered by Stephenson. During the latter part of the nineteenth century many railway viaducts and stations were built. Amongst these,

Durham's railway station and viaduct were constructed in 1857; Darlington's Bank Top Station was opened in 1887 and remains in use today.

Horse, steam, electric and petrol powered transport

Since those early days of railway engineering, the years have seen many changes in ownership, routes and development of trains and rolling stock. However, local transport services also needed to be improved in the main centres around the Tyne, Wear and Tees. Newcastle's suburbs had expanded to an extent that it was time for a new transport network. As a result in 1879 the Corporation formed the Newcastle and Gosforth Tramways and Carriage Company. Initially rail tracks were laid for horse drawn trams which operated from Scotswood, Jesmond and Gosforth to the City. Additional routes were then leased on twenty-one year contracts to private operators. In addition, horse buses were becoming more established in the main town centres. By the early 1880s steam trams were operating in quite a number of localities. The Hartlepool Steam Tramway Co. Ltd.,

Horse drawn buses operated across the High Level Bridge, Newcastle, 1880–1931

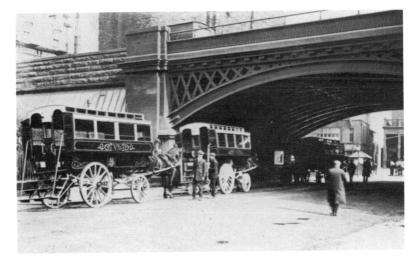

Opposite page:

1. *Solid wheel Northern buses in County Durham, C.1922*

2. *Sunderland steam tram with trailer car No.21, 1879*

3. *South Shields Electric Tramways, opening day in 1906*

4. *Horse drawn carriages at Kings Head Hotel, Darlington C.1912*

5. *Race day special electric tramcars at Gosforth Park, 1912*

commenced its service between Hartlepool and West Hartlepool in 1884. The steam trams pulled double decker bogie cars which seated 48 passengers. The trams would only operate at speeds of 4–8 mph and had shifts limited by the capacity of their engines to carry fuel and water. The company ceased trading in 1889. Steam trams were introduced the following year in Tynemouth but electric traction was soon to take over. Horse buses were also increasingly popular. A service in Newcastle took people to Gateshead across the High Level Bridge at a fare of one half penny. Each bus could carry 26 passengers. The service began in 1880 and continued until 1931, even after the electric trams commenced their route across the bridge in 1923. The advent of electricity brought electric trams to the streets. The first of these tramcars operated in Hartlepool in 1896. Others followed, notably Stockton and Middlesbrough in 1898, Sunderland and Tynemouth in 1900, Newcastle 1902, Darlington 1904 and South Shields in 1906. Trolley buses were introduced to Newcastle in 1912. Powered by overhead electricity they did not require tracks as they used conventional vehicle wheels. The yellow and white trolley buses became a familiar site around the Newcastle area with 160 of these vehicles operating until they were withdrawn in 1966 due to their restricted overhead routes. A fleet of 303 new buses replaced the trolley bus services to speed traffic flow across the city. The North Eastern Railway Co., opened the first electric train service (coast circuit route) outside London during 1903. This service ran successfully until 1918 when a fire in the sheds at Walkergate caused tremendous damage. It took nearly four years for the

service to completely recover. A further line from Newcastle to South Shields was electrified in 1938 and electric trains remained in service for many years.

1900 – First chase of criminal by car

With a regional background of pioneers in railways and shipping, communications by land and sea had developed dramatically by the beginning of the twentieth century. As well as developments in power through steam and electricity, there were developments with the internal combustion engine. Motor transport became increasingly popular in the 1890's. In Newcastle on 15 August 1900, the world's first chase of a criminal by motor car took place. A policeman borrowed a car and ordered the driver to pursue a drunken horse rider. The chase lasted for a mile. By 1908 there were 18,000 motor cars and 21,000 motor bikes in Great Britain. The cost of petrol was seven pennies per gallon. Public transport had become widely used in the region with motor bikes and trams being a familiar sight in all the main towns.

Prestige motor cars made in Newcastle

At the Armstrong Whitworth factory the first crude two cylinder paraffin powered vans were produced in 1902. With just one van per week coming out of the factory only a few believed the new vehicles had much future. However, in 1906 the first of the hand built luxury private motor cars was built for the very rich. Its hallmark was solid and reliable with the provision of a sophisticated tool kit for any repairs. Although ten variations of body styles were available, a customised version with a personal monogram could be made to order. The new motor cars had an unusual engine, four cylinders cast in a single block

33

Right: *Motor cars
manufactured at the motor
department of Armstrong
Whitworth & Co Ltd*

Below: *Armstrong
Whitworth manufacturing
aircraft at their Aerial
Department, Newcastle*

with exhaust valves on one side only. The vehicles were fitted with Dunlop detachable spoke wheels and pneumatic tyres. The footbrake acted directly onto the prop shaft and ignition was by magneto. With a price range between £125 and £550, the least expensive was known as the Eshott. Some Armstong Whitworth's were exported and one five seater ordered by the Emperor of Japan (never delivered due to the impending war), may be viewed in the museum at Beamish. Also, at Newcastle's Discovery Museum there is a 1911 Armstrong Whitworth 15/20 h.p. model. Ironically, it was the advent of the First World War which curtailed the growth of motor manufacturing when a rapid switch to full scale military equipment production was necessary. In addition to motor transport the skies were also being commercially exploited both abroad and in this country.

1913 – Town Moor built fighter aircraft

On Tyneside in 1912 Armstrong Whitworth engineers were already making aircraft engines designed by Granville Bradshaw for the All British Engine Co Ltd. By 1913 Armstrong Whitworth had developed expertise in building both airships and aircraft, the aircraft being built in Newcastle and airships at Selby in Yorkshire. The War Office awarded Armstrong Whitworth many contracts for B.E.2 series aircraft. These were built at their Aerial Department based in a former skating rink at the western end of Duke's Moor, (part of the Town Moor), Gosforth. It was from this site that early aircraft were both built and tested, and by 1917 an average of 35 a month were produced. Armstrong Whitworth employed designers to make better aircraft, the first of these included the F.K.3 and the F.K.8 conventional aircraft and some unorthodox triplanes and quadruplanes. Later the Armadillo and the Ara, both good single seat fighters were among the last aircraft to be manufactured in Newcastle. After the war, by 1919 a lack of contracts caused them to close having built three rigid airships and 1,275 aircraft. Although aircraft had used the Town Moor as an air strip, the Corporation was to prohibit this practice on

the basis of public safety. After this, Cramlington was chosen as a better facility, and an Aero Club was officially opened there in 1925.

1920 – A re-start for aircraft manufacture

The story of Armstrong Whitworth's aircraft manufacture was to continue but this time emerging at Coventry through being connected as a sub contractor of motor car engine parts for the Siddeley Deasy Company. By 1920 a new business evolved known as the Armstrong Siddeley Motor Company. During the same year a subsidiary company, The Sir W G Armstrong Whitworth Aircraft Co Ltd., was established at Coventry and this was to become world famous for its aircraft design and manufacture for the next forty years.

1935 – Newcastle Airport opened

The Lord Mayor of Newcastle, Sir Stephen Easten believed in the importance of better facilities for aircraft. From 1929 he campaigned for a £35,000 investment to open an airport in Newcastle. He achieved this and Sir Phillip Cunliffe-Lister, Secretary of State for Air, opened Newcastle Airport on 26 July 1935. The airport covered 345 acres of land, which included a 600 yard approach road and a hardy grass airfield. The new airport was managed by Newcastle Aero Club with the facilities of a club house and hanger. In the war years it was requisitioned as an auxiliary base and the RAF added some huts and a wooden control tower. Everything was basic, and even the runway landing lights were simple torches made from rags soaked in oil and lit as planes approached. Passengers were weighed, together with their luggage, and boarded the aircraft by step ladder. After the war the airport was managed by an ex-fighter pilot, James Denyer who worked continuously for improvements until his retirement in August 1989. Development finance was a major obstacle, but eventually this was resolved at a meeting in

The Alan Cobham Flying Circus at Newcastle Airport's opening day in 1935

Inset: *Ft/Lt James Denyer*

35

1958 between Newcastle Corporation and John Boyd-Carpenter, Transport Secretary. A new Regional Airport Committee was established with seven local authorities and the airport was at last seen to be a spring board for regional development. By the new millennium with the status of being an international airport, it was managing nearly three million passengers a year with three thousand on site employees.

The construction and opening of the Tyne Tunnel

From 1961 work on a new traffic route beneath the Tyne commenced between Howdon at the north and Jarrow at the south side. The construction was completed in 1967 and the Tyne Tunnel was officially opened by Her Majesty The Queen in October of that year. It was designed to be a link to join the A1 (M) motorway.

1970s – Plans for an electrically operated transport system

For many years there were no significant developments to the transport network until the advent of Tyneside's Metro system. However, on the main lines from 1963 diesel trains were introduced in a belief that they would be more economical than their electric counterparts. Within twenty years they were being phased out in favour of electric trains once again. Also during 1963, on the advice of a railway report undertaken by Doctor Beeching, many of the region's branch railways were to be axed. Following the Transport Act of 1968, an area Passenger Transport Executive was established in 1970, and within three years corporation transport in Newcastle and South Shields came under its wing. The main initiative was to provide an efficient, integrated transport system. By 1971, having considered various options, the one that gained favour was a Rapid Transit System. In July 1973, the Tyneside Metropolitan Railway Act, giving the PTE statutory approval to build the Metro received Royal Assent. Ironically, the coastal route for the new system was the same one used by the North Eastern Railway Company in 1904 for their first electric train service.

1981 – The Metro, opened by Her Majesty Queen Elizabeth II

The civil engineering work for the Metro was immense. It involved years of tunnelling between new stations that were built in massive caverns carved out beneath Newcastle's famous landmarks. The tunnelling was completed using a round-headed cutting machine but the conditions were far from ideal. Huge amounts of

The Queen Elizabeth II Bridge designed for the Metro

boulder clay were excavated and the tunnels were prone to problems from running sand. Once they were ready, pre-cast concrete or cast iron-lined segments were moved into the tunnel. Concrete was then poured between the segments and the surrounding clay to make a solid tunnel. A new bridge had to be built to take the Metro across the Tyne. After two years with 500 men working on its construction the bridge was complete. It was named after and opened by Queen Elizabeth II on 6 November 1981. The Metro was also officially declared open although the first trains had been operating between Newcastle's Haymarket and Tynemouth since August 1980. As an achievement it was Britain's greatest single piece of 20th century rail engineering, a revolution for transport on Tyneside. It had cost £280 million with 41 stations over 34 route miles forming the core of the UK's first integrated transport network. By the turn of the century a staggering average of 40,000 people were using the Metro system every day. The expansion of the network continued and by 2002 a link to Sunderland was officially opened by the Queen. Together with the north Tyne circuit, a route to Newcastle International Airport, and south of the river from Gateshead to South Shields, Sunderland and South Hylton, a total of 58 stations have been linked to the system. The Metro now carries over 37 million passengers a year.

Moving transport in Tyne and Wear into the 21st century

Tyne and Wear Passenger Transport Authority is responsible for overseeing the co-ordination of the provision of the area's public transport. This includes the Tyne ferries and river tunnels. The PTA comprises

of fifteen members drawn from its five constituent authorities with Newcastle City Council providing financial, legal and administrative support. Funding is raised through a levy on each of its constituent authorities. In order to implement its policies, the PTA has an executive body known as Nexus that is committed to delivering the PTA's objectives and providing plans for future developments. Although public use of the Metro grew in the 1980s, patronage suffered during the 1990s. There were a number of contributing factors: the effects of a recession, population decline, lower levels of economic activity, unemployment, increased competition with buses (due to the de-regulation of bus services), and growth in car ownership. However, on the positive side, after the first full year of operational services to Sunderland the net Metro patronage had increased by almost ten per cent. Plans and developments for the future are considered very seriously. As the Director General of Nexus, Michael J Parker has instigated a key strategy for future transport in the area. The plan named Project Orpheus outlines

Gateshead Metro/bus Interchange

developments needed in Tyne and Wear's local public transport to meet the aspirations of the 21st century traveller. One of the first phases of Project Orpheus is the reinvigoration of the Metro. Funding initiatives for this will entail some private sector involvement. New technology is proposed for issuing tickets on the Metro together with new station entry systems. These will be designed both to make the purchasing of tickets easier and dramatically reduce fare evasion. For all concerned, as transport plays such a major part in daily life, any new initiatives to make journeys easier particularly at peak times will be seen as an enormous benefit.

Masters of Conveyances – A profile based on a works visit in 1894

Written in the style of the time. – Messrs. Atkinson and Philipson. Coach-builders and Harness Manufacturers. 27 Pilgrim Street, Newcastle upon Tyne.

The roots of this successful coachbuilding firm went back in time to 1794. In 1825 the works in High Friar Street built the first passenger coach to George Stephenson's order, for the Stockton and Darlington Railway. In 1840 John Atkinson took his brother-in-law George Hare Philipson into

partnership to form Atkinson and Philipson, and moved to premises in Pilgrim Street (where the former Odeon Cinema was situated). The business flourished until 1919 when the advent of mass produced motor cars forced it to close. In the year 1894, this house celebrated the centenary of its existence. Apart from the practical and theoretical qualifications of Mr John Philipson, the senior partner, and his two sons, Messrs. William and John Philipson, the greatest pains were taken to kindle enthusiasm in the employees. Careful attention was given to the education of the mechanics and apprentices, and the works could have been designated as a training school for coachbuilders. For over a quarter of a century classes had been instructed in the technique of the business, and some of the prizes won and medals awarded would have done credit to a much more pretentious educational institution.

A vast expanse of workshops and offices

Completing a visit to one of the best equipped carriage building establishments in the kingdom, the tour covered more than a mile. The house was established by the great uncle of the present managing partner

Mr John Philipson. The premises of the firm were well situated and the entrance was through a large covered gateway. On the left were the counting house and the private and drawing offices. In the principal's room there were many quaint sketches of old coaching days by distinguished artists, valuable books of history and reference about the craft and harness making, diplomas and awards of medals from numerous exhibitions. The first place to visit was the timber yard. It contained every description of timber for coach building. In the timber drying stores there was a stock of birch, pine, elm, mahogany, second growth hickory and other woods, in process of maturing. The smithy was exceedingly lofty and well ventilated. There were many processes such as wheel making, axle forging, and several departments of timber sawing and coach body making. There were coaches and carriages in all stages of painting, from the first coat to the finish. Sometimes as many as twenty coats in addition to the coats of varnish imparted that delightfully brilliant and glassy appearance. The heraldic work enlisted the services of special artists. Entering the showrooms there were superb designs, in carriages, dog carts, coupes, cabs, broughams, hansoms, waggonettes, landaus, victorias, stanhopes, phantoms, etc. One of these, a sedan chair used by ladies, was being packed for despatch to the World's Fair at Chicago, together with a series of pictures descriptive of the progress of coach and carriage-building. Since 1876 the firm devoted a great portion of its energies to the construction of ambulances and stretchers. Utility, lightness, and comfort were combined in their designs for hospitals, colliery companies, police, and to

private establishments at home and abroad. With all its accessories, the carriage only weighed about ten cwt., and was considered rapid, noiseless, and almost frictionless in motion. The showrooms were lofty and well lighted, containing from 500 to 600 carriages. There were stores for every branch of the business – fellows, naves, spokes, shafts, poles, etc., and for accessories such as lamps, cloth trimmings, buttons, flannel, horse hair, flock, paints, varnishes, iron, steel, brass and brass fittings, handles, hinges, and the hundred and one articles necessary to equip a conveyance. In the spring and axle department, Messrs. Atkinson and Philipson being practical engineers, these parts were always of their own construction. A large stock of manufactured harness was splendidly arranged in the warehouse, to meet the requirements of both home and foreign trades. Besides supplying private individuals, the firm had orders for the trade and sent harness to the East and West Indies, the Cape of Good Hope, and other British Dependencies and Colonies. Messrs. Atkinson and Philipson were singularly successful in securing awards at the great exhibitions of the world. With a special

Atkinson and Philipson's offices and workshops, Pilgrim Street, Newcastle

warrant of appointment as coach-builders to H.R.H. the Prince of Wales, the firm had also long been recognised as designers to Her Majesty's Post Office, and the Metropolitan Police.

Steel forging tracks for the railway industry

A profile based on a works tour in 1895. Written in the style of the time. John Spencer and Sons Limited, Manufacturers of steel. Newburn Steel Works, Newcastle upon Tyne.

John Spencer began manufacturing steel files in 1810 at Fighting Cocks Yard in the Bigg Market, Newcastle and moved to new works at Newburn in 1822. These works could be described as a record of gigantic development in the history of the steel industry. Founded at Newburn, on the north bank of the Tyne, about five miles west of Newcastle, the locality abounded in particularly interesting associations. It had been the home of George Stephenson, Hedley, Locke, the Hawthorn brothers and other pioneers of engineering science, while many places in and around the works were equally interesting to the historian and antiquarian.

Scene of bloody pursuit, battle and marriage

Newburn village church, dedicated to St. Michael and All Angels, was built on Saxon foundations with a perfect Norman tower, and mentioned in history as early as 1071.

Then, William the Conqueror, having deprived Osulph of the Earldom of Northumberland, had conferred it upon Copsi, the Uncle of Earl Tostig. Osulph, obliged to take refuge in the woods, collected a band of followers, then beset a house at Newburn where Copsi was feasting, and pursued him to the church to which he had fled for protection. Osulph immediately set the church on fire and slew Copsi in the porch as he escaped the flames. In August 1640, the church and neighbouring ground lying towards the river was the scene of the battle between the Scottish Covenanters under General Lesley and the Royal forces under Lord Conway; the Scots on that occasion placing their pieces of cannon in the church steeple. The church was also where George Stephenson was married.

Works situated near the oldest railroad

Within the boundaries of the steel works Newburn Hall was situated and used as a works store house and chemists' laboratory. The works showed an industry of vast resource and spread over an area of sixty acres. Favourably situated, the grounds were traversed by the Scotswood, Newburn and Wylam Branch of the North Eastern Railway, and contained a river frontage of upwards of 3,000 feet. The site was close to the Wylam

Above: *W J Spencer, Managing Director*

Right: *John Spencer and Sons Ltd., Newburn Steel Works, Newcastle*

waggonway being the oldest railroad in the world, and was for many years traversed by Hedley's Puffing Billy. This waggonway was at first only a wooden track, and ran close past High Street House, Wylam, where George Stephenson was born. It was later laid with iron plates, the waggons being horse drawn until 1812 when the line was replaced with rack rails and worked by Hedley's cogged wheel locomotive. Some of these wheels and rails were to be seen preserved at the steel works. It was first demonstrated on this line that the friction on plane surfaced rails was sufficient to move a train without rack and pinions.

Probably the 1st steam driven rolling mill

Through the older portions of the works, and along the east side of the more recent additions was a stream alongside of which was Jolly's Close, where Stephenson once lived. On this stream there was a water wheel from which power was supplied for the first rolling mill. This rolling mill was later driven by a horizontal engine made by Messrs R & W Hawthorn in 1845 and was probably the first steam engine to directly drive a rolling mill. For some years the principle industry of the steel works was the production of steel and files. Before being cut or re-cut the files were ground by grindstones driven by a water wheel at the side of the stream and formerly used for milling flour and originally erected in 1500. With the introduction of the locomotive, and consequent demand for springs and other items required in the development of railways, additions were made to the site. Probably no other works better illustrated the early history of steel manufacture and engineering progress from the time when the only steel used was made from Cemented Swedish bars.

Increasing demand for springs in railways

The approach to the works consisted of an adopted and elegant structure which was the refreshment pavilion at the 1887 Newcastle Exhibition. This was a neat two story building. The frontage was enhanced by pillars supporting an upper and lower verandah. It afforded a splendid view of Newburn occupying a lovely nook, the adjacent foliage and vegetation being uncontaminated due to the great height of the chimneys. From here was the entrance to the file and spring making departments. Messrs. Spencer were the original manufacturers of volute springs under Baillie's patent, and supplied these to Stephenson and Hawthorn for their locomotives. Spencer's springs were supplied to all the principal railways and shipping companies throughout the world. They produced approximately 1,200 tons of spiral and volute springs per year. At this time 2 1/2 in. square bars of steel were being coiled into helical springs. Several were being made for the purpose of checking the recoil of guns. Applications for volute and spiral springs were various and some were supplied to relieve sudden strains on towing ropes or cables on inclined places, and also for relieving the shocks on forge cranes and for colliery locomotives, etc.,

Water wheel near Jolly's Close

where the space available would prohibit the use of laminated springs.

In the adjoining workshop laminated bearing springs were made, tempered, and tested. In close proximity to this were eight cementation furnaces, for the manufacture of lister steel from Swedish iron bars, used in high class tool and shear steel manufacture. Then there was a department for the manufacture of buffers for railway waggons as well as general smiths' work, and a machine and fitting shop. Crank and other axles, wheels, and other parts could be seen in various stages of progress, while Foster's patent built crank shaft, of which many hundreds were supplied to marine engine builders and shipping companies gave employment to a number of hands. The steel forge, operated with steam hammers, augmented by a hydraulic press of 2,000 tons was capable of forging the largest marine cranks and shafting and much smaller items. The heating furnaces worked on Siemens' regenerative principle, gas being generated in a range of producers supplying both the forge and steel foundry. In the steel tilting department all sizes and sections of tool steel were forged into shape. The crucible

Rack rails and wheels used for William Hedley's locomotive

steel melting house was specially arranged for the manufacture of tool steel and the smaller classes of steel castings. A magnificent range of buildings known as the steel foundry covered an area of approximately 7,000 square yards, and was worked by eleven overhead steam travelling cranes, varying in lifting capacity from five to eighty tons each, besides several hydraulic swing cranes. The divisional sections comprised of machines that were labour saving and increased the total productive capacity to between 5,000 and 6,000 tons of steel castings per annum. The Siemens' Martin steel smelting furnaces heated by gas, produced steel for the foundry.

Steel castings included ships anchors

The firm promoted steel castings being less expensive than iron and steel forgings. Their successful adoption by the Board of Trade and Lloyd's Register was chiefly due to the persistent advocacy of Mr. J W Spencer, the Managing Director of the firm, supported, of course, by the very excellent castings with which he substantiated his arguments. One of the main products manufactured in this department was Wasteney Smith's patent stockless anchor. Some thousand of these soley produced anchors were supplied worldwide to mercantile fleets. Adjoining the cast steel foundry was a large cast iron foundry which supplied the firm's own requirements. The foundries were lighted by 3,000 candle power electric arc lamps. After this was the electric welding shop, where welding operations were performed using an improved version of Benardo's process. With the exception of the pattern shops for the castings, and several storage houses in the enclosure, this completed a tour.

In the newer part of the works were the rolling mills. These were on level ground over forty-six acres in extent, bounded on one side by the North Eastern Railway and on the other side by the Tyne. The covered area of the mills amounted to over four acres. The mills themselves consisted of plate, bar and angle mills, and guide mills for round, square and other sections. These mills were supplied with steel from a large range of Siemens Martin gas furnaces, each one capable of casting upwards of twenty five tons, the gas being generated in sixteen gas producers and then transferred to the furnaces. In front of the gas furnaces was the casting pit in which the ingot moulds were placed. By way of spouting, a ladle received the molten steel which was delivered through an orifice at the bottom into moulds with capacity varying from one to twenty tons, the soaking process being in vast pits. From the soaking pits the ingots were delivered to the cogging mill, impressive with the ease with which the hydraulic machinery would first seize huge slabs of metal of many tons weight, then lift, reverse, turn and pass them backwards and forwards. The works were careful in their selection of ingots. The most rigid scrutiny and tests were implemented throughout the processes including rolling out to the requisite degree of thickness of plates. The average output of plates in one shift (there being night and day turns) was 100 tons. Adjoining the plate mills was a magnificent wharf complementing the firm's great transport operations. There were also the test offices, having the most modern labour-saving tools for the preparation, and subsequent testing and recording of results. Finally there was the plate and bar shearing

and delivery departments, with powerful shears and circular saws, together with extensive railway sidings and docks in conjunction with the main railway line.

Spencer's strong in community spirit

In whatever part of the works there could be seen manifestations of industrial precision creditable to the managers, and the skill of the staff and of 1,800 employees. The village of Newburn thrived through the firm which took a keen interest in the community. The local Working Men's Club Institute was built and endowed by Mr. Thomas Spencer and other members of the Spencer family. Also as the works expanded, the firm erected, on Newburn West Estate, 178 workmen's dwellings and four shops. Messrs. Spencer were actively connected with the erection of the bridge over the Tyne, at Newburn, opened on Whit Monday, 1893. The company derived a large share of business from British and foreign governments, the controllers of marine, railway, colliery and mill concerns, and from general and agricultural engineers.

Spencer's volute springs were used in steam locomotives

The excellence of their ship, bridge and boiler plates, steel propellors, bosses, blades, stern tubes and stern and rudder frames were indisputably noteworthy, but Messrs. Spencer were also pioneers in the manufacture of products for the railway industry supplying demands worldwide. Eventually by 1929 in the face of changing markets and after more than a century of business, the company went into voluntary liquidation.

Engines for the Stockton and Darlington Railway

A profile based on a works tour, early 1900s. Written in the style of the time. The North Road Locomotive Engine Works, Darlington.

Established in 1863, these works were owned by the Stockton and Darlington Railway Company and managed by William Bouch and David Dale. Rivalled by few locomotive works in the north of England for extent, the facilities were unmatched for symmetry and arrangement. Originally constructed on a much larger scale than the Shildon Engine Works which they were largely intended to supersede, they attained the rank of producing nearly the whole of the engines required for the purpose of the Stockton and Darlington Railway. The firm also turned out some of the largest and handsomest engines that were ever built. The works was constructed over an area which consisted of seven spans, each 40 feet by 120 yards in length. With three six-ton cranes, supplied by Sampson Moore, each fitted with two crabs, the mechanical ability was such that it was not unusual to lift an engine of thirty to forty tons weight in six minutes. The workshops were well lit and had roof ventilation and all the floors were boarded with the exception of the smithy. All of the walls were scrupulously whitewashed, whilst the milling, turning and engineering machinery had been painted a lavender colour giving the works a light and agreeable appearance. The main shafting throughout the works (5 inches diameter) was turned and polished with metal couplings and runs in brass plumber blocks. A patent chain was fitted for the purpose of lubricating the journals. The works covered an area of four acres whilst the offices

North Road Station Railway Museum, Darlington

44

fronted 150 yards along the North Road. At the back of the works there was a round building capable of containing twenty-four of the largest engines. This was furnished with a central turn-table to facilitate engine access to the line of rails running through the main works. The firm employed over a thousand hands and it was a testimony to their merits that the goods engines constructed at these works were frequently in use for eighteen months without repairs. The North Road Works eventually changed from building steam trains to diesel. The first main line diesel train, a class 24, was built at Darlington and left the works in January 1960. The works finally ceased production of locomotives in 1966. The former station at North Road has been converted into a railway museum. Among the exhibits include George Stephenson's *Locomotion*, an 1846 passenger carriage and many relics from the age of steam.

A business that just keeps motoring

Reg Vardy plc. Houghton House, 3 Emperor Way, Doxford International Business Park, Sunderland.

Ford's Model T was only 15 years old years old and balloon tyres for cars had just been introduced when Reg Vardy began his own transport business just a few miles from the cathedral city of Durham. Reg Vardy was only 14 when he left school in 1923 but his entrepreneurial skills were apparent even then. He began by selling fruit and vegetables from a cart pushed around by hand and soon took his first commercial decision. This was to buy a horse named Kitty to enable him and his brother Ted to sell and deliver coal around his neighbourhood in Houghton-le-Spring. Seven years later, the partners invested £38 in their first truck and began in the haulage business. By 1939, they were operating with seven vehicles that were to be commandeered for the war effort. After the war, at Stoneygate, Houghton-le-Spring, Reg bought a commercial site that consisted of a tin shed and two petrol pumps. This site was to be used for the haulage business and for Reg's first car sales. Today, it is still in use and has seen some major redevelopment over the years.

The haulage business diversifies into car sales

While he continued to build up the haulage business, Reg soon decided to branch out into motorcar retailing and in 1946 he sold his first car. Four years later, the company was appointed as an official retail dealer for the Ford Motor Company. As the retail operation grew, the haulage business was moved to another site and Stoneygate was developed as a large car showroom. Sadly, after more than 50 years work in establishing successful road haulage and car retailing businesses, Reg Vardy died in 1976. The business continued as Reg would have wished and in the same year Aston Martin, one of the most famous names in luxury cars was introduced into the Stoneygate sales showroom. Three years later Ferrari cars were available on sale, followed by Rolls Royce in 1981and

Reg Vardy pictured with a prestigious Bentley motor

then Jaguar and Daimler. The company's innovative finance schemes made such cars affordable and made Reg Vardy one of the most successful specialist dealers in the UK. The commitment behind Reg Vardy's 'Making Cars Affordable' slogan remains one of the company's priorities today.

Reg's legacy was to be kept in the family

Reg's three sons, David, Peter and John, joined the family business after leaving school but six years after their father's death they each decided to go in different directions. John was to emigrate and start a new life in Australia whilst David took control of the haulage business. Peter, who liked cars and had always shown a flare for the motor trade, took over the retail side. He quickly began to emulate and even exceed his father's success. During the 1980s when most households owned at least one vehicle, he expanded the company's innovative finance scheme to volume cars, initially with Ford, Rover and Vauxhall, and later with European and Japanese marques. Reg Vardy's name as a motor dealer was well established in the North East of England. However, it was to expand its interests out of the region for the first time with a BMW franchise in Harrogate and a Jaguar and Rover business in Aberdeen. By

1988, the company had 12 dealerships and a turnover of £100 million. It was at this time that Peter proudly received the North East Businessman of the Year award.

Reg Vardy is floated on the stock exchange

As the potential for development grew, and so that Peter's aspirations for the company could be realised more quickly, it was decided to float the company on the stock exchange. The flotation raised £6 million and in 1989 the company became known as Reg Vardy plc. A rights issue in 1991 raised a further £13 million, allowing additional expansion. In 1995, Reg Vardy plc was awarded the prestigious Used Car Retailer Award. Vardy Contract Motoring, the contract hire and personal leasing arm of the business was established in 1998. This currently has a fleet of more than 10,000 vehicles. It was a time for major acquisitions at the end of the 1990s. These included the Trust Motor Group in 1999 and 11 dealerships from Caledonia Motor Group a year later. As the business continued to expand it was contending with greater publicity costs. In order to gain a better return and have greater control, Vardy Marketing, their own advertising and marketing agency was established. With a strong sense of pride in the area and the company's roots, in 1999 a sponsorship agreement was signed with Sunderland Football Club. This sponsorship promotes the Reg Vardy name on players' shirts and on advertising at Sunderland's ground at The Stadium of Light.

Education, and business training and development

In 1990, Peter established a charitable trust, the Vardy Foundation. This is a wholly independent charitable trust which embodies the ethos and values of Reg Vardy plc, and serves to augment the company's charitable and community work. The Vardy Foundation became a major sponsor of Emmanuel College in Gateshead, Tyne and Wear. This city technology college has 1,250 pupils aged between 11–18 years, and 60 per cent of these are from areas of high deprivation. Other educational establishments, The King's Academy, in Middlesbrough, and Trinity Academy, Doncaster have been opened in 2005. Both King's and Trinity are City Academies. The Vardy Foundation has donated £1 million to Sunderland University Development Trust and the University Business School was named the Reg Vardy Centre in honour of Sir Peter's father. For Reg Vardy's own employees (approximately 6,000 working colleagues), The Vardy Academy was launched in 2004 to provide professional training and career development. In recognition of his services to business and education in North East England, Peter received a knighthood in the 2001 Queen's Birthday Honours List. Sir Peter Vardy gained a further accolade in 2003 when he was awarded the Industry Personality of the Year.

Purpose built headquarters, a stone's throw from Stoneygate

Less than a mile from Reg Vardy's original site at Stoneygate, a purpose built head quarters was planned at Doxford International Business Park, Sunderland. Construction was completed in 2001 and by July of that year the company's support services had moved into the new complex. Situated there at the hub of the business are human resources, training, property, finance and IT departments. It also houses Vardy Marketing, Vardy Contract Motoring and Vardy Group Fleet, as well as meeting rooms and a 130 seat capacity lecture theatre. Over

the years, the business has been characterised for its appetite for growth and its success in remaining profitable. Reg Vardy plc has built a network of 98 dealerships stretching from Reading to Aberdeen, selling around 200,000 new and used cars every year. In 2005, the annual turnover was approaching £2 billion making it one of the largest motor retailers in Europe. Everyone who works for Sir Peter Vardy knows that he has his fingers firmly on the pulse of the business. He works as hard as ever and is well respected for his achievements, and any ambitions and plans he has for the future will almost certainly be fulfilled.

Sir Peter Vardy outside the company's headquarters at Doxford International Business Park

Inset: Reg Vardy plc, headquarters, Sunderland

Taking a logistical route through time into the 21st century

Fergusons Transport Ltd., Kitty Brewster Trading Estate, Blyth, Northumberland.

Above: *Matt Ferguson (left), brother Will and Jimmy Gaff, in front of the "Chevs", 1930s*

Below: *Eddie and son, Alan, pictured in their rare 1926 Bean truck*

Wherever enterprise has developed there has always been a driving force behind the movement of raw materials, partially complete or finished products. In one of the most difficult times for trade, during the 1926 Miners Strike, Matt Ferguson left his work at the local colliery, sold his home and bought a Bean commercial truck to operate

in general haulage. It must have been a very worrying time and a tremendous risk. As an indication of the local difficulties, in 1925 the Port of Blyth shipped 4,424,795 tons of coal. This plummeted to less than half of this amount in 1926, which must have made life almost intolerable for people relying on work from Cowpen and Newsham, its doorstep collieries. This was the year Matt began transporting his first truckloads between Blyth and Newcastle. Matt's haulage business remained steady through the 1930s by which time he had three Chevrolet trucks. His ambitious son Eddie eventually joined the family firm in 1947 and developed the business during the 1950s and 1960s. This involved buying out either single vehicle haulage operators or small fleets to acquire their important carriers licences. Thompson's of Blyth was one of these. They started in furniture removals with a horse drawn wagon and grew to have three trucks, a hearse and a taxi. Another was BRS, not British Road Services, but Baird Road Services who had two Vulcan trucks. Although Fergusons was also to diversify into longer distance and heavier haulage, because it was beneath the threshold, the company was saved from nationalisation.

Company acquisitions, property development and retailing

Eddie's son Alan joined the firm in 1971 and became Managing Director in 1986. Tragically, Alan's father and brother Stuart both died in a helicopter crash in 1989. However, Matt's legacy and resolve to achieve in business has continued through Alan who is now Executive Chairman. Through his direction there have been greater acquisitions. One of these, Redpath's of Wooler that specialised in agricultural transport was particularly interesting. Having bought the business in Wooler, Alan's relationship with Eileen Redpath blossomed and took them along the road to marriage. It was purely coincidental but Alan received more than his money back from this acquisition. Other purchases included Hewitt's of Morpeth who in their early days specialised in forestry transport, Broads Transport of Plymouth, and H J Cutter of Poole, Dorset. Their depots have been retained in the South West to supplement others in Tilbury, Yorkshire and North East England. The transport operations have a base in Sunderland with activities covering general haulage, logistics, warehousing and distribution services. Strategic partnerships have also been formed with major European haulage companies. In another part of the business, for more than 75 years, Fergusons Removals have been assisting people on the move in this country and

abroad. With the purchase of land, the company has built a commercial property development portfolio, which includes several business parks. Fergusons also have interests in motorcycle and bicycle retailing.

Fergusons extend welfare into the heart of the community

Alan Ferguson has an incessant motivation to expand and diversify company interests, but at the same time he retains a family run business ethos. As a result, the welfare and skill of every employee is always at the top of his agenda. His belief in people is extended into community support through Fergusons of Blyth charitable fund (administered by the Community Foundation), and by being a main partner in the regeneration of Blyth. Today, the company's original entrepreneur Matt Ferguson would have been proud to see the expanse of his family's enterprise.

Above: *Alan Ferguson, Executive Chairman*

Left: *A section of the transport fleet, 1980s*

Chapter Three

North East coal fuels the industrial revolution

It is believed that the Romans probably knew the value of coal for unburnt pieces were found in many of their excavated sites. However, for hundreds of years after their departure from Britain, coal mining was a latent industry. In the reign of Henry III (1216–72), coal from Plessey (near Bedlington, Northumberland) was being shipped to London, where it was called sea coal because it arrived by sea. There are records in 1314 that Bishop Kellaw appointed a keeper to look after his coal mines as well as his forests; and in 1313, the Monks of Jarrow were buying coal for their own use. In those days the amount of coal excavated could not have been great, for in 1348–49 the Monks of Finchale Priory received nineteen shillings and six pence for coals sold during that year from their mine at Lumley. In the year 1366–67, King Edward III bought 576 chaldrons of coal (nearly 750 tons) from Winlaton for use in the fires at Windsor Castle. By the end of the fourteenth century mines were being worked in Durham at Ferryhill, Lanchester, Heworth, Rainton, Cockfield and Evenwood, and in Northumberland at Ryton, Whickham, Elswick, Benwell, Denton, Plessey, Hartley, Earsdon, Marsden, Tynemouth, Whitley, Monkseaton, Cowpen, Shilbottle, Beadnell and Bamburgh. An impetus had been given to the industry by the serious demand on the forests for timber for smelting iron and lead. Newcastle outstripped all its rivals in trade. The first licence to mine coal was granted by Edward III in the year 1350, the places specified in the charter being the "Frith" (which became Forth) and the "castle-field" (which became the Leazes and the Town Moor). Before his death the King also made Newcastle one of eleven English

towns in which wool and cloth might be bought and sold. An export rate of 40 shillings a sack also proved to be a stimulus to the wool trade. From the middle ages, coal rapidly surpassed trade in other industries. Around Newcastle and Gateshead coal reserves lay near the surface where it was of high quality for both domestic and industrial use, and being close to the river it was well placed for supplies to London.

Monks export coal from Tynemouth

As far as we know, the Tyneside pits were the first to be worked in the country and ideally situated for export. Some of the first exported coal was taken from Tynemouth where it outcropped on the shore. The Monks of Tynemouth shipped coal from their own port near their monastery and were amongst the first colliery owners establishing pits in Northumberland. They managed some mines themselves and leased others, until the dissolution of the monastery in 1539, when their Elswick pit had a daily output of forty tons. Tynemouth and North Shields had a staggered trading history due to restrictions imposed by envious and powerful Newcastle merchants. North Shields had a prosperous community where the Priors of Tynemouth built boats for fishing (every house having its own small landing place), boats for trading in coal (for the river trade with collieries beyond Newcastle), and also wine and wool. In 1267 led by the mayor of Newcastle, Nicholas Scott with a band of merchants attacked the Monks, burnt their mills, the houses of their tenants, and seized a boat laden with coal. This was certainly extreme action but the friction continued over the subsequent years. Then much to the pleasure of Newcastle's

Opposite: *Causey Arch, the world's oldest surviving railway bridge was built for carrying coal*

Above: *A coal drop, on the River Tyne*

merchants, in 1290, a blow was struck at the trade of North Shields. The Monks had over-reached themselves and the Prior was found guilty, before the bar of Parliament, of founding a new town at North Shields and encouraging his tenants to set up in business as fishermen, bakers and brewers and to take tolls which belonged to the King. From 1303 the port facilities were banned for fishing and trading in coal and other commodities. Despite this and the opposition from Newcastle's merchants, the fishing trade went on and was fully restored in 1390, although coal trading was restricted until a few years later. By 1429 North Shields had 14 fish quays and 200 houses. It became a centre for fishermen

venturing as far as Iceland in cobbles and fishing boats. In 1446 coal was permitted to be shipped from North Shields and Tynemouth Priory, but was banned once again in 1530. By 1378 Newcastle shipped 15,000 tons of coal per year both to southern England and to many parts of Europe. Transport of coal was restricted to cart, wain or pack horse and by wooden barges known as keels and lighters. In 1452 trades included the keelmen who ferried the coal to collier ships in the centre of the Tyne. Keelmen formed a community outside Newcastle's walls at Sandhill and wore distinctive clothes, including border style blue bonnets as recalled in the famous Keel Row ballad.

Collier Brigs loading at Shields

THE KEEL ROW

As I came thro' Sandgate,
Thro' Sandgate, thro' Sandgate,
As I came thro' Sandgate,
I heard a lassie sing.
"O weel may the keel row,
The keel row, the keel row,
Weel may the keel row
That my laddie's in.

"O who is like my Johnnie,
Sae leish,* sae blithe, sae bonnie;
He's foremost 'mang the mony
Keel lads o' coaly Tyne.
He'll set and row sae tightly,
And in the dance sae sprightly
He'll cut and shuffle lightly,
'Tis true, were he not mine!

"He has nae mair o' learnin'
Than tells his weekly earnin',
Yet, right frae wrang discernin',
Tho' brave, nae bruiser he!
Tho' he no worth a plack† is,
His ain coat on his back is;
And nane can say that black is
The white o' Johnnie's e'e.

"He wears a blue bonnet,
Blue bonnet, blue bonnet,
He wears a blue bonnet,
And a dimple in his chin.
O weel may the keel row,
The keel row, the keel row,
Weel may the keel row
That my laddie's in."

*Leish = lithe, nimble.

† Plack = a small copper coin, worth about one-third of a penny.

Sandgate Shore,
Newcastle

53

The phrase 'Coals to Newcastle' was first recorded in 1538 and given to mean an unnecessary pursuit. Due to the restrictions of transport, for coal to be economic, reserves needed to be relatively close to the Tyne. Between Newcastle and Wylam various sites were developed with stages known as staiths for loading coal into the keels and lighters.

Newcastle roads were waggon ways

The introduction of the wooden-railed waggonway was seen as an important innovation in making it possible to work pits further away from the waterfront. The early colliery waggonways were known as Newcastle roads. Horse drawn coal waggons, or chaldrons conveyed coal to the staiths along these railways. A single horse was able to draw five or six tons at a time along these specially made wooden roads. They were the world's first railways and the earliest recorded (in 1620), was called The Whickham Grand Lease Way. It ran from Whickham via Lobley Hill to the staiths on the Tyne. Eventually the staiths which were

built at Dunston (by NER from 1890–93), were reputedly the world's largest wooden structure. As well as to the Tyne, a railway supplied coal staiths on the Wear near Washington and a railway existed near Blyth from at least 1693.

The world's oldest surviving railway bridge

At Tanfield in north west Durham, a railway was opened in 1725 and has the distinction of having the world's oldest surviving railway bridge, Causey Arch, built in 1727. It was the largest single span bridge in Britain and remained so for thirty years. Without any previous examples, the builder Ralph Wood, a stone mason by trade, relied on Roman technology. Linking both sides of a deep gorge, the huge arched stone bridge is a lasting testimony to this major civil engineering project built in 1725–26. It was constructed for a group of coal mine owners, known as the Grand Allies. Once completed two sets of wooden railed tracks crossed the arch. Nine hundred and thirty horse drawn waggons crossed the arch in each direction everyday. Effectively this

Benwell Staith, Newcastle

meant that a waggon crossed the arch every twenty seconds (with 50 yards on average between waggons). By the 1770s the arch was hardly used. Its heyday was during the years before the closure of the nearest pits (between 1733 and 1738), and the Tanfield Colliery which ceased to operate after a fire in 1740. The line, originally constructed as a waggonway from Tanfield to Dunston-on-Tyne was eventually adapted for steam locomotive haulage and continued until its final closure in 1965. The chief markets for coal were London, East Anglia and abroad in northern France, north west Germany and the low countries. Ships from the Baltic brought timber for pit props or pitch, hemp, flax, iron ore and materials needed in ship building whilst taking coal for a return shipment.

The company of Hostmen control coal trade

In 1547, Newcastle's population was 10,000 and the Tyne coal trade was exclusively maintained by the Company of Hostmen. These were Newcastle's merchants who, through right of the Crown, levied one shilling tax on every chaldron of coal shipped, a chaldron being equivalent to 53 cwt. All coal had first to be sold to the Hostmen before being resold to reach other markets. Many Hostmen became rich as the demand for coal increased and subsequently held high positions in Newcastle's municipal affairs. The period after the Restoration witnessed a great development in the coal trade. Pits were leased at Whitley on condition that the rents from them should be used towards the cost of making a pier and quay at Cullercoats. The pits at Lumley Park near Chester-le-Street were considered to be amongst the most important in the region.

In the year 1675, the Tyne Valley produced 570,000 tons of coal and by the end of the century 175,000 tons were being shipped on the Wear. Coal that cost at the pit head four shillings a ton, sold in London at seven shillings a ton. There were many industries which benefited from coal as a cheap alternative fuel and it replaced charcoal as a fuel in industries such as brewing, pottery, glass, brick making and hardware. As a result of the expansion of traditional industries, skills were also needed and imported for making salt, paper, glass, and cannon-founding. By the end of the seventeenth century the country had won the unique position of being a land of manufacturers. This was a transformation from being one of the most backward countries in Europe only 150 years earlier. The industrial revolution was already on the doorstep and most manufacturing industries were coal based.

Centre of the salt pan industry

With plentiful supplies of coal, ideal for the salt pan evaporation process, this fed the fires of salt pans which were well

Replica of chaldron waggon at Causey Arch

steady demand for salt in the fishing industry. Howdon, between Wallsend and North Shields, was originally known as Howdon Pans because of its association with salt making.

There appear to have been local customs in the manufacture. The brine water when lukewarm was clarified with the whites of eggs or the blood of sheep and black cattle, then boiled. The salt was eventually raked out of the pans and left for a number of days to dry. Equipment appeared to be expensive and the duty high; hence it became unprofitable as well as unlucky to spill the salt. A tradition continues to this day to cancel the bad luck of spilling salt on a table by taking a pinch of the salt and throwing it over the person's left shoulder.

In Roman times it was believed individuals had good and bad sides. The left side of the body being good and the right side bad. Romans would enter a house with their left foot, putting their best foot forward to bring luck.

The industry created terrible fumes and pollution. On Teesside at Billingham salt had been manufactured since the fourteenth century. The peak of the industry rapidly declined after 1800 when rock salt discovered in Cheshire replaced the poorer quality salt produced by the evaporation of sea water. Some salt continued to be made at South Shields, no longer by using coal but by dissolving Cheshire and Irish rock salt in sea water and evaporating brine through the waste heat of coke ovens. When pitmen killed their pigs, it was said that they would only use Shields salt for curing.

established along the coastline. As early as 1290 Robert de Brus granted one of his tenants at Hart near Hartlepool permission to make salt, and Salt de Gretham from the same locality was well known in the fifteenth and sixteenth centuries. In 1533, the Abbot of Newminster leased seven pans at Blyth. Salt pans were established at Seaton Sluice, Cullercoats and Sunderland with the main centres at North and South Shields. Early in the seventeenth century 430 workmen were employed making salt in Northumberland and Durham, and 120 keelmen were employed conveying coal to the salt makers. In 1708 the salt pans of Cullercoats yielded 2,180 tons of salt, at a profit of £535. The two towns at Shields had approximately 200 salt pans in 1767 consuming 1,000 tons of coal a year. However, by this time many salt pans were being dismantled although there was a

Salt making

The method of obtaining salt was to imprison the sea at high tide in huge vats, draw it off into smaller vessels, and evaporate the moisture partly naturally in hot sunshine and partly artificially by means of several boilings. The salt left behind was then purified. The boiling pans measured about 20 feet by 12 feet by 14 inches deep, built of plates of iron rivetted together with iron nails and the joints filled with a cement. Across the top of the pan were placed several strong bars of iron, and from these, at regular intervals, iron hooks hung down to support the shape of the pan bottom. In 1722 the cost of building a new Pann and Pannhouse was recorded at almost £145 of which more than half was for iron plates and bars. A series of grates beneath the pans boiled the brine. As this evaporated, salt was skimmed and shovelled off and packed into conical shaped wicker baskets to drain. Travelling in the north of England in 1725 Lord Harley described a visit to South Shields. "... which is the chief place for making salt. The houses there are poor little low hovels, and are in a perpetual thick nasty smoke. It has in all 200 salt pans, each employs 3 men. Each pan makes one tun and a quarter of salt at 8 boilings which lasts 3 days and a half. Each consumes 14 chaldrons of coal in 7 days in which time it makes two tuns and a half of salt. The wages for Pumpers, ie; those who pump the salt water into the pans is 5 d. per diem. The watchers, ie; those who continually have an eye to the pans and the fire stoves have 6 d. a day".

Tees and Wear emerge as trade centres

At the beginning of the 17th century, along the river Tees, Stockton and Yarm

were emerging as trade centres. However, during the previous century Stockton had become a casualty of a general British economic downturn. This had effectively run down the town's small industry, markets and fairs. By the late 1600s the river's ports had significantly increased prominence. The stimulus was the result of the demand for northern coal for the expanding London area. On their return voyage colliers would sail into the Tees to purchase rum, tobacco and tea. Locally

Illustration of mid 18th century Stockton, and Cecil Wren & Co Ltd,. sauce factory

produced butter had become Stockton's major trade to the capital. As the ports grew busier, the river's shipyards began to prosper, and associated trades required imported supplies of timber, flax, hemp and iron from northern European countries. Such was the emphasis of trade on the Tees, that in 1680 the customs office was relocated from Hartlepool to Stockton (a new customs house was built and opened in 1730). As a result of the Wear Valley coal industry, Sunderland saw the most notable urban development growth of the century. From being a little used port before the 1600s, Sunderland was to increase its coal trade sufficiently for Newcastle's merchants to feel threatened and they petitioned the King to raise a levy on Wear shipments. They were successful and in 1610 James I ordered that part of Sunderland's coal revenue had to be paid to Newcastle's merchants. From two or three thousand tons a year in the 1590s, by 1610 Sunderland's coal shipments had risen to approximately 14,700 tons. Sunderland continued to grow and was incorporated as a borough in 1634 by Bishop Morton. Coal shipments were also stimulated in the

1640s during the civil war when trade was cut off from the Tyne through a blockade. By the beginning of the 1680s the borough's population had reached 2,490 and the port's coal shipments had risen to 180,000 tons. Sunderland had become a major rival to Newcastle. North of the Tyne, Blyth and Seaton Sluice had been developed as ports in the 1600s. In 1609, 855 tons of coal were exported from Blyth and conveyed there on the Plessey waggonway which was five and a half miles long. The Delaval family had established a coal mine at Hartley and developed Seaton Sluice as a port specifically for their mining interests.

Captain James Cook born near Middlesbrough

Although Whitby in North Yorkshire was outside the coalfield, it also benefited from the coal trade. Whitby was a busy shipping port and in 1746, James Cook (born at Marton, near Middlesbrough 1728), worked on Whitby colliers, shipping coal from the Tyne and Wear to London. Later, in 1769 James Cook was made captain of the H M Bark *Endeavour* to explore new lands. He sailed across the world to explore Tahiti,

Coal drops on the River Wear, Sunderland

New Zealand and Australia where he named the famous Botany Bay. In 1772, in search of the great southern continent, he voyaged to the Antartic Circle, but it was while he was on his third trip in 1779 when he died. Captain James Cook was murdered on the island of Hawaii following a skirmish between the ship's crew and the natives. This was also a notorious time for press gangs who would take able-bodied men by force to work aboard the ships. In January 1760, press gangs captured sixty men from North Shields who managed to take control of the ship and sail into Scarborough where they escaped.

The Grand Allies control coal trade

By the eighteenth century the northern coal trade was controlled by a cartel of wealthy coal owners called the Grand Allies. The families associated in the cartel were the Brandlings of Gosforth, Liddles of Ravensworth, Gateshead, the Russells of Brancepeth, Durham and the Bowes family (the Earls of Strathmore). There were many merchants who had made their fortunes from owning collieries. They were often unscrupulous in their dealings with pitmen's wages and conditions and would often evict any protesting tenant miners from the homes they provided. Down and outs, known as candymen, from riverside or dock areas would frequently be given the task to assist with evictions. The Marquess of Londonderry was one of the unpopular aristocratic colliery owners.

1615 – Looking at glass through coal

Glass was introduced to Northumbria in Saxon times by Benedict Biscop, a Monk who founded Wearmouth and Jarrow, and who brought makers of glass from France so that his churches could have glazed windows. However, glass making only

Gosforth colliery and railway

In the early days of manufacture, glass was considered to be valuable. At times when Alnwick Castle was not being used as a residence, the Steward used to remove the glazed windows and put them safely away until the family returned. The growth of glass manufacturers around the Ouseburn to the Tyne was particularly favourable. The tributary afforded both wide and deep anchorage for the shallow draught keel boats. Soon the industry grew to a point where there were eleven glass based operations and this area of the Tyne became known as The Glasshouses and a bridge built across the Ouseburn was called Glasshouse Bridge.

1745 – An Act which smashes the glass industry

It was not until 1684 when the Dagnia brothers (from the Forest of Dean area near Bristol) established a works at Closegate, Newcastle, that fine quality glassware was produced. This was known as flint glass, containing a greater lead content and giving a brilliant clarity. Following the founding of Beilby and Company Engravers in 1760 (detailed in the first chapter), William and Mary Beilby took a keen interest in the glass making industry based only a mile or so from their own premises. A year or two earlier William had been an apprentice enameller to John Hezeldine of Bilston, near Birmingham. It soon became William's obsession with experimentation to fuse enamel pigments into glass, creating a new art form. In 1761 he achieved his objective, and then with his wife Mary began to produce decorated glass which was to give them immortal fame. Newcastle had become the largest glass

became a significant industry through the Crown granting a patent in 1615 to the company of Sir Edward Zouche permitting the manufacture of glass with any fuel for the furnaces other than timber. A growing shortage of timber in England had led to restrictive usage legislation and therefore Tyneside was well placed for the glass industry with coal as an alternative fuel for the furnaces. Sir Robert Mansell (then the Treasurer of the Navy and later an Admiral of the Fleet), soon joined Zouche's company buying out all the partners. Mansell's glass works were established in 1619 at Byker and at Ouseburn, Newcastle in 1623, with skills imparted by Huguenot refugees from Lorraine who had fled religious persecution. These families and their descendants, the Tyzackes, Tittories, and Henzells, were involved in the business of glass making on the Tyne for several generations. The Henzells founded glass works at Howdon, near North Shields, which remained in operation until the First World War. Mansell's works made bottles, window glass, mirror glass, tumblers and spectacle glass.

Top: *Sir Robert Mansell*

Below: *The Glasshouse Bridge, Newcastle*

producing centre in the world. It had approximately thirty glasshouses within half a mile of the main town. This was to increase to more than forty for the area by 1827. There were also other glassworks established in the region. The Sunderland Company of Glassmakers set up at Southwick in 1698 and Thomas Delaval founded a glassworks at Hartley near Blyth in 1763. By 1850 there were between 40–50 glassworks based on the banks of the Tyne. There were various types of glass manufactured which included plate, crown, sheet, blown and flint or crystal glass. Plate glass was produced by throwing molten glass on an iron or copper table and rolling it to an even thickness. By 1845 South Shields was manufacturing more plate glass then any other centre in England. Crown glass, the main type for windows was made with a large central bullion shape.

Glass for Crystal Palace made in Sunderland

After 1850, the demand for larger glass panes was provided through sheet glass extensively manufactured at Sunderland, particularly by the Wear Glass Works established by James Hartley in 1836. Hartley's firm made glass for the construction of Crystal Palace in 1851 and later became famous for its coloured glass. By 1865 one third of the sheet glass in the country was produced in Sunderland by The Wear Glass Works. As well as locally produced salt (which for a long period had been used in glass production), it was cheap coal and local sand and lime that became the catalyst for the glass industry. The demise of the glass industry was largely caused by The Glass Excise Act of 1745 which levied a 20% tax proportional to the glass metal weight. This was eventually

raised to 40% which resulted in the loss of almost two thirds of the industry. One of the longest surviving glass works was at Lemington, originally founded by the Northumberland Glass Company around 1780. The company was eventually taken over by the General Electric Company who produced light bulbs and television tubes until the 1960s. The largest remaining brick

Above: *Interior of James Hartley's glassworks, established 1836 at Sunderland*

Below: *Lemington Glassworks, Newcastle, 1915. The large cone remains today*

built cone shaped structure of this glassworks may still be seen on the north side of the Tyne at Lemington. Within the cone, pots of molten glass were heated ready for the glass to be blown into shape. It is the last visible link with a once famous glass industry.

1685 – Crowley's iron works forges ahead

Coal was used for smelting lead, copper, tin and brass but had not replaced wood in the smelting of iron. Although experiments had been made to smelt iron with coal or coke, no reliable method had been found to prevent sulphur from entering the iron and making it brittle. It was for this reason that iron was originally made by heating iron ore in simple furnaces using charcoal. In 1306 a petition was handed to Parliament against the Bishop of Durham for the destruction of Weardale forests for charcoal used in the iron furnaces. A lease was granted in 1368 by which John de Shotlington, forester to the Bishop of Durham, gave John de Merley and others permission to place an iron furnace near Bishop Auckland at Evenwood

for a weekly rent of sixteen shillings. Formerly iron-stone was worked on Waldridge Fell and Shotley Bridge and later more extensively in Weardale. Ambrose Crowley's family came from Worcestershire where they were ironware manufacturers. Sometime before 1685 he founded a business in Sunderland manufacturing nails. By 1691 Crowley moved to Winlaton where from a disused cornmill he extended production to include nails, files, knives, hammers, chisels and hinges. Later he opened works in Swalwell and Teams with forges and foundries making chains, pumps, anchors and cannons from imported swedish pig iron. The quality of Swedish bar iron was such that it was used in the production of Newcastle steel for cutlery and edge tools. At this time steel was made through a lengthy process of heating iron in the presence of charcoal so that the red hot iron absorbed carbon content. It was discovered that when the iron bars were packed in charcoal in sealed earthenware

Remains of 1750s steel making furnace, near Rowlands Gill, County Durham

containers, these could be then heated by coal fires to make steel. A sword manufacturing industry was established in Shotley Bridge by William and Nicholas Oley using skills imported from Solingen, the main sword making centre in Germany and Thomas Bewick was commissioned to etch designs on many of these swords. This industry continued until the last Shotley Bridge sword maker died in 1896.

Industry goes hammer and tongs with local iron works

It was an ability to smelt iron with coke introduced in 1709 by Abraham Darby, an iron master of Coalbrookdale, that almost certainly saved the English iron industry from extinction. Some years afterwards in 1745, the first blast furnace to use coked coal in Northumbria was installed by Issac Cookson at Whitehill near Chester-le-Street. Two years later in Gateshead, William Hawks, a

working blacksmith, started with a few forges to make ships anchors and chains from disused iron ballast. This business was established as the Gateshead Iron Company and became one of the largest iron concerns in the north. Then great rivalry developed between Crowley's Crew and Hawks Blacks. In time the iron industry was to stimulate local ship building, although ships were still wooden, and those built were usually colliery vessels or sometimes a man of war. The building of railways stimulated the demand for iron bridges and viaducts and encouraged the growth of constructional engineering. One of the first in this market was Hawks, Crawshay and Company (originally established in 1747 as the Gateshead Iron Company), and whose engineering achievements included the construction of the Tyne's High Level Bridge, completed in 1849. With changes in the

Above: *The High Level Bridge, Newcastle, constructed by Hawks, Crawshay & Co., 1849*

Below: *Blacksmiths hammer and tongs, repairing anchor chains*

industry Hawks, Crawshay closed in September 1889 but ensured every creditor was paid in full. The height of iron manufacture around Newcastle was between 1800–42. During this time iron works were opened at Lemington, Walker, Jarrow, and with the most successful Derwent Iron Company being established in 1840. This followed the discovery of iron ore deposits at Consett in 1837. The Derwent Iron Company became the Consett Iron Company Ltd in 1864 and became the largest local steel works and main producer of ships plates. Imports of ore landed at Jarrow provided the bulk of rail traffic between there and Consett with plates for shipyards passing in the other direction.

1804 – Thomas Bewick makes an impression with birds book

Together with coal based industry and a growing population, the advent of publishing was to leave some lasting impressions. In 1712, The Newcastle Courant was the first weekly newspaper to be published north of the Trent. Daily newspapers were introduced some years later, the Newcastle Journal in 1739 and the Chronicle in 1764. Newcastle was to become a centre of the printing trade. John White, son of Royal Printer to William III established his printing business in 1711, publishing sermons, histories and ballads.

Path Head Water Mill, Ryton

When Thomas Saint became a partner in this concern fifty years later, he commissioned Ralph Beilby's engraving business to produce illustrations for books which included fables and educational works for children. It was Beilby's apprentice, Thomas Bewick who used his talented craft to engrave the wooden printing blocks. In 1777, Bewick realised his potential and went into partnership with Beilby to publish a range of books, including A General History of Quadrupeds issued in 1790 with copy written by Beilby and his own illustrations. Bewick's understanding of wildlife, particularly birds and their habitat became the hallmark of his work. In particular, two volumes published in 1797 and 1804, the History of British Birds, and Birds are acknowledged as his masterpieces. Thomas Bewick was described by Ruskin as 'the Burns of painting'.

1808 – The last of the local water wheels given the push by steam power

During the seventeenth century one of the most noticeable features of the landscape around Newcastle was the large number of assorted shaped windmills. These were used mainly for grinding corn but also powered the wheels of numerous industries. The wheels of industry were

soon to turn faster through improvements generated by steam power fuelled by coal. In the iron industry water wheels had been the only power to work blast furnace bellows and great forge hammers. As a result this made production impossible in dry weather spells. Often, metal workers had plots of land to cultivate when through periods of drought the water wheels had ceased. Then in the late seventeenth century there was a development towards a reliable power source when simultaneously, two inventors, Thomas Newcomen and Thomas Savery designed a steam engine. By 1712, Newcomen applied his engine to pumping water and over a period of twenty years its use in coal mines was common place. It was not until 1782 when James Watt invented a rotary steam engine that the final push was given to the power of the water wheel, locally the last of these being at Greenside 1808 and Path Head Mill, Blaydon in 1828. (Locally this was the first mill used to grind corn and with extensive restoration has been re-opened for visitors to see the elaborate gear system working once again). It is probable that the grindstones once used in this mill were produced at Eighton Banks, Windy Nook. The manufacture of grindstones was an industry which had been carried out since the middle ages both at Windy Nook and Heworth. Richard Kell and Co., had their own quarry and had a large trade in exporting grindstones and also pulpstones used in the paper industry. However, the transformation of traditionally powered mills had begun and Watt's rotary engine was now turning the wheels of industry.

1753 – Coal wound to the surface by steam

Once steam engines were utilised to pump water, applications ensued for lifting

coals through the descent of heavier buckets of water, the water being pumped back to the surface. This was a way forward to replace hauling coals to the surface by gin horses. The first of these adaptations was a machine made by Michael Menzis and installed at the Chatershaugh Colliery on the Wear in 1753. The Menzi could lift

1. Grindstones being hewn to size at Richard Kell and Co., Gateshead

2. Steam locomotive working at Hetton Colliery

3. Hartley colliery near Seaton Delaval, also showing a glassworks cone

about 600 pounds weight from a pit 50 fathoms deep in two minutes. Twelve years later Joseph Oxley invented a steam engine to wind coal to the surface. This was installed by Thomas Delaval at his Hartley pit and successfully brought a corf (of over 600 pounds) per minute to the surface. Unfortunately, it had no flywheel and with an irregular action became unreliable to the point that eventually it was reverted for use as a water pumping engine. Mining was to gain greater benefit through improved application of the steam engine. At this time coal mining was concentrated around the Tyne and the Washington area of Wearside. It spread to the Hetton area after 1800 but the South West Durham coalfield was not developed until after 1825. In 1787, the region employed 7,000 pitmen, growing to 10,000 by 1810. Together with coal mining, the carbonisation industry had developed in the late 1700s. There were 81 coke blast furnaces operating in the country by 1790. Even from the early days smoke abatement was sought and coke was the fuel which

enabled the steam locomotive and the railway system to become established. Coke had to be used, as a clause prohibiting the emission of smoke in built up areas was included in most of the Railway Acts. However, with the introduction of an improved type of locomotive fire box in the 1860s, the proportion of coke used fell to approximately one third by 1871.

A century of great expansion in the coal industry

By 1816 the total production of coal in the United Kingdom is estimated to have been about 15 million tons and fifty years on, the combined production of all of the collieries in Northumberland and Durham had exceeded this figure. Thereafter, coal demand increased dramatically and within a hundred years these coalfields were producing over 56 million tons of a United Kingdom total of nearly 290 million tons. Following an initial impetus during the reign of Elizabeth and James I, expansion of industry had never been so great. Although

Finished grindstones ready for transporting at Kenton Quarries, Newcastle

originally coal for domestic use was supplied to the south, it was a demand for industrial use that accelerated the growth of the coalfields. In Northumberland, the Killingworth Pit, where George Stephenson worked, was sunk in 1802, Netherton in 1818 and Bedlington in 1837. However, south of the Tyne expansion of the coalfield was more difficult. Great sections of magnesium limestone covered the coal seams. This limestone formed the coastal cliffs from South Shields, stretching southwards and making the coal deposits less accessible than the shallower seams in west Durham. Coal was first mined at east Durham when the Haswell pit was sunk in 1811 and was followed by several deep pits. During the period 1800–1900 over 200 pits were sunk in County Durham.

Clarence railway carries coal to Tees

In 1824 a bill was introduced into parliament for the formation of a railway to extend from Stockton to the outlying districts. Unfortunately, owing to some informality it was thrown out. In 1828, however, it was reintroduced, passed and given royal assent in 1829. This meant that the proprietors were authorised to form a line of railway including branches from 47–49 miles in length. The main line, from Port Clarence on the Tees, was laid to Heighington with branch lines to Stockton, Coxhoe, Chiltern and Byers Green. The colliery at Byers Green was particularly noted for the quality of its coke manufacture. A facility for coal and coke drops at Clarence on Tees rapidly developed as a result of the new railway.

1822 Hetton has largest colliery railway in the world

In 1821 a new pit was sunk at Hetton, reaching the Hutton seam at 147 fathoms (over 1,000 ft). As well as becoming one the most productive pits it is notable that Hetton

Clarence coal drops on the River Tees

was used by Stephenson in 1822 to build the largest colliery railway in the world. This served as a model for the Stockton and Darlington Railway. During the next twenty years other pits were sunk at Murton, Harton, Thornley, Shotton, Castle Eden, Trimdon, Seaton and Monkwearmouth. Of these, Harton, at South Shields was the deepest pit sunk in 1841 (1,290 feet). However, Monkwearmouth colliery, which had been shipping coal from a depth of 1,590 feet since 1835, became the deepest mine in the country at 1,700 feet in 1846. There were immense difficulties in establishing the workings of these pits. This was due to huge levels of water present at the base of the magnesium limestone which poured into the new pit shafts. At its worst, 9,000 gallons of water per minute poured into the Murton pit shafts. Without the developments to Newcomen and Watt's inventions, mining many of these pits would have been impossible. The expansion of the coalfields increased traffic at the ports and a number of new docks were opened on the Tyne, Wear and Tees from the 1830s.

The development of new ports at Seaham and Hartlepool

In 1820, Lord Londonderry commissioned engineer William Chapman to prepare plans for a new coal port development at Seaham, on the Durham coast. Construction work on the port commenced in 1828. Other plans were also being prepared. Hartlepool was no more than a fishing community which had seen better days; but in 1823 plans were discussed to extend Durham's south eastern waggonways to reach and develop Hartlepool into a coal port. Hartlepool's trade was to be stimulated through Christopher Tennant's plans for a railway link to the port from Stockton and outlined in 1831. Before the construction was complete in 1839, regrettably, Tennant died, and the project was taken over by Ralph Ward Jackson, a Stockton solicitor. New port facilities were completed and the Victoria Dock, Hartlepool was opened by Jackson in 1841. Being linked to the railway network, the port soon became a focal point for local collieries. The new railway transported more coal than any other in the region and Hartlepool became the top

George Stephenson's railway at Hetton Colliery

northern port for shipments. However, Ralph Ward Jackson realised the limitations of The Victoria Dock and in 1844 obtained an act for the formation of Hartlepool West Harbour Dock Company. Once constructed, the new Union Dock was the first part of the development of West Hartlepool. Records show that in 1862, shipments from both docks were more than three times the combined total of Newcastle, North and South Shields, Sunderland, Stockton and Middlesborough. Hartlepool was busier than Liverpool, London and Hull and had become the fourth most industrious port in the country. The newly born West Hartlepool had a population of 28,000 in 1881, whilst the old town had a population of 12,361. Gradually, coal production spread south to Bishop Auckland and Hartlepool, enhancing the region's importance and also giving problems associated with large scale development. As a result, the area became a centre of experiment in mining technique and transport methods.

1816 – The Davy Lamp and Geordie Lamp invented for mining safety

From the early eighteenth century, Tyneside pits were being worked at increased depths, most averaging 33 fathoms with some being worked to double this depth. It was with the advent of deeper mines that ponies or galloways led by small boys were employed in the larger collieries. They had to draw coal sledges along underground railed tracks. By 1765, a colliery at Walker was being worked at a depth of 100 fathoms. Working at these depths air circulation was extremely difficult. Eventually, between the years 1810 and 1813, John Buddle introduced an improved system of double or compound pit ventilation, known as spitting the air. This was used at Percy Main, Wallsend, Heaton and Hebburn until 1880. In 1812, following a mine disaster at Felling where 92 men and boys died through a fire damp or marsh gas explosion, the Sunderland Society for the Prevention of Mining

A fishing community at old Hartlepool

Above: *Miners safety lamps – three Geordies against one Davy (left to right)*

Accidents sought help from Sir Humphry Davy. The result was the invention of the miners' safety lamp. Although George Stephenson designed a safety lamp in 1815 at the same time as Davy, it was the Davy lamp which gained acclaim. An explanation for the nickname Geordie may have derived through the pitmen who used the safety lamp devised by George Stephenson in favour of the Davy lamp. They used Geordie Stephenson's lamp. Use of the miners' safety lamp reduced the dangers of explosion so that deeper pits could be mined. The colliery cage, introduced for the safer movement of miners underground, was first used in 1834 and by 1862 an Act of Parliament made it law for every colliery to have two shafts for safety purposes. During the nineteenth century there were approximately thirty major mining disasters claiming the lives of over 1,500 men and

boys, and many pit ponies. Some of the disasters were caused by gas explosions, but others were the result of collapsing mine shafts.

Agriculture, fishing and associated industries

Despite the influence of coal in the period 1500–1800, the north was heavily dominated by agriculture and associated industries. In medieval time, monasteries controlled and farmed vast areas whilst farming villages practiced an open field system. This usually involved three large arable fields centred around the village. Using crop rotation, each year one field would be left fallow for soil recovery whilst wheat, rye, barley or oats would be grown in the other fields. As servants to the local Lord, bonded men cultivated the land using teams of oxen for ploughing. Pasture land beyond these fields would be used for grazing cattle and woodland provided fuel in the form of charcoal. Village greens may have provided shelter for livestock during border raids. During tudor times lawlessness ruled and many border reiver families raided and thieved from each other. Many northern communities developed into small towns with markets; Hexham was the agricultural market for a large area of Northumberland. With a trade in cattle and grain, the town had been granted the privilege of having a weekly market by Henry III. It possessed guilds of weavers, tanners and shoemakers, skinners, glovers, and hatters. There were also a body of people known as scalerakers who were responsible for keeping the market place clean. One of the scalerakers rang a bell for the opening of the market.

Darlington's growth through wool, leather and milling

Darlington had a wool trade from at least the fourteenth century when John and William Durham exported wool for the King through Hartlepool. The town developed with weaving, leather, tanning and milling industries. Darlington suffered a setback in 1585 when a huge fire destroyed 273 houses and left 800 people homeless. From 1706 the West Yorkshire Pease family developed a wool combing business and established a mill at Darlington in 1752. During 1749, a writer in the Universal Magazine referred to Darlington as "the most noted town in the whole world for the manufacture of linen of the sort called huckaback, so much used for table cloths and napkins". John Kendrew invented and patented new ways of manufacturing flax in 1787, whilst he also designed and produced a spectacle lens making machine. At nearby Barnard Castle, there was a history

of making leather goods and carpets. The town's mills also made shoe laces and rope.

1749 Cullercoats – England's best northern fish market

All along the coast there were fishing harbours. These included Whitby, Hartlepool, North and South Shields, Cullercoats, Blyth, Craster, Seahouses, Holy Island and Berwick. By 1749, Cullercoats was described as the best fish market in the north of England. Cullercoats had also gained a reputation for smuggling. This

Darlington in 1885

1749, Cullercoats, England's best northern fish market

trade had grown to augment legal incomes and in particular through running brandy. Opposite St George's Church at Cullercoats is a headland called George's Point and at its foot there used to be an inlet known to the locals as Smuggler's Cave. This has almost disappeared through coastal erosion but it was put to good use by smugglers who also found St. Mary's Island ideal for their purpose, and had arranged an intricate system of signs and signals amongst themselves. In 1722 Anthony Mitchell, Customs Officer for Cullercoats, was murdered by two villains who used to run brandy.

The growth of the North Shields fishing industry

Despite difficulties caused by the early opposition of Newcastle merchants, the North Shields fishing industry prospered progressively. It was to become the most important centre for the fishing industry between Hull and Aberdeen. In 1832, the

The Union Fish Quay, North Shields

Union Quay, North Shields, was constructed to connect the Low Street with the bridge over the Pow Burn. The industry was to owe its prosperity to natural advantages coupled with local initiative. The natural advantages were the proximity to good fishing grounds, having plentiful coal supplies and a densely populated hinterland to act as a local market. These factors were seconded by the energy of both municipal and private enterprise. The Corporation began to interest itself in the provision of marketing as early as 1866 and progressively developed the facilities for fishermen at the Quay. Before 1870 nearly all the fishing was done in sailing smacks or sailing trawlers. When the weather was calm the smacks were towed by steam tugs to the fishing grounds. Near the surface, herring, mackerel, sprats, pilchards and salmon could be caught in drift nets by drifters and the bottom fish caught by trawlers and line fishing boats. Between May and December, in the herring season, there were many drifters in the North Sea. Herrings generally feed and become active at night so the drifters nets were usually "shot" in the evening, and the boat then drifted at her nets. About dawn the net was hauled in and the drifter returned to port. At North Shields the fish could then be salted and cured, or sold as fresh herrings, or turned into kippers and bloaters. The industry also owed much to the initiative of the Irvin family and the acumen of businessman William Purdy who in 1877 saw the advantages of converting his steam tug, *Messenger*, into a trawler. The importance of this innovation was national rather than local, since, generally adopted, it brought the Icelandic Bear Island grounds within reach of all the fishing ports of the British Isles.

A firm whose female employees were known as angels

Messrs Haggie Brothers. Hemp and wire rope manufacturers. Gateshead.

An enterprise to rise in fortune from the industrious coaly river was rope manufacture. A name remembered for its notorious female employees was R Hood Haggie & Co Ltd. The firm was originally established in 1789 as Haggie Brothers, based at Gateshead. In the early part of the twentieth century the company merged with a Wallsend based manufacturer to become R Hood Haggie & Co. Ltd. In the early days when ropes were made from hemp, the work force was predominantly female. They gained the nickname Haggie's Angels because of new worker initiation ceremonies they instigated and the hard time they gave to any men working around them. These ladies were employed from the age of fourteen, were very poorly paid and often suffered terrible industrial injuries. Whilst at work Haggie's Angels swore, fought and generally struck fear into others' hearts. Haggie's Angels reigned through until the 1950s when industrial diversification and new technology replaced traditional skills.

Left top: *Ropes ready for despatch from Haggie's warehouse*

Left bottom: *Flax bales being unloaded for rope manufacture*

A firm entwined in tradition

At the end of the nineteenth century Haggie's production capacity for wire rope amounted to almost two thousand tons per annum. The factory produced hemp and wire rope of every thickness including manilla rope, both round and flat, white hempen rope, white and tarred spun yarn, galvanised wire rope for ships' rigging, galvanised steel hawsers for the towing and mooring of vessels, improved steel ropes for steam ploughing, wire rope pulleys (flat and round), wire rope springs, best chains specially made for use in collieries, wire

strand for fencing and signal cord, lightening conductors, picture cords, sash lines, and much more. A considerable part of their work was in supplying local ship builders, ship owners, collieries and railway companies. The firm had a reputation for exceptionally fast execution of orders. This was partly due to the large stocks always kept in the warehouse, but mainly to the efficiency of the management and staff. Their efficiency and output made this business the foremost supplier of wire rope in the United Kingdom.

Haggie's industry continues through Bridon International

With an increasing demand for steel cable manufacture, Haggie's firm eventually changed hands and became part of Bridon International of Doncaster whose Tyneside operation at Willington continued into the new millennium. A contract for 80 km of cabling and fittings for the construction and support of the domed roof of the Millennium Experience at Greenwich was completed by Bridon's factories in Doncaster and Willington Quay. At that time the company employed 150 people at Willington Quay, Wallsend and manufactured twenty thousand tons of steel wire rope a year. The main markets were offshore, fishing and mining industries, whilst they exported to USA (Houston, oil industry), South Africa, Russia, Poland, Iceland and Norway.

Coal at a famous battlefield – 19th Century Profile

Written in the style of the time. The Stella Coal Company, Towneley, and Stella and Whitfield Collieries. Offices: Queen Street, Newcastle upon Tyne.

The history of this company is useful due to its early link with the Battle of Newburn in 1640. It may be mentioned that in Queen

Elizabeth's reign the Bishop of Durham made to Her Majesty a grant of an extensive coal working district, comprising Whickham, Winlaton, Ryton and Stella, and that the Queen sub-let all of this to the Stella Coal Company. Previous workings were opened in 1667 to discover numbers of dead bodies which had been thrown into them during the great civil war, the Battle of Newburn having been fought on Stella Haugh which adjoined the colliery. The early coal workings covered about five thousand acres and based around three drawing shafts, the Stargate pit, sunk in 1800, the Emma pit, sunk in 1845 and the Addison pit sunk in 1845 with depths up to eighty three fathoms. The coal seams varied from 2 feet to just over 6 feet thick. In the early days, coals were sent into the London market for domestic fuel under the Whitefield brand, but also had a reputation for glasswork and sugar refining processes. Markets were later developed for other uses, each coal seam differing slightly in character. Gas making, accounted for one tenth of production, with Newcastle and other coastal district gas companies being customers whilst regular shipments went to France, Italy, America, and other countries.

Twelve tons of water for every ton of coal

The Stella Company collieries were remarkable for their complete and efficient equipment. In 1894 the latest one hundred h.p. pumping engine was used to drain water from the Addison pit moving an average of twelve hundred gallons per minute. About eight thousand tons of water were drawn daily, averaging twelve tons of water to each ton of coal. The ventilation of the shafts was accomplished by two Guibal ventilating fans, one sixteen feet in diameter, the other thirty feet in diameter, together replacing a hundred thousand cubic feet of air per minute. The Addison pit was situated on the public railway line to which all coal from the other pits, except that sent to the Stella Staith on the Tyne, was conveyed by means of a three mile private railway line owned by the colliery. The company kept several keels or lighters to transport coals from the Stella Staith to

Colliery locomotive, Wylam

ships and industries down the river. In 1884 the company purchased the Blaydon Main Colliery, with an output of one hundred thousand tons of coal per annum, and having a hundred coke ovens which produced forty thousand tons of coke annually. The Ramsay Condensed Coke brand won a gold, and a bronze medal (at Newcastle, 1887), and in 1888 a silver medal at the Barcelona Exhibition. Its main markets were abroad, with Russia, Spain, Italy, and others who used it for foundry, blast furnaces, and locomotive purposes. This coke was extensively used in blast furnaces producing Bessemer iron in West Cumberland. In total the collieries of the Stella Company had an annual output of 500,000 tons of coal, and 110,000 tons of coke whilst employing more than 1,300 hands of all classes of labour. In July 1893 they opened Clara Vale colliery near Wylam station. After overcoming difficulties with water, they found several seams of coal, potentially yielding 2,000,000 tons per annum for at least fifty years.

Impressions of a growing newpaper – 19th Century Profile

Written in the style of the time.
The Chronicle Newspapers, Westgate Road, Newcastle upon Tyne.

The Newcastle Chronicle was founded in 1764 as a weekly and sold for seven pence halfpenny. It was published by Mr Slack, a printer whose premises were situated close to the old Town Hall on Union Street. After the ownership of the paper passed to the Hodgsons and Lamberts, it was then acquired by Joseph Cowen (junior) who published it from printing works on Grey Street. His association with the publishers began prior to the Chronicle becoming a daily newspaper in May 1858. It was then

that the paper advanced from being produced on an early flat bed printing press to a cylinder machine. This press had a type bed capable of printing some 1,500 copies per hour and was driven by a hydraulic engine built by Armstrong's at Elswick. Soon the demand for the newspaper grew faster than their production capability and the hydraulic engine was replaced by steam power.

New premises and presses to meet demand

From Grey Street the Chronicle moved its operations to St Nicholas' Buildings and in 1863 two (Kircaldy type) four-feeder cylinder presses were installed. To satisfy demand these presses increased the printing capability to 6,000 impressions per hour. Within the next three years the facilities still proved to be too modest and new premises were bought in Westgate Road. The departments within the new buildings which were described at the time as "the grandest home of any provincial newspapers". Overlooking Westgate Road, it had a magnificently decorated advertising office with four beautiful chimney pieces being of artistically chiselled marble. Demand for the newspapers kept increasing and in 1874 a decision was taken to install a much greater capacity printing press. This was ordered from Messrs. R Hoe and Company, London and the Pioneer Press as it became known took four years to build. It was soon supplemented by two more presses, the Tyne and the Wear. The new installation enabled either two full size eight-page papers to be printed at one revolution of the cylinders, or four four-page papers. Both The Daily and Weekly Chronicles were printed on these presses for several years.

Reputation attributed to Joseph Cowen

When the Evening Chronicle was first issued, the advantages of a further press to meet demand was quickly apparent. A press known as the Champion was, therefore, next to be commissioned, and with the addition of Hoe's patent folder, this could produce 44,000 copies of the Evening Chronicle per hour. Together with a much improved printing capability and new linotype machines for the fast setting of type, editorial could be news much earlier than it was possible ever before. The success of the Chronicle newspapers was attributed to Joseph Cowen's great European reputation and his active sympathies with the oppressed in every quarter of the globe. It was through this background and a relentless quest in obtaining exclusive and singularly interesting foreign news that has made the influence of the Chronicle felt far beyond the limits of this Kingdom, and setting the standards for regional newspapers into the twentieth century.

Pioneers of fire bricks and coke ovens – 19th Century Profile

Written in the style of the time. The Swalwell Fire Brick Works and Colliery. Messrs. G. H. Ramsay and Company. Manufacturers of Fire Bricks, Gas Retorts etc. Offices: Mansion House Chambers, Quayside, Newcastle upon Tyne.

One of Newcastle's oldest businesses trading into the twentieth century was Messrs. G H Ramsay and Company, also known as the Swalwell Fire Brick Works and Colliery. This enterprise with 400 employees, the largest of its type in the north, had been founded 1789 by Mr. George Heppel. A policy of progression prevailed and Mr. George Heppel Ramsay, the founder's grandson, later earned himself the unquestionable right to be considered the pioneer of fire brick manufacture in the north. Indeed he introduced fire clay retorts for gas works, to become almost exclusively used by gas corporations on account of their economy. He and the last Marquis of Bute were the first builders of coke ovens, and it was with a pardonable ambition to excel his noble contemporary that when the Marquis

Left: *The Chronicle's linotype composing room*

Right: *Chronicle Buildings, Newcastle*

77

built three ovens at Derwenhaugh at the mouth of the river, Mr. Ramsay at once built six, supplementing even these by another twenty. This was much to the surprise of the people of Tyneside, who appeared apprehensive that the coke trade would be ruined by too great a supply.

Horsing about on business and pleasure

Mr. Ramsey died in 1879; he was a typical Tynesider, and it was related of him that when the occasions of either business or pleasure called him to the Newcastle side of the water, he would frequently swim his horse across the Tyne rather than seek the Wylam or Tyne Bridge (low level) – in those days when there were only two bridges crossing the Tyne. Of course the Tyne at that period was much shallower as dredging operations had not commenced. The great inconvenience Mr. Ramsay thus experienced no doubt quickened his interest in the erection of the Chain Bridge at Scotswood with which he was chiefly instrumental. During these days horses were almost exclusively employed for travelling, and riding was necessarily a general accomplishment. The aristocracy of the district held annual races on the Town Moor at Newcastle, and returning on one occasion from these races a wager was laid amongst several gentlemen of note as to who should first arrive at the Mansion House Hotel, Quayside, where they usually dined. To more surely win the bet Mr. G H Ramsay actually rode his horse down the steep steps from the Castle, called the Long Stairs. Beyond these personal characteristics – born of a love for sport and recreation – Mr. Ramsay was a man of first rate business capacity. He was a Justice of the Peace for the county of Durham and held a wide local influence, carrying into all his dealings the same frankness, geniality and manly vigour from which his business so largely benefited. The Mansion House, Quayside was used as a hotel after the municipal quarters were moved higher into the town in 1837. Later, the building was used as a timber warehouse and was destroyed by fire in 1895.

A railway transports coal and fire clay

By 1895 the Swalwell Colliery had reached a productive capacity of something like 3,000 tons of coal and fire clay per fortnight. A large steel boiler of the Lancashire pattern by the Hebburn Boiler Company had been installed together with new winding engines. The coal seams being mined were the Brockwell and Stone Seams, the merits of which were well known for heating and cooking purposes. The North Eastern Railway Company also used a great deal of round coal for their

The Swalwell Fire Brick Works, Gateshead

locomotives, and the slack was conveyed to the brick works, as was the fire clay, by a short line of railway. A very short walk led to the brick works, alongside of which a siding of the North Eastern Railway Company ran connecting the works with the main mineral line. Here could be seen some of the firm's operations. The Swalwell locomotive tugged its burthen of chaldron waggons, some laden with coals, others with fire clay and, entering the yard, it would halt alongside the main building. Then the false bottoms of the waggons opened, and the coal and fire clay were dropped into their proper places. Over the whole of an extensive area of five acres of works a bogie railway traversed the grounds. The situation of the works being on a peninsula of the Derwent was seen as a particularly advantageous one.

Processing fire clay in the works

Towards the centre of the works was a large mill containing two boilers, a beam engine having a capacity of eighty horse power and two pairs of grindstones with one pug mill to each pair. The grindstones, which were seventy inches in diameter were the largest on the Tyne. During the initial processes the fire clay fed to the grindstones was pulverised, elevated, sieved, or more technically riddled, and then the fine particles passed into the pug mill where the material became plastic with the addition of water. The bogie, placed under the pug mill, was loaded with clay and ran to the first or second drying floors as required. The enormous capacities of these drying floors were such that no less than seven million bricks could be dried in the course of a year. The boy here passed the clay to the moulder who, with a brass mould, rapidly formed the material into the particular shape wanted. Another boy quickly removed the shaped mass to the drying floor. Thirty six hours here rendered the slabs so formed ready for the burning kilns, thirty six in number, all quite new and constructed to the firm's own design.

Consignments for various parts of the world

A tour along the loading quay some 500 yards long gave some idea about the business. First there were orders ready for dispatch to a British cement works and an iron works at Montreal. Next, there was a pile of shaped cupola lumps for a Swedish smelting works. Then there was a varied range of bricks, lumps and quarls or square slabs for blasts, puddling, chemical, smelting, glass and other works, all bearing the famous Ramsay brand. During a survey of the works there were also some hundred casks of ground fire clay for shipment to Calcutta, China and Japan. Indeed, it might be easier to say to which places these productions were not consigned. The excellence of the firm's work received compliments both at home and abroad.

The Mansion House, The Close, Quayside, Newcastle

Chapter Four

A century of great industrial trade expansion

In 1801 the region's population was 645,000 and this was to increase three fold in just over a century. However, the warring years with France which followed brought a mounting debt, heavy taxation, inflation and with wartime shipping demands, a lower volume of international trade and restricted imports. All of this led to a considerable rise in prices, especially in food. In towns beside the rivers, food scarcity was aggravated by press gang activities. With threats of a French invasion first in 1797 and then between 1803 and 1805, volunteer regiments were established throughout the region and particularly in Newcastle, Gateshead, North Shields and Tynemouth. At Newcastle, an armed association or home guard was formed with nearly 1,200 men and about 160 waggons and carts. It was only after the Battle of Trafalgar and the defeat of the French and Spanish fleets in 1805 that peace was to reign for a century. First into the onslaught at Trafalgar was Newcastle born Vice Admiral Collingwood, commanding *HMS Royal Sovereign*. During the battle, on his ship *HMS Victory*, Lord Nelson received a fatal wound from a musket shot. After Nelson's death, Collingwood took command and led the fleet to a final victory. For this, his finest hour, he was awarded a peerage. Above the Black Midden Rocks at Tynemouth and overlooking the Tyne's estuary is Collingwood's monument, erected in honour of his memory. From this time of peace, Northumbria began to shape itself into its height of industrialism. John Scott was appointed Lord Chancellor of England (1801–27) and became Earl of Eldon.

The start of the chemical industry

The chemical industry began to develop in the 1700s. In 1798 William Losh and the Earl of Dundonald took a lease on a rich supply of brine pumped from the Walker pit. Once salt was extracted, it was used in the manufacture of alkali. This became an important industry because alkali, when mixed with fat, could be used to produce soap, and with lime and sand was used to make glass. Alkali production was also linked to cloth manufacture with a demand for dyes and bleach. Losh, Wilson and Bell established an alkali works at Walker on Tyne in 1807. Production of bleaching powder began in 1830. The business was so successful that Losh was soon manufacturing 50% of the country's soda. In 1814 the Le Blanc process was introduced to this country. It made alkali production easier through use of rock salt. Between 1822 and 1834 alkali works were founded at Tyne Dock, Felling Shore and Friars Goose, Gateshead. At Gateshead a business which was established by Charles Attwood in the 1830s was bought in 1840 by Christian Allhusen, and Allhusen's expanded to eventually occupy 137 acres of the South Shore. The firm was incorporated as the Newcastle Chemical Works Company in 1872 and later bought by United Alkali in 1891. There were 1,200 employees in 1889, mainly producing caustic soda. Gradually business declined and after the First World War chemical production transferred to Teesside. In the meantime, generally the chemical industry had expanded, with copperas being produced at Felling, coal tar, sal ammoniac and prussate iron at Heworth, while oil of vitriol was produced at Walker and Bill Quay. The chemical industry grew naturally from the utilisation of the by-products of coal, and many old collieries and iron works were being converted into chemical works. This was

Opposite: *Admiral Lord Collingwood's monument with cannons from HMS Royal Sovereign at Tynemouth*

Above: *Friars Goose Pumping Station*

assisted by the development of the coking industry and new methods of distilling pitch, resin, tar oils and sulphate of ammonia. By 1844, the Alkali Works at Jarrow was producing sulphuric acid, soda crystals, epsom salts and bleaching powder. Although soap making began in 1770, it was not until 1841 when Messrs. John Green and H. Hedley established a soap manufacturing business that their products were developed to eventually bring the company into the Proctor and Gamble empire. From Lemington to North Shields the banks of the Tyne were lined, not only with collieries, but with factories and forges, breweries, glass houses, refineries and shipbuilding yards. There was a pottery at St. Anthony's, coal tar ovens, a coke making plant, a brown paper mill at Scotswood and at Low Elswick, an extensive lead works, lead shot being manufactured in a specially built 175 foot high round tower. In the area of the Close in Newcastle was a sugar refinery, a glass house, a large soap works, and a foundry owned by Issac Cookson.

Roman lead industry origins

At Bill Quay there was a large lead refinery supporting a very active lead

Above: Elswick works shot tower

Below: Lead refining, early 20th Century, Cookson's, Newcastle

mining industry with origins probably from Roman times. For a century onwards from 1750 the lead industry was most prosperous. At peak times there were some 86 local mines supplying lead works on the banks of the Tyne at Elswick, Hebburn, Blaydon, Bill Quay and Byker. The most important lead producing area in the country was Northumbria. The industrial revolution had stimulated the demand for lead with many construction based applications. Mines stretched throughout the north Pennines, covering the Yorkshire Dales, Weardale, Teesdale, the Derwent Valley and south Tynedale. The Tyne based Blackett family, which had extensive interests in coal mining, were also involved in lead mining. Among their lead mines, the Blacketts had operations at Allenheads, near Hexham from 1684, and Burtree Pasture, Weardale and Coalcleugh in the West Allen. The London Lead Company established their northern headquarters at Middleton in Teesdale from 1880. It had already been mining at Weardale in 1692 and Alston from 1696. During the next century the company mined extensively in the north Pennines area from Alston to Teesdale. The London Lead Company was mining lead at Teesdale until it ceased production in 1905. Newcastle was the main centre for exports, although Stockton was used as a local port for lead from the Yorkshire Dales. At Blanchland, Allenheads and Weardale, the lead ore was rich in silver and Allenheads was once the largest silver mine in the world. Blackett's lead works at Blaydon developed a crystalization process for extracting the silver from the lead ore. The mine at Alston was eventually exhausted and closed in 1896. By the 1870s much of the lead ore had been mined.

There was cheaper overseas competition particularly from Spain, resulting in many mine closures, leaving the remaining interests to smaller operators.

A lasting legacy of three centuries in lead

A company which has one of the longest trading histories in Northumbria is Calder Industrial Materials. Originally this Newcastle business was established in 1704 as The Cookson Lead and Antimony Co., Ltd. The founder Isaac Cookson had begun several businesses at this time including an ironworks, colliery, saltpans and a glassworks. His nephew, also called Isaac (a famous Newcastle silversmith), was to take an interest in mining lead ore at Teesdale in 1742. Cookson's business refined lead and antimony (an element used especially in alloys). The smelting and refining works produced metallic antimony and its compounds which gained recognition for being the brand standard in the world antimony markets. By 1851 Cookson's was one of the largest local employers with a workforce of 160 people. It was then that the Cookson family, together with a partner, William Cuthbert, commissioned new lead and chemical manufacturing plants at Hayhole and later at Willington Quay near Wallsend. The firm manufactured lead pigments and oxides, white lead, red lead, orange lead, lead ingots, pipes and sheets. Customers for their products included construction, glass, paint, printing (ink and hot metal type), enamel, rubber, pottery and battery accumulator industries.

The Cookson industry and workers welfare

By 1884 Cookson's Newcastle Works had a 930-foot frontage along the river. In the works there were 33 white lead stacks, two

sets of red lead furnaces, a steam de-silverising process, six hydraulic pipe presses and a 35 horse power beam engine. Within the site complex there were workmen's cottages, and general workers' bath and dining facilities. Also well separated from the works was the Cookson's large Partners' house. This had stables, tennis courts, greenhouses and extensive gardens. The business produced a huge 25% return on capital. In 1892 it provided Clive Cookson with a £42,000 income. In later years, discussions with ten competitive local companies brought about a group amalgamation in 1949 to become Associated Lead Manufacturers. One of the longest established of these companies was Walker, Fishwick and Ward. At their works in Elswick they had constructed a 192-foot shot tower in 1792 and this remained a landmark on the riverside until 1969. In their early days (established 1778), they were commissioned to de-silverise lead from the Cookson mines for use by Cookson's silversmiths. However, from 1949 they were part of Associated Lead Manufacturers,

Sheet lead manufacture at Cookson's, Newcastle

which was to re-brand in 1984 as Cookson Industrial Materials, bringing into use again the famous family name. The last Cookson to have an involvement with the business was Roland Cookson, who actively held an office until he died in 1991, aged 82 years. Change is inevitable and a change of ownership in 1994 brought the business under the Calder Industrial Materials banner. Newcastle became the headquarters of the Calder Group, operating from nine sites across five countries. From the early days many of the markets for its products had also changed. Although the construction industry remained important, there were new customers in automotive, chemical, medical, steel and nuclear industries. Following Calder's investment in the latest technology, production was increased to 15 tons per hour of finished product. At the beginning of a new century, from the headquarters of that original business, Calder remained Europe's largest supplier of lead sheet and speciality fabricated lead products.

A lead refining shop, 1949

Many of the Tyne's chemical industries prospered until the 1860s and 1870s when new processes were developed and there was overseas competition. There was then a shift from the Tyne to the Tees for the chemical industry. In 1859 huge rock salt deposits were found at Middlesbrough, and within a year William James established an alkali works. By 1869, Sammuel Saddler also based a new chemical works at Middlesbrough. It manufactured aniline and alzarine dyes, and distilled tar. The Solvay process, introduced in 1872, made the Teesside alkali production more economic through using electrolysis and local rock salt deposits. In 1874 natural salt deposits discovered by Bell Brothers at Port Clarence were sufficient encouragement for them to eventually establish a works at Haverton Hill, near Billingham, in 1882. Salt production was on a large scale and in 1890 Brunner Mond and Co., of Cheshire, bought Bell Brothers' salt making interests. At Greatham, between Hartlepool and Billingham (which was a famous medieval salt making centre), George Weddell re-established the industry in 1894 with the Greatham Salt and Brine Company. In 1903, the famous salt manufacturer Cerebos bought the Greatham works which by then had become an industry giant. Another kind of chemical process which increased by demand was brewing, and the market for beer also supported glass and bottle manufacturing. At Sunderland, Vaux Breweries was established in 1837, and in 1890, Newcastle Breweries.

John Walker invents matches

A growing population had stimulated the demand for products which would make life easier. One example of this was the invention of the friction match. The inventor was John Walker, born on 29 May 1781 at 104 High Street, Stockton. During his school life he became very knowledgeable about chemistry, botany and mineralogy. After leaving school he chose to become a surgeon and lived in London where he qualified. Eventually, he returned to Stockton and changed his career to work for a firm of druggists. Having worked in Durham and York, he established his own druggist business at 59 High Street, Stockton, in 1819. John Walker believed that he could find a means of igniting a suitable compound by a single friction match. He continued to experiment until 1826 when he produced a flame on three-inch splints dipped in a chemical mixture. John Walker's friction lights were sold for one shilling per hundred including a piece of glass paper (to be used as a friction surface), and his first recorded sale was on 7 April 1827. Within 30 months, sales of friction lights had exceeded 23,000. He had no patent for his invention and died a year after his retirement in 1859. John Walker was buried near his home at Norton Church.

Iron industry switches to the Tees

With the gathering momentum of the railway network and the beginning of a swing in the shipbuilding industry away from wooden vessels, locally produced iron was in demand. By 1850, there began a pronounced shift of the iron industry to the Tees area. There were already 38 blast furnaces in existence in Northumberland and Durham, of which more than one third were situated at the Consett works of the Derwent Iron Company. The switch was triggered in 1850 when the company Bolckow, Vaughan and Co., began mining

the richest iron deposit in the United Kingdom at Eston, in Cleveland. The established iron manufacturing centres around the Tyne and Northumberland found it increasingly difficult to compete with the new centres at Witton Park near Stockton, Consett, Darlington and Middlesbrough. There had been no smelting in Cleveland before 1826, but within fifty years there were 139 furnaces producing twenty per cent of the United Kingdom's pig iron. Many smaller iron producers in Northumberland and Durham for a time bought Cleveland ores to replace worked out local supplies. Eventually the older Tyneside iron works centred at Bedlington, Swalwell, Winlaton and Wylam ceased production in turn. The longest survivors were furnaces at Beamish, Gateshead and the Walker ironworks of Bell Brothers (established in the early 1830s). Teesside had immense advantages over all other regional iron producing centres.

Dramatic growth of Middlesbrough

Middlesborough had made a remarkable transformation from a hamlet, consisting of a few houses in 1830, to a small town with a population of 7,631 by 1851, 18,892 by 1861 and 39,563 by 1871. Middlesbrough's

Middlesbrough in the late 19th Century

Coal drops on the Tees at Middlesbrough

growth began in 1828 when Joseph Pease and Partners bought the hamlet's farmland to develop it into a town and coal port. Initially, the impetus came with the extension of the railway from Stockton in 1830, and the construction of a new port and staiths for coal shipments. It took a few years for Middlesbrough to become established as a trading centre, although a pottery was established there in 1831. At this time the population was 154, whilst neighbouring Stockton had a population of 7,000. The town's development was boosted by the construction of Middlesbrough dock, which was completed in 1842. It covered an area of 9 acres and had ten staiths. Although it shipped 151,000 tons of coal during its first year of operations, as the decade progressed, iron replaced coal as the main export. The railway link with the Durham coalfield and facilities for importing ore or pig iron made Middlesborough an ideal centre for industrial development. In 1840, John Vaughan, an iron works manager at Walker, near Newcastle, and Henry Bolckow, a German accountant who was living in Newcastle, became business partners. Henry Bolckow had retired from a partnership with Christian Allhusen and Company where he made a fortune of about £50,000. John Vaughan was the son of a welsh ironworker and understood about

the production of iron. They listened to Joseph Pease's advice about setting up a business in Middlesbrough. Within a year of purchasing land from Joseph Pease, their iron rolling mills and puddling furnaces were in production at Middlesbrough. Other new iron works were founded both at Hartlepool and Thornaby whilst in 1842, Losh, Wilson and Bell erected blast Furnaces at Walker, and The Weardale Iron Company was also established.

Teesside makes tracks and founds locomotive works

A firm in Middlesbrough, The Tees Engine Works, was purchased in 1844 by Isaac Wilson and Edgar Gilkes. They changed their operations so that the Gilkes and Wilson Works became well known for building iron railways. Also in the same year Robert Stephenson constructed an iron bridge over the Tees to replace the one originally used by the Stockton and Darlington Railway. Then, in 1845, a locomotive works was founded by Timothy Hackworth at Shildon, the place where Locomotion Number One began its historic journey to Darlington and Stockton in 1825. With a good supply of coking coal, Whitton Park, near Stockton, was Vaughan and Bolckow's next choice of location for blast furnaces. By 1846 the furnaces were in production using ironstone from Whitby.

The pig iron they manufactured was then dispatched to be processed in Middlesbrough's forges, foundries and rolling mills. From 1847 the North East production of iron expanded from 20,000 tons to 2,400,000 tons in 1880.

Rich iron ore seams found in the Eston Hills

The iron ore used in North East blast furnaces had been partially supplied from Scotland and supplemented by Whitby stone. This was found along the Whitby shoreline in a band 4.5 feet thick and, although not popular with ironmasters, other local sources were scarce. However, in 1850 when large blocks of rock had fallen from the cliffs at Skinningrove in Cleveland, they were discovered to be ironstone from a 14–15 foot thick bed which had a 31% iron content. The same seam, richer than the Whitby stone, stretched inland to the Eston Hills overlooking the flat shorelands of the Tees estuary. Cleveland's newly found iron ore deposits now made the industry self sufficient. By the end of 1850, the Eston Mine had produced over 4,000 tons of ore. Within four years the mines in the Cleveland district were dramatically increasing their output. In 1854, they produced 650,000 tons, in 1855 this rose to 970,300 tons, to an amazing 1,197,517 tons in 1856. Within a year of opening the Eston Mine the first blast furnace was blown in, beginning production at Middlesborough. Both John Vaughan and Henry Bolckow had quickly become highly prominent personalities in the Teesside community and in 1854 Henry Bolckow became the first mayor of Middlesbrough. By 1859 the number of blast furnaces operating in Middlesbrough, Eston, Cargo Fleet and Port Clarence had increased to thirty. As a general rule, it was calculated that each furnace would require a total of

over 160 ironstone miners, coalminers, cokemen, limestone quarrymen and labourers to prepare the raw materials, then at least another 50 men to look after the iron in production.

Clay Lane Ironworks, Middlesbrough, 1884

Bessemer steel brings set backs to Middlesbrough

The North East was not the only centre for iron manufacture, although Teesside was fast becoming a major producer. By this time practically all London's water piping was made of Teesside cast iron. However, in 1856, the Bessemer steel making process was developed and this became a setback for Middlesbrough. (Rather exceptionally in the 1860s Bessemer steel was being made at the Tudhoe works of the Weardale Company). Locally mined iron ore was believed to be unsuitable due to its phosphoric content and the demand for steel was fulfiled by Sheffield which dominated the market for a time. The Malleable Iron Works of South Durham Steel and Iron Company was opened in 1860 and the number of blast furnaces in Teesside had now reached a total of thirty two.

The original hour bell, Big Ben itself, was cast on 6 August 1856 at Norton, near Stockton-on-Tees. A pair of furnaces each able to take ten tons of metal had been specially prepared. Pouring in the metal took an hour, and fusing it another two and a half hours. The sixteen ton bell was sent by rail to West Hartlepool and then by schooner, which it badly damaged when it dropped too suddenly on the deck. Once it arrived in the Port of London, it was pulled across Westminster Bridge to its destination, on a truck drawn by sixteen white horses. Such was the attraction that the crowd was similar to those seen during a public execution.

From iron to major steel production

Between 1855–75, the Teesside ironmasters dominated the British industry in production, technology and organisation. Cleveland ore had risen to provide approximately 40 per cent of national output. By this time almost a hundred blast furnaces existed in Middlesbrough. There were several leading firms. One of these based on the north bank of the Tees was Bell Brothers at Port Clarence. Bolckow and Vaughan had established a Bessemer steel plant at Eston (to compete with Sheffield steel), using high grade iron ore from Cumberland and Lancashire and imports from Spain. Also, Arthur Dorman and Albert de Lande Long founded an ironworks in 1875 which was to take a major role in Middlesbrough's steel making industry. (Dorman, Long and Co., was to become famous for its structural steel construction work). Increasingly from the 1870s, steel superseded iron, with much of the output supplying local shipbuilding and heavy engineering industries. New steel making methods were introduced in 1879 using locally mined Cleveland ore. This again gave a great boost to Middlesbrough's industry. Following initial difficulties, the Thomas Gilchrist process of steel making from phosphoric ores was successfully developed during the 1880s. The early experiments were conducted at the Bolckow Vaughan works by two cousins, Sidney Gilchrist Thomas, and Percy Carlyle Gilchrist. Together these men were responsible for the breakthrough. Until the end of the century the steel industry grew rapidly using the acid and basic Bessemer processes and the open-hearth method. Local shipbuilders took longer to change from iron to Bessemer steel materials and were persuaded only reluctantly to use basic Bessemer steel produced from Cleveland ores. Large imports of Spanish hematite made acid Bessemer steel as cheap as basic steel from local ore.

Demand for blast furnace coke

As a result of the increase in Tees produced iron and steel, there was an equal demand for coking coal from the Durham mines. Economies of scale were sought and the larger iron and steel works soon acquired their own collieries. By 1911, Pease and Partners of Darlington owned eleven and Bolckow, Vaughan and Co., a staggering sixteen collieries. From the 1870s coke

The Spawood Iron Mines, Cleveland, owned by Dorman Long & Co Ltd

producing beehive ovens were installed at many collieries in the Northumberland and Durham coalfields. By 1877, there were 14,000 beehive ovens in Durham producing more than 4 million tons of coke annually. The coalfields of Durham also saw further expansion as gas lighting became a universal standard for streets and industry. However, the early beehive ovens were not designed to collect gases or other valuable by-products. The first recovery ovens installed in the UK were built at Crook, County Durham in 1882 and remained in operation until 1953.

Milling stands the test of time

The concentration of Tyneside's main industries, coal, shipbuilding and engineering led to the decline of many older established manufacturing companies. Those firms which survived into the twentieth century had considerably diminished in number. Subsidiary industries to shipbuilding, such as rope manufacturing continued. Firebricks were made at Blaydon and Scotswood, whilst grindstones from Ayton Banks, Gateshead Fell, Windy Nook and Kenton still continued to be exported. However, glass, pottery, alkali and wrought iron production had ceased almost entirely. In other trades there was an immense increase in Baltic timber imports required for pit props, railway sleepers and shipbuilding. Growth in the population also brought greater demands on agriculture and fisheries resulting in a greater dependence on foreign food imports. On a local basis, important fish supplies were provided through the ports of North Shields and Blyth, whilst new found steam power aided local corn mills to increase grain output. One of the steam corn mills which replaced the early wind powered mills was run by John

Davidson and Sons, whose Phoenix Mill was based near the Mansion House in the Close, Newcastle. This mill found its name by being a replacement to an earlier Davidson mill which was destroyed in Gateshead during a great fire in 1854. The Co-operative Wholesale Society built a large scale mill at Dunston on the opposite bank of the Tyne in 1891, known as the Phoenix Mill and in 1896 it was taken over by Spillers Ltd., who refurbished it with the latest machinery. Over a hundred years later in 1998 another Spillers flour mill formerly owned by the CWS on the Quayside changed hands when Dalgety sold its flour milling division and food ingredients business to the Irish based Kerry Group after a £335 million deal. In 1998 the Spillers Milling Tyne Mill in Lawrence Road, Newcastle had 80 employees.

Establishing trade union movements

As industry had grown with the expansion of the coalfields and shipbuilding, there was a great contrast between the wealthy coal lords and

The Jubilee of Bolckow Vaughan & Co Ltd., 1891

CWS Flour Mills, Dunston-on-Tyne

shipbuilding magnates and the lifestyles of the common workers. A Combination Act did not allow the establishment of trade unions. However, they were determined and courageous in their efforts to provide for those who were sick or with hardship. Even before the repeal of the Combination Laws in 1832, the shipwrights organised hardship assistance in the form of sick and travelling relief. The boiler makers formed a union in 1832 which gradually grew to appoint paid officials (in 1875), when local branches became very strong. The Amalgamated Society of Engineers was founded as a national union in 1851 and although it became powerful, its influence on Tyneside was not so great.

Miners Union movement gains momentum

Coal miners had difficulty in establishing unions, mainly through failure of their action at the start. In 1830, under the guidance of a mining leader Thomas Hepburn, the region's coal miners established a union. The following year they successfully negotiated a ten per cent increase in wages and a reduction in working hours for boys. The Northumberland and Durham miners did

strike shortly afterwards in 1832 but it was not until the 1840s that they gained strength on a national basis. Then, from 1843, they became part of the Miners Association of Great Britain and Ireland, with headquarters at Newcastle. By 1848 the union had been weakened through successive depressions. The Durham Miners Union was established in 1869, after a meeting of mine leaders at the Market Hotel, Durham. Their annual gala was to become a major regional event, the first of these being held at Durham's Wharton Park in 1871. The venue was changed to the racecourse in 1873. The gala became so successful that in 1875 it was claimed that the local railways could not cope with the huge number of passengers travelling to the event. As a result, or for inferred political reasons, the LNER railway temporarily withdrew its local services. At the beginning of the twentieth century 100,000 coal miners were working in the Durham coalfields, and in Northumberland a further 37,000 miners were employed. Coal mining reached a peak in Durham by 1923 when 170,000 miners were employed. More than a quarter of Tyneside's employment had become involved in coal mining, and with this came exposure to the continual risk of personal injury and death. Their strengths were consolidated when they joined the national association, the Miners' Federation of Great Britain. From this, the National Union of Mineworkers developed to become a very powerful force in the North East until the closure of many of the mines in the 1970s and 80s, over 100 years later. The turning point for the industry was in the mid 1920s, when two thirds of the region's output was being exported to alternative markets abroad.

In an effort to combat poverty caused by low wages, workmen pooled their resources to own their own bakeries and shops where goods would be reasonably priced. This was known as the co-operative movement, which began in Lancashire in 1844, with the Rochdale Equitable Pioneers' Society. Initially stores were opened during evenings to suit the times of committee members who acted as shopkeepers, selling butter, sugar, flour, oatmeal and a few candles. In Newcastle, Joseph Cowen took interest in the co-operative concept and by 1858 opened a society at Blaydon. The principle of returning a dividend to its members as an incentive for purchasers proved to be highly successful. Society stores were soon opening in all of the main towns under the organisation of the Co-operative Wholesale Society. At the end of the 1800s factories were established where foodstuffs and raw materials were imported and manufactured. At Dunston the C.W.S.

manufactured soap. It also had large flour mills where grain from ships was taken in an endless belt to storage bins ready to be milled into flour. Near Gateshead, Pelaw was almost entirely the creation of the C.W.S. By the 1930s most of its 3,500 inhabitants were employed in their Pelaw factories. Drugs, polishes, clothing and furniture were made, and books printed and bound. In Newcastle C.W.S. had building and engineering works, leather goods and picture framing concerns. Lard was refined at West Hartlepool, and at Birtley milk churns and tins for polish were produced. C.W.S. banks also took their place on the high street whilst members of Co-operative Insurance Societies insured their lives, houses and motor cars. By 1998 the North East Co-op was quoted as one of Northumbria's largest businesses with a turnover of £452 million and employing a workforce of nearly 6,000 people. Their interests are now mainly in convenience stores, although their funeral homes were arranging some 12,000 funerals in a year.

CWS Birtley Tin Plate Works

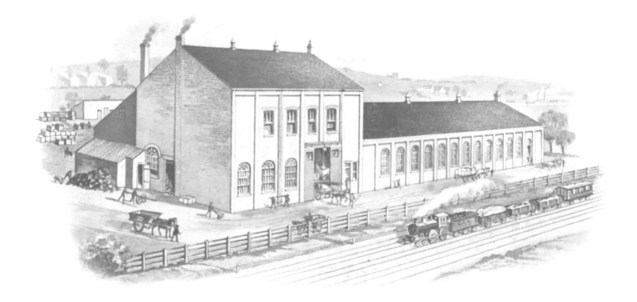

C. T. MALING & SONS LTD.

FORD POTTERY · NEWCASTLE UPON TYNE 6

Potters since 1762

SPRINGTIME
A design of charm
and colour

An advertisement showing Maling's summer design tableware, 1952

Over two centuries in the pottery business – a profile based on a works tour in 1894

Written in the style of the time. Messrs. C T Maling and Sons, Earthenware Manufacturers, Ford Potteries, Newcastle upon Tyne.

The business of Messrs. C T Maling and Sons, at the Ford Potteries, Newcastle, owed its origin to Christopher Thompson Maling, who with his brother, John Maling, commenced manufacture of earthenware at Hylton, near Sunderland, in 1762. Fifty five years later, Mr. Robert Maling, having succeeded to the proprietorship, removed the works to the Ouseburn Bridge Pottery. In 1853 he was succeeded by his son, Christopher Thompson Maling, who built the works known as the Old Ford Pottery in 1859 and in 1878 the New Ford Pottery. By 1891 he took into partnership his four sons, and thus constituting the firm of C T Maling and Sons. At the Old Ford Pottery, the business was centred on machine production of jelly pots or jam jars for their main customer Keiller & Sons of Dundee.

However, Christopher Thompson Maling's vision also led to the domination of a market in affordable kitchen and tableware. Maling had invested the huge sum, at the time, of £100,000 in the construction of the New Ford Pottery at Walker which doubled their product output. There were over a million and a half finished pieces of pottery leaving their new Walker based production lines every month. Such was their efficiency that everything was handled on site with raw clay being unloaded at the factory's own huge railway junction, second only in the country to that at Newcastle Central Station.

Production extended from jars and pots

For many years Messrs. Maling had devoted themselves almost exclusively to manufacturing jars and pots for wholesale confectioners, extract of meat makers and druggists. In the 1880s they diversified production to general earthenware, sanitary ware, electricians' porous goods, dinner, tea, and toilet ware in white and ivory bodies, and enamelled decorative ware in gold and colours. They much advanced the beauty, quality, and finish of this ware that their name was amongst the first in their trade. With variety they had far reaching markets, both home and abroad, and contracting largely with H.M. Government and public bodies, sanitary authorities, hospitals, etc. During a visit there could be seen a stack of preserve jars, thirty yards long by sixteen yards wide, and eighteen jars deep, which must have been over a million jars, all standard, and for the use of a jam manufacturer in Dundee. This was only one stack out of many, as there were several others nearly as large of different kinds of pots.

By 1894, the pottery buildings exhibited proportions of unusual magnitude, covering five acres of ground, and being supplemented by another ten acres of spare land, partly utilised by the storage of straw, flints, crate rods, and gardens for the workmen. The whole works were arranged so that each successive stage connected. The entrance frontage had no fewer than 280 windows. To the rear of the two principal wings, were the glost and biscuit kilns or ovens, between which was the dipping or glazing house. At the rear there was three-quarters of a mile of railway sidings, and a private railway station where the ware was packed into trucks. They packed a large quantity of their wares and confectioners' jars loose in trucks, and as many as eighteen trucks were packed and sent off in a single day, each containing over 900 dozen of pots. At the high end of the yard, in a large warehouse, capable of containing over 1,500 tons, the ground flint not used for making into clay, was dried and stored. The flint here was ground as fine as the finest flour, almost as white as snow. Messrs. Maling were renowned for this material, and supplied it to some of the leading houses in England and Scotland, and also some of the main earthenware and china makers on the continent. The facilities included flint kilns and grinding mills, engine and boiler houses, subsidiary sheds and buildings, offices, warehouses, and employees' kitchens and dining rooms.

Flint mill one of the largest in the UK

Over a thousand hands were employed at the two works in 1894, and two hundred tons of clay converted weekly into ware, and the stock of flints on hand in the yards generally averaged six thousand tons. All the flints used at the Ford Potteries were imported direct from France, whilst the Kaolin or China clay, Cornwall stone, and ball clay came from some of the most noted Devonshire and Cornish mines. Large quantities of Devonshire and Welsh chert stone were used for grinding purposes. Further up the yard towards the flint mill there were a long range of coal depots, a range of boilers, and an engine which drove the flint mill, worked by Corliss valves, and developing over 300 horse power. The flint mill was one of the largest in the kingdom, capable of turning out 150 tons of ground material per week. The flints, having been

Below: *A works department at Maling's Old Ford Pottery, Ouseburn*

Bottom: *An aerial view of Maling's New Ford Pottery, Walker*

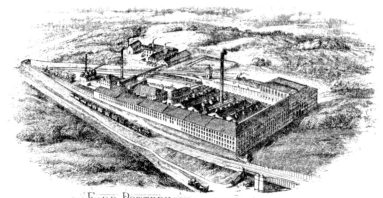

FORD POTTERY NEWCASTLE ON TYNE

thoroughly washed with the aid of swinging frames and cold water, were passed into the flint kilns – four in number, and each capable of calcining forty tons at a time. Within forty eight hours the flints would turn from a dark brown to a snowy whiteness, and having been carefully picked and riddled, they were ready for the crushing mills, where the rough fragments underwent rapid pulverisation. The product, afterwards was ground in large tubs, with water, to the consistency of thick cream, to become known as slop.

A variety of appealing designs

The firm manufactured every kind of pottery, from the plainest to the most artistic descriptions – in which were included their celebrated Jesmond blue, and Indian red or Armstrong wares. Great attention was also given to the design of dinner, tea, dessert and toilet services; many of the patterns in ivory and gold, enamel bronze and relief, being regarded as standard. Specialised production included photographic, chemical and electrical ware; white earthenware; hospital and sanitary fittings; and goods intended expressly for the use

and comfort of invalids. Continual additions were regularly made to an almost illimitable series of useful receptacles the firm introduced, and without equal in the country.

The largest pottery in the world

Export and home sales of Maling pottery remained strong until the 1920s and the time of the Wall Street Crash which virtually finished any American trade. Maling then formed a partnership with Ringtons, the local tea company, to supply the blue and white tea caddies which quickly became collectors pieces. At Maling's peak, employing two thousand people it was the largest pottery business in the world, producing universally renowned designs from the 15 acre Walker works site. This factory produced some of the finest decorative pottery in the world from a succession of talented designers. These included Charles Miguet (known as Mr Miggy) in the 1880s, followed by Harry Clifford Toft, Lucien Boullemier and later his son. Maling was famous for its blue and white ware and from the 1920s saw the arrival of the highly valued lustreware

Left: *Maling's potters working on belt driven wheels*

Right: *Tableware painters in the Decorating Department*

pieces with their luminescent glaze. These bowls, vases and tableware found a place in fashion conscious homes for three decades. By the early fifties the company was owned by the furniture removal company Hoults. After the death of Managing Director Fred Hoult, business declined along with investment and eventually the business closed in June 1963.

The early years of a giant in engineering

19th Century Profile. W. G. Armstrong & Co. Engineers, Elswick, Newcastle upon Tyne.

People are apt to forget the difficulties and anxieties which attend the earliest efforts of the pioneers, and which increase as business increases – all the financial requirements, the search for orders, the organisation to be perfected, the policy to be pursued. The late Lord Armstrong in his old age, recalled an occasion when he paced up and down Grey Street, turning over in his mind how he could find more capital to keep his engine works afloat. He finally had to cease walking the pavement, because the soles of his boots became so hot that it was painful to continue his promenade. He established W G Armstrong and Company early in 1847 and having already patented designs for "apparatus for lifting, lowering and hauling", started manufacturing hydraulic cranes. It was the Crimean War in 1854 which highlighted the need for improved artillery, which hadn't progressed since the times of Napoleon. Soon he had developed the Number One Gun with a breech-loading mechanism and a rifled barrel; the steel being supplied from Sheffield by two brothers called Vickers. The gun was competitively tested by the war office and was selected against a rival from Joseph Whitworth of Manchester. Armstrong presented his patents for the gun

to the government and for his patriotic generosity received a knighthood which by the end of the century was elevated to peerage. In 1876, already with world fame, W G Armstrong was exporting the largest guns ever produced, of some 17.7 ins. calibre and 100 tons. Thirty of these were unloaded at their destination in Italy by a 180 ton hydraulic crane, also the largest in the world, and manufactured by Armstrong's great works. They also developed interests in shipbuilding of which a separate account is given.

Above: *Span of Soan Bridge, Elswick Works, 1857*

Below: *W G Armstong & Co., Elswick Works, 1860*

A good location with over 5 acres

The founders of the business were William George Armstrong, former Lord Mayor Addison Potter, Armorer Donkin, George Cruddas and Richard Lambert. When the owners looked for land to house the machine shops, they bought five and a half acres from the Elswick Estate which at that time had been owned by the Hodgson family since 1720. The Estate had been developed by Hodgson's son who succeeded him, took the name of Hinde, and became John Hodgson Hinde. He was an active and energetic man who represented Newcastle in Parliament for some years. We owe him that picturesque thoroughfare which is so familiar to us, the Scotswood Road. It bisected his estate and

ended in what was called an elegant suspension bridge opened on 12 April 1831. The Newcastle and Carlisle Railway opened a branch line from Blaydon to Newcastle in 1839, crossing to the north bank of the river and traversing the Elswick Estate. Therefore, the site offered conspicuous advantages with access both by rail and river.

Armstong had a bed in his office

The first machinery purchased included machines from Smith, Beacock and Tannett., Buckton & Co., Joseph and James Fox., Lawson & Sons., Andrew Shanks., and so on. There was a single large lathe from Whitworth & Co., which at the end of the century remained in the machine shop where it was installed fifty years earlier. A lathe by Smith, Beacock and Tannett was used to turn the barrel of the first Armstrong gun. Altogether, for the new machine shop fifty machines of various kinds were housed, though additions were soon made. There were three buildings divided by a line of rails, which started at the west and joined the main line. On the north side of this were two buildings, the smithy and the machine shop, with boilers in between. On the south, and under one roof, were the joiners shop, the pattern shop and an erecting shop. The offices were situated in a small two storey building. On the ground floor,

Above: *Machine shop No 1 with Whitworth lathe installed 1847*

Right: *The Flying Dutchman built at Elswick in 1848*

George Cruddas presided over the accounts office, and on the upper floor were the offices of W G Armstrong, and George Hutchinson (head of the drawing office and assistant manager) with the drawing office. In those heroic days the drawing office started work at six o'clock, and Mr Armstrong had a bed in his office, where he frequently spent the night.

Two years profits lost on Flying Dutchman

In the beginning, it was the intention of the business to develop in the manufacture of hydraulic equipment and general engineering. With Mr Armstrong's inventiveness (deriving from his first hydraulic crane patents), the new locomotive scene was attractive to him. Soon he had a novel design for a locomotive called the Flying Dutchman, but it did not fly very far or for very long. The intention was to gain 40% more steam power by exhausting into a condenser, an ingenious idea but creating a constant cold water supply for condensing proved insurmountable. Building the locomotive, with all of its experimentation, cost the company the first two years' trading profits and represented that rare phenomenon, a failure on the part of Mr Armstrong. In the early 1860s the Elswick works did produce some locomotives but this was only when the cessation of War Office orders made the company very slack. These were regular design locomotives but the results of the order bore a great resemblance to the earlier efforts and they became the last of the line.

John Thorburn, the original Hydraulic Jack

Initially business came in for hydraulic cranes and Lord Armstrong used to credit Mr Jesse Hartley, the engineer at Albert

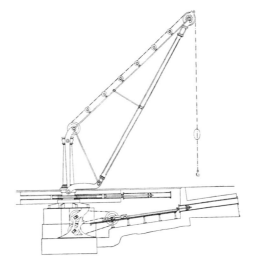

The No. 1 Crane erected on Newcastle Quay, 1846

Docks, Liverpool for being the earliest patron. A demonstration of a hydraulic crane was organised for Mr Hartley on the Quay at Newcastle. The crane was in the charge of John Thorburn, known to his friends as Hydraulic Jack, and who was remarkably expert at manipulating the crane. He gave for the benefit of the famous engineer an extraordinary display of its powers. Jesse Hartley was so bewildered and taken aback, that he could hardly employ the picturesque language which seems to have usually seasoned his conversation. He briefly introduced himself to the inventor, and declared the crane was just the thing for his docks. There were other orders from docks but for the first few years the main business came from a growing number of small railway companies. One leading expert of the day, Isambard Brunel, the celebrated engineer of the Great Western Railway, gave the company many orders. However, there were also orders for hydraulic machinery, one of which included a hydraulic system for working the gates for Great Grimsby Docks, hydraulic machinery for the lead mines at Allenheads and some coal mines.

In 1850, a hydraulic machine was ordered by Newcastle Chronicle to power the printing press.

Artillery testing range was back garden

Then business was overtaken by events which were to reshape production at the Elswick Works, namely the Crimean War in 1854. At an early stage the works were entrusted with an order for submarine mines, intended to blow up Russian ships which had been sunk in the entrance of Sebastapol Harbour. These infernal machines were never used for their original purpose, but the fuses of one or two of them were exploded by Mr Armstrong in his garden at Jesmond for the amusement of the employees whom he invited to witness the spectacle. In a characteristic manner Mr Armstrong turned his attention to the task of constructing field guns which would be more powerful and easier to handle than those already in service. In December that year he had a meeting at the War Office with the Duke of Newcastle, the Secretary of State for War. He received authority to make a number of guns and there followed three years of development until his field guns were tried and it was pronounced that the Armstrong system of Artillery was superior on every possible count. Mr Armstrong was investigating entirely new problems with his usual thoroughness and enthusiasm. He tested his first gun from his garden at his home in Jesmond, firing towards the adjacent hillside in the dene. There was no science of artillery or knowledge about the pressures that metals would stand, and for his perilous pioneering courage he deserves great credit. Certainly there were many exciting adventures during these firing trials, as well as the narrow escapes from blowing himself to pieces. Pictured is a 5 pounder gun designed for use with a concussion fuse and lead coated projectile. The guns for which he gained the first orders were 18 and 12 pounders. Once successful, Mr Armstrong decided to make over his patents to the nation, and also entered the service of the Government as Engineer of Rifled Ordnance, with the duty of superintending the manufacture of his guns. His appointment was dated 22 February 1859, and at the same time he was knighted. In January 1859, a separate company was formed, under the title of the Elswick Ordnance Company with three partners, George Cruddas, Richard Lambert and George Rendel.

Above: Armstrong Whitworth's locomotives were built and shipped worldwide, 1920s

Below: 5-pounder Armstrong field gun, 1855

To make the new Ordnance Works, additional land was purchased and several new buildings were built. Within four years there were about 15 shops housing vast numbers of new machinery. The works manager was George Rendel and in August 1860, Sir William Armstrong appointed the position of joint manager to Captain Noble, a young artillery officer already distinguished for his scientific attainments. He was responsible for developments in the most powerful types of gun and became a top authority in the science of gunnery. In the first three years business was worth £1.06 million in Government orders but during 1862 the Secretary of State wrote detailing that he would be placing no new orders with Elswick. Under the agreement, Elswick could not accept other ordnance business and although there was some compensation (£65,000), Sir William found his position with the Government unendurable and resigned. An amalgamation of The Ordnance Company and the Engine Works then followed to form Sir W G Armstrong & Company in 1864. Between 1864–78 Government business only totalled about £60,000.

In 60 years there were 25,300 employees

A resumé of these facts highlights business growth from the beginning to a point at the turn of the century. In January 1848 owning five and a half acres, the company had 20–30 employees with about three orders in hand and capital of about £40,000. By the end of that year there were 180 employees and the wage bill was £8,661. Sixty years later owning 312 acres, the company averaged some 25,300 employees with a wage bill of £1,672,000. At

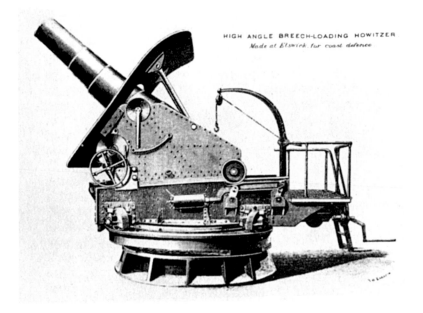

HIGH ANGLE BREECH-LOADING HOWITZER
Made at Elswick for coast defence

the same time for one year, in energy and resource terms, the business consumed 124,000 tons of coal, 225 million cubic feet of gas, 9 million units of electricity and 425 millions of gallons of water. Also between £30–£40,000 was payment on profits both to the Imperial and Local Revenue, and about £13,000 in rates.

1917 – First hundred Mark IV tanks ordered

Although the bulk of their work was in the production of armaments and ship building, having merged with their Manchester rival in 1896 to form Armstrong Whitworth, locomotives, motor vehicles and aeroplanes were also manufactured in Newcastle. By 1916, Armstrong Whitworth had developed six pounder guns for the world's first tanks. These were adopted by the British Army to give an advantage on the Western Europe front during the First World War. The following year, tank manufacture on the Tyne was established with its first order for over a hundred Mark IV tanks. By 1919 Armstrong Whitworth

A coastal defence howitzer gun

had manufactured 13,000 guns and a collective total of 54 million shells, fuses and cartridge cases. In addition the company had built forty seven warships, twenty two merchant ships and had provided armament to 583 vessels. Vickers of Sheffield had also expanded with similar interests in tank building and gun manufacture, particularly the famous Vickers machine gun. The defence interests of the companies were brought together in 1927 as Vickers-Armstrong.

Vickers-Armstrong works on a huge re-armament programme

The new combined business was greatly involved in the re-armament programme prior to the Second World War. Wartime naval production comprised 225 naval ships, including 8 aircraft carriers, 1 battleship, 1 monitor ship, 36 destroyers, 123 submarines and 51 assault craft. For the Royal Airforce, the company manufactured 21,676 Spitfire and Seafire fighters and 11,461 Wellington bombers. The army was equipped almost completely by Vickers-Armstrong weapons. Its automatic infantry weapons were the Vickers and Lewis machine guns. The main army tank was the Vickers Medium. The new tanks of the re-armament period were the Vickers Light Tanks, the Vickers A9 and A10 Cruiser tanks and the Vickers

Valentine Infantry Tank. After the outbreak of war the company produced about 20,000 machine and gas operated guns and two-thirds of the national output of field artillery. By 1940, Vickers-Armstrong was producing a range of tracked armoured vehicles. These included Light Tank Mark VI and VII, Cruiser Mark 2(A10), Infantry Tank Mark I (Matilda I) and Mark III (Valentine). The years following the war, the main areas of manufacture were in aircraft, steel, shipbuilding and general engineering. The first three of these business interests were subsequently nationalised. Then, with a change of name to Vickers Defence Systems, the Royal Ordnance fighting vehicle factory at Leeds was acquired in 1986. With manufacturing now centred on fighting vehicles and main battle tanks, the Centurian, Chieftain and Challenger 1 tanks were produced both at Newcastle and Leeds. In 1990, the UK MOD order for the first driver training tanks was completed. Then Challenger Armoured Repair and Recovery Vehicles (CRARRV) together with Challenger I tanks were both used in the Gulf War. Without any losses, the Challenger I tank destroyed over 300 enemy tanks, armoured personnel carriers and artillery pieces. As the world's most formidable battle tank Challenger 2 won the British Army contract in 1991 against strong competition from America, France and Germany. During 1993, The Royal Army of Oman made the Challenger 2 its choice as a main battle tank. By 1999 Rolls Royce acquired Vickers and the Newcastle factory became the single centre of excellence for heavy armoured vehicle manufacture and design. Within three years Alvis Limited, (a Coventry based company established in 1919 to

Above: *A 12" Mark 9 Armstrong Whitworth gun being despatched*

Below: *25 pounder field gun production line, 1942*

manufacture motor cars and later light armoured vehicles) was to acquire the business interests of Vickers Defence Systems.

Other great names in engineering

From the 1840s there was a tremendous growth in engineering. Many businesses were driven by demand to supply the particular needs of existing industries. In 1840 Head Ashby and Company began a foundry and general engineering business at Thornaby on Teesside. Thomas Wrightson was an engineer who trained at Armstrong's on Tyneside. He joined Head Ashby and Company in 1866 and the firm then became well known as Head Wrightson and Company. In 1864 Messrs Clarke Chapman established a business in Gateshead to make colliery winding gear and auxiliary appliances for the marine trade. Another example of meeting the demands of the time was a firm founded to serve the gas lighting industry. In 1873 William Ashmore established the Hope Iron Works at Stockton to manufacture gas holders, boilers and bridges. Gas lighting was introduced to the streets of Stockton in 1822 by the Stockton Gas Light and Coke Company. Ashmore's gas holders were so well made that Middlesbrough and Stockton's were still in use in the latter half of the twentieth century. In the interests of company development a number of businessmen brought additional capital into the firm and in 1885 it was incorporated as Ashmore, Benson, Pease and Company Ltd. The works were extended and renamed the Parkfield Works and in later years chemical and ironworks plants were constructed. Such was the reputation of the company with the rapidly expanding chemical industry that during

MEETING THE CHALLENGE

Challenger 2 is a world-beating new tank designed by Vickers to be the next main battle tank for the British Army.

Stabilised commander's and gunner's sights, a laser rangefinder and a thermal imager combine with a highly-advanced fire control computer and refined crew ergonomics to provide exceptional day and night combat capability, using a single engagement sequence. A databus provides growth potential.

The new, 120mm high-pressure gun provides firepower able to meet all known and anticipated threats.

Protection is provided by British Chobham armour augmented by stealth technology in the hull and turret design. An auxiliary power unit supplies electrical power during silent watch. Solid-state electrical drives avoid the use of hydraulics in the crew compartment and all explosive ammunition is stowed below the turret ring.

New standards of mission reliability have been achieved with Challenger 2's fighting systems and automotives, yet the hull retains significant commonality with Challenger 1.

Challenger 2 is backed up by advanced commander's and gunner's simulation systems and a driver training tank. In the field its effectiveness is increased by an Armoured Repair and Recovery variant.

FIGHTABILITY

MAINTAINABILITY

RELIABILITY

Challenger 2

Vickers Defence Systems
Scotswood Road, Newcastle-upon-Tyne NE99 1BX, England. Tel: (091) 273 8888. Fax: (091) 273 2324. Telex: 53104. Manston Lane, Crossgates, Leeds LS15 8ST, England.
A Vickers PLC company · **Engineering Success**

the 1914–18 war, the company acted as consultants and advisers to the Ministry of Munitions for the construction of chemical factories and power stations. Eventually in the early 1960s the old Ashmore foundry changed hands and became known as Parkfield Foundries (Teesside) Ltd. At the same time part of the original Ashmore site was sold to Whessoe Ltd., engineers of Darlington.

A good clean business – a 19th century profile

Written in the style of the time.
Messrs. Thomas Hedley and Co. City Soap
Works, Newcastle upon Tyne.

The firm, Messrs. Thomas Hedley and Co., the City Soap Works was established in 1841 by Messrs. John Green and H. Hedley. Twenty-three years later the firm passed into the hands of Mr. Thomas Hedley and his brother, Edward Armorer Hedley, and they were subsequently joined by Mr. Armorer Hedley, the son of Mr. Thomas Hedley. He continued the business as Thomas Hedley and Co., and despite the severe competition, conducted a very substantial and steadily increasing trade.

Extensive works for manufacturing and warehousing

The works in City Road had a frontage of about fifty yards to the thoroughfare, and extended to the rear as far as the Quayside Granaries. There were six spacious floors, variously used as warehouses or for manufacturing. The two lower stories contained facilities for a heavy floating stock of oil, resin, tallow, soda, and other raw materials. The boiler house had a couple of large Galloway Lancashire type boilers sufficient to generate steam for heating and melting purposes. Further reserve supplies of material were housed on the two top floors, where there were quantities of alkali, caustic soda, resin, etc. In this section was housed the steam blower, by means of which tallow could be removed from the casks without the necessity of breaking them. The steam blower was capable of dealing with two and a half tons of tallow per hour. The link with the boiling tanks beneath was through a feed and service gutter. The boiling room was fitted with thirteen copper tanks, varying from three to twenty tons capacity. Here the preliminary processes of melting and mixing were completed. After being properly manipulated and heated to the required degree of consistency, the contents of the coppers were allowed to settle. The soap, in a semi-liquid state, was then subsequently ladled into coaches and transferred to the frame rooms, where it was cooled and cut into slabs. Upwards of 120 frames were continually in use, and as each frame held eleven hundred weight, the output was considerable.

Hedley's soaps favoured in woollen mills

Messrs. Hedley made about fifty kinds of soap, including pale, brown, cold water, special, mottled, and scented goods. Some of these were put up in 3 lb bars, others in three, four, five, six or seven tablets to the pound, and so on, special machinery being used for moulding and stamping. The process of making mottled and curd mottled soaps was interesting as these lines were highly favoured amongst the Scottish

Thomas Hedley and Co.,
City Soap Works,
Newcastle upon Tyne

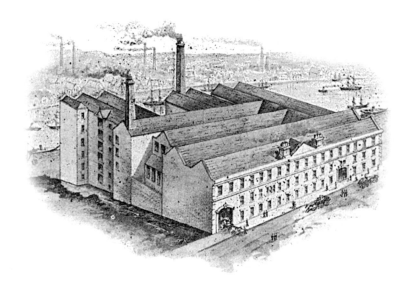

and Yorkshire woollen manufacturers. They used them in the mills particularly for scouring and kindred purposes. The care and accuracy with which the whole of the manufacturing process was conducted, not only with respect to the special and scented soaps, but also with the cheaper kinds, was interesting to observe. Through their unremitting endeavours, coupled with careful selection of staple material, Messrs. Hedley maintained consistent soap quality. The warehouses contained large reserves of finished soaps. These were kept in suitable bins so that orders of almost any magnitude could immediately be fulfilled. Loose wrappers were supplied with many of the items, and the steady activity which prevailed in the packing and forwarding departments was ample testimony to the strength and regularity of the demand. They produced all their own boxes and cases, having dedicated wood stores and joiners' shops. There were also extraordinary precautions against fire with the soap works' own fire brigade. Throughout the works, the arrangements were organised so the risks were always minimal.

A genuine demand for Hedley's quality soaps

Messrs. Hedley dealt almost exclusively with the home market, and doing it in a way that may be described as an old fashioned business. Reliance for trade was on the quality of the name, rather than on advertising. The firm concentrated largely in the production of genuine soaps for household and ordinary toilet use. As well as the principle brands, they were manufacturing two noteworthy cold water soaps, and a number of cleansers, such as Hedley's Eclipse Cleanser, First Extra Anti-rubber Paraffin, and City Cleansers, etc., all of which gained a widespread reputation.

More than 150 years of brewing in Hartlepool

J. W. Cameron and Company Limited. Lion Brewery, Hartlepool, Teesside.

In 1852 William Waldon bought some land to build a brewery in Hartlepool. This was the site of the Lion Brewery. Sadly, two years later he died, leaving his wife Jane and son and namesake William to take over the business. In 1865, the Waldons engaged a young brewer named John William Cameron to work for them in the brewery. Although he was only 24 years old, he was an experienced brewer and maltster having served his six years' apprenticeship at Barnard Castle. By 1872 John Cameron was running the brewery, and in the following year he reached an agreement with the Waldon family to assign him a lease of 21 years for the brewery, its malting facility and sixteen hostelries. John Cameron soon extended the size of the brewery after buying some adjoining land and he also purchased other taverns. When his lease came to an end John Cameron bought the

instrumental in obtaining a Charter of Incorporation for the town of West Hartlepool in 1887. After becoming a prominent figure in business and local government, Colonel John William Cameron died in December 1896, aged 55 years. His family built and endowed a hospital in his memory, opened in 1905. The brewery was taken over by the Colonel's younger brother, Captain Watson Cameron, who maintained growth in the business by extending the site and targeting other local breweries for acquisition together with their managed inns. As a supplement to the existing drinks production, in 1899 he began manufacturing mineral waters. When Captain Watson Cameron died in 1920, his son was too young to take over the responsibility of running the brewery and the family appointed Joint Managing Directors, A J Morgan and H J Hewlett. The years from 1922 to the early 1930s were difficult at the brewery. Trade was affected by the General Strike and the depression particularly when the shipyards and other local businesses were going through slack times.

Cameron's Strongarm quickly became a brand leading ale

In 1935 the Captain's son, John Watson Cameron, took control of the business and trade began to improve. Cameron again went on the acquisition trail, increasing the portfolio with more companies and inns. Constraints during the Second World War restricted further development although they did their best to supply as much beer as they were allowed. In 1944, the company responded to a trend for wine and spirits off licenses and formed a subsidiary company, Goldfinch Wine Stores. From the 1950s another great era of expansion ensued and

A picture of Colonel John William Cameron situated in the brewery visitors centre

brewery outright for £34,442 and established it as a limited company in 1894. In less than 30 years J W Cameron had turned the brewery into a thriving business.

Cameron joins the ranks succeeding in business and public life

John Cameron had joined the Artillery Volunteers as a Sub Lieutenant in 1871 and after 14 years of service had risen to the rank of Lieutenant Colonel. In public life he played a prominent civic role and was

more local breweries were purchased and a bottling factory was opened close to the Lion brewery. In response to public demand, a new brand called Strongarm was introduced in 1955. Stronger than any draught beer available for the same price, it proved immensely popular and became the company's flagship ale. John Watson Cameron was well liked by the brewery employees and followed in his uncle's footsteps to serve Hartlepool in local government. John was invested with an OBE at Buckingham Palace in 1960. His son, John Martin Cameron, joined the company in 1957 and became a director in 1962. After lorries became more widely used for deliveries, the last two dray horses were presented to a local farmer in 1960.

Trials and tribulations lead to a rebirth of the brewery

During the 1970s, the business was subject to new commercial pressures due to changes in licensed trading patterns. During 1975, Cameron's business was itself the subject of a successful takeover by the shipping company Ellermans. In the 1980s, the brewery changed hands twice, first when the Barclay Brothers purchased it in 1983 and then by the Brent Walker Group in 1989. With each new owner, the company was restructured and downsized from a business that had supported Cameron's 4,000 employees in a self-contained supply chain from malting and brewing, to bottling and delivering by dray, and from bar fitting and furnishing to public houses and off licenses. In 1992, the Wolverhampton and Dudley Breweries plc acquired the company with its remaining 51 public houses. David Soley, a local businessman who previously led the buyout of the closure threatened Castle Eden Brewery, purchased the Lion Brewery in 2002. The historic Castle Eden plant was closed and production was centred at Hartlepool, where a new company retaining a connection to the famous family name was incorporated. David's son, Chris Soley, is Managing Director of the family business and once again there are extensive expansion developments with the purchase of licensed premises. Although not on the same scale, today Camerons Brewery Limited produces some of those original beers as well as some new ones. For those people with a sense of nostalgia, the management have opened a centre for visitors at the Lion Brewery. Ready for new challenges in a market that has changed the face of many old style pubs, one of the oldest established businesses in West Hartlepool has regained its independence so that the lion can roar once more.

The heart of Camerons fine ale, the Brew House

Chapter Five

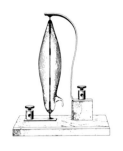

Pioneering electricity – new lamps for old

Tyneside played an important role in pioneering electric power when in 1879, Joseph William Swan in his home laboratory at Underhill, Gateshead, invented the incandescent lamp. He first demonstrated his electric lamp before 700 people at Newcastle's Literary and Philosophical Society some nine months before the American, Thomas Edison sought to take credit for the invention. The following year he used an electric lamp to illuminate Mosley Street and the premises of Messrs. Swan and Morgan, making Newcastle the first town in the country with electric lighting. During the same year Sir W G Armstrong, keen to appreciate its benefits adopted the new lighting in his Rothbury home. A water turbine situated in the grounds generated the power to make Cragside the first mansion to have electric lights installed. Together, in 1881, Joseph Swan, Armstrong, Spence, Watson and Merz founded Swan's Electric Light Co. Ltd., and with a factory in Benwell it was the first company to manufacture electric lamps. The business was a great success and this influenced a decision to move its headquarters to London with a factory in Middlesex.

1884 – Holmes' electric switch is patented

In 1883, John H Holmes founded an electrical engineering business in Portland Street, Newcastle. During the same year, he fitted electric lights in his father's house Wellburn in Jesmond, the first privately owned property to have an electric installation. His business developed quickly with many contracts for lighting sets. Learning from an unfortunate incident at a Wallsend installation, Holmes invented a quick break switch with snap-off action, which he patented in 1884. His first dynamo was manufactured in 1885, and using the Castle brand name, it gained a reputation for reliability and was supplied to customers both at home and abroad.

1885 – John Holmes manufactures the famous Castle dynamo

John Holmes was an exceptionally skilled craftsman. As well as making a market for his patent switch through the granting of licenses to sixteen other manufacturing companies, he designed one of the earliest

Top: *Swan's experimental lamps*

Above: *Sir J W Swan*

Below: *Lord W G Armstrong*

Bottom and Opposite: *Cragside at Rothbury was the first country mansion to have electric lighting*

Constant Reyrolle's company employed fifty eight people in a vacant dye research works standing on a five and a half acre site. To assist in the business two other pioneers joined Reyrolle, Norbert Merz, and Henry W Clothier who had designs for what he described as ironclad switchgear. This revolutionary control equipment for electrical power circuits proved to be reliable and entirely safe for operatives. The benefits of this new switchgear were quickly recognised for both domestic and industrial electrical supplies. At Wallsend, the first high voltage metal clad panels were erected at a sub station situated at Swan Hunter's shipyard, and at the Rising Sun Colliery, the first all-electric colliery in Britain. Interestingly, Reyrolle's was based only a few miles across the river Tyne from Parsons, a company with which it later became famous for building and equipping power stations throughout the world.

1884 – Parsons invents a turbo dynamo

Following the pioneering of these electric inventions, Tyneside reached a new landmark in history when Charles Parsons revolutionised the production of cheap bulk electric power with his invention of the turbo-dynamo. Parsons career began when he served a four year apprenticeship at Armstrong's Elswick works after finishing at Cambridge University in 1877. He then spent two years with a Leeds company before moving to become junior partner and head of the electrical department of Clarke, Chapman, Parsons and Co., in Gateshead. By 1884 he had invented a working turbo-dynamo developing 7.5 kw at a speed of 18,000 r.p.m. The main application was for electric lighting on ships.

Top: *Parsons first condensing turbo generator 1891*

Bottom: *Parsons first practical steam turbo generator 1884*

dynamos, developed train lighting sets, electric drives for printing presses and portable navigation lighting sets for shipping. Seven years before John Holmes' death he incorporated his business into A Reyrolle & Co Ltd. This firm was established on 14 June 1886 when A C Reyrolle started a small workshop in London making switchgear with six employees. In 1901, the business was incorporated as a limited company and transferred to Hebburn. Initially, Alphonse

1889 – Half a century of power breaking records

Charles Parsons partnership with Clarke and Chapman was dissolved in 1889 when he was able to establish his own works at Heaton, Newcastle. This gave him the flexibility to work on the first condensing turbine, a unit of 100 kw capacity which was built for the Cambridge Electric Light Station. Gradually, electric supplies companies invested in the new turbines which proved to give much better economies in fuel consumption than traditional steam engines. A few years later Parsons constructed the first 350 kw turbo generator which could drive a single phase non-condensing alternator at 3000 r.p.m.. Parsons consistently produced larger and more economical generators, breaking all previous records of steam machines. By 1900 Parsons had manufactured a pair of 1,250 kw turbo-alternators, followed by the first three-phase turbo alternator. His name had become synonymous in the field of power generation and was soon famous throughout the world. In 1928, his company manufactured the first turbo-generator to produce 36,000 volts and in 1937 made a pair of 50,000 kw turbo alternators, the largest ever made in the country. Sixty years later, Parsons was manufacturing turbine generators to meet the demands for power up to 700 megawatts.

A powerful association is formed

Parsons formed an association with Reyrolle in a company called Parolle Electrical Plant Co., which was to provide the market with fully constructed and equipped power stations. Reyrolle's specialised products covered all applications for switchgear and for reasons of safety they pioneered the enclosure of all electrical conductors in metal. The company had also developed excellent facilities for research, including a 1,500,000 volt impulse-voltage generator (for simulating lightning conditions), and a high power circuit breaker testing station. These facilities were the first of their type to work in conjunction with the National Physical Laboratory at Teddington. Reyrolle built switchgear for controlling high voltage plant, welding sets, electric motors, precision electrical instruments, and electrical control equipment for mines, printing presses and ship propulsion. The electric motors and the electric drive for printing presses manufactured in the Hebburn Works were developments of

Below: *Parsons at the Great Exhibition 1929*

Bottom: *Reyrolle circuit breaker testing station commissioned in 1926*

steadily extended to cover 43 acres with facilities for research on contacts, insulation, mechanism, experimental model production, mechanical and electrical testing, batch production of components and wherever possible, mechanical handling of assemblies. As demand increased, voltages for transmission also increased, together with greater distances for power to be transmitted. Reyrolle's metal-clad switchgear was being exported throughout the world.

1889 – A Newcastle electricity company is established

Both Parsons and Reyrolle's cultivated a working relationship with the North Eastern Electric Supply Co., (NESCo), one of the earliest electric supply companies, formed in January 1889. Originally incorporated as the Newcastle upon Tyne Electric Supply Co., it was established to supply the eastern half of the city with electric light from a small power station at Pandon Dene. The company's chairman was Alderman T G Gibson and among the co-directors were Dr. J Theodore Merz and Dr. Robert Spence Watson. Initially the generating station at Pandon Dene consisted of two small 75 kw generators. These were supplemented by installations of larger generators, up to 500 kw. The coal that powered the steam generators was delivered by horse and cart at a cost of three shillings and sixpence per ton. During 1900 the governing body of NESCo initiated the first United Kingdom scheme for the supply of electrical energy in bulk for industrial power. A year earlier the Walker and Wallsend Union Gas Co., had secured a parliamentary sanction to sell electricity within its supply area and by agreement a new power station was commissioned. This was already under

types first designed by J H Holmes. The provision of Reyrolle's insulating materials was established through an association formed in 1929 with the Bushing Co Ltd., (part of the General Electric Co), also based at Hebburn.

Reyrolle is a world leader

Within 50 years the original staff of fifty eight became a team of 7,000. Then during the 1960s Reyrolle employed nearly 12,000 people. The factory departments were

Reyrolle metal clad outdoor switchgear CEB, Tongland

construction at Neptune Bank, Wallsend and following the opening ceremony on 18 June 1901, NESCo began supplying electricity to consumers.

Local contractors used for Power Station

Neptune Bank was celebrated for being the beginning of the era of electric power utilisation throughout the United Kingdom. It was the first power station to supply three phase electricity, operating at a pressure of 5,500 volts. This was a form of power best suited to industrial applications where higher voltages were required, whilst power at lower voltages was supplied for domestic use. Three phase electricity supply gave the region an enormous advantage for increasing productivity with industrial plant and machinery. At the same time Neptune Bank Power Station was the beginning of a rapid expansion of NESCo, leading the world in power for the next thirty years. Among the contractors for the Neptune Bank Power Station, there was the Darlington Wagon and Engineering Co., supplying steel, Reyrolle for the low tension switchboards, Wallsend Slipway and Engineering Co., and Wigham, Richardson and Co., providing marine type engines whilst two 1,500 kw three phase alternators produced to supplement these machines were driven by Parsons steam turbines. The fine results from these alternators, then the largest in the world, were to influence the same type of propulsion installation in the Mauretania owned by the Cunard Steamship Co.

More power – more power stations

Soon additional power stations were required to cope with a surge in the demand for electric power. In 1904 a new station with steam turbine plant was

erected at Carville, Wallsend and this was the largest public generating station in Europe. It was a landmark in power station design, and secured the reputation of Newcastle's consultants and designers Merz and McLellan. Powered solely by Parsons steam turbines, these were ten times the average size being installed in other British stations. In 1906, to improve reliability and continuity, NESCo became the first supply company to adopt balanced electrical protection gear. This was the Merz-Price system, the principle of which was to be used in every other form of automatic electrical protection. During the same year NESCo led the installation of Reyrolle's metal clad switchgear into substations, one of which was situated at Swan Hunter's shipyard at Wallsend-on-Tyne. NESCo's operations were also extended through the construction of a transmission system consisting of underground cables and overhead lines initially operating at 6 kw. Also in 1906, to minimise losses over long distances, NESCo was the first in the country to begin transmission at 20 kw. This was followed by a much improved power station at Dunston in 1910, and another plant at Carville in 1916. In order to save the waste heat and

Newcastle Corporation Manors Power Station (closed in 1936)

gases lost from traditional coke ovens and blast furnaces, many of the larger iron and steel works and collieries installed new generating machines. Later NESCo took over some of these operations to supplement output, whilst the new market demands created increased orders for Parsons turbo alternators and Reyrolle metal clad switchgear.

Switches in ownership for power giants

In 1977, Reyrolle, Parsons, Clarke Chapman and Peebles amalgamated to form NEI. Reyrolle had built a reputation as the Rolls Royce of Switchgear and this became a matter of fact when NEI became part of the Rolls Royce Industrial Power Group in 1989. It had supplied more than half of the switchgear for the National Grid. Having exported to over 100 countries, exports accounted for a substantial part of the company's business. In 1998, the Rolls Royce Power and Distribution Group, Reyrolle's parent, was taken over by VATECH-ELIN, part of a technology based Austrian engineering group. During the

previous year in April 1997, Siemens Power Generation Group (KWU) acquired the extensive service business for turbines and generators supplied by Parsons, Newcastle. This involved Siemens taking over around 800 employees.

A new century sees the introduction of electricity to transport

From the beginning of the twentieth century, electricity rapidly changed the face of industry and commerce. Electric power was introduced to transport, mining, ship building and engineering. There were electric cranes, winches, pumps and equipment, coal cutters, conveyors and lighting. An electric tram was introduced by Newcastle Corporation in 1901 and by 1904 the North Eastern Railway Co., opened the first electric train service (coast circuit route) outside London. Initially, trials for this service were completed on the line between Carville and Percy Main in September 1903. This was 78 years to the month after the first steam train operated on a public line between Darlington and Stockton. Although the region had become unique in the scale and integration of its electricity supply arrangements, there were several local authorities that began operating municipal lighting and industrial power stations. For example Newcastle Corporation built a power station at Manors to supply the tramways, whilst the smaller authorities such as Middlesbrough and Tynemouth linked their requirements to NESCo. The early supplies of electricity were provided by NESCo at four pence per unit but by 1905 this had been reduced to a fraction over one penny per unit. Between 1900–1910, NESCo's business had increased thirty fold with an average load factor of 45 per cent. This was much greater

Electric tramcar on the Gosforth and Central Station route, 1901

than any other industrial area in the country where averages were around 20 per cent. A report in the Times newspaper in 1905 had a comparison between North America, where new industrial loads had developed around the cheap hydro-electric power of Niagara, and Tyneside. Similarly with power rates among the cheapest in the world, the North East's economy was growing significantly and attracting new industry to the area.

A power boost for the chemical industry

By the beginning of the twentieth century cheap electric power revived the declining chemical industry. The Solvay process originated in Belgium did not require coal to evaporate the brine for caustic soda manufacture, it worked by electrolysis. A major producer was The Allhusen Works at Gateshead. Also, to take advantage of Tyneside's cheap electricity, the Castner Kellner Alkali Company relocated its sodium operation from Runcorn to Wallsend in 1906. In the same year, a company to benefit from the revival of the chemical industry and use of electricity was Wallsend based Thermal Syndicate Ltd. With research by consulting engineers Merz, McLellan and electricity from the Neptune Bank power station, Thermal Syndicate commenced manufacture of fused silica electrical insulators and vessels for the chemical industry. By the outbreak of the First World War NESCo's electric power network covered 1,400 square miles and the conversation to three-phase 40Hz AC was about to become the largest integrated power system in Europe at the time. This had made it possible to construct large central generating stations, requiring small reserve plant margins. The rise in demand for electricity during the war

resulted in an extension of the existing generating plant to a new Carville B operation. The steam pressures obtained by this plant were the highest then used by any UK supply authority. Carville B installed the first system control room, a principle pioneered by NESCo for displaying, controlling and operating the high voltage electricity network. The control display covered 960 square feet indicating generating stations, substations and the network of transmission and power distribution. The operation was linked to NESCo's own private telephone system and the new control room attracted visitors from around the world.

NESCO becomes a role model for the new national grid

Following the 1st World War and during the depression years, demand for electricity was considerable with the advent of new street lighting, illuminated shop signs and theatre and cinema lighting. NESCo was seen to be prominent in both industrial and social progress. By 1924 it

An electric train coastal service operated north of the Tyne from 1903

Carliol House, Pilgrim Street, Newcastle

was the first electricity authority in the country to introduce transmission of as high a pressure as 66,000 volts. Where overhead installations were difficult in built up areas, they were the first to make commercial use of underground cable operating at 66 kw. NESCo had become the model for co-ordinating and interconnecting widespread power distribution when the government planned to establish a national electricity grid.

NESCO's new HQ – Carliol House

Between 1924 and 1927, NESCo built Carliol House for their headquarters in Newcastle. L J Couves of Newcastle were the architects and it was the city's first office development in the modernised classical style of the inter war period. There were many technical innovations which made Carliol House architecturally important. It was constructed using a method of reinforced steel construction imported from the USA. The building's electric heating system was built into the ceilings for the circulation of 60 tons of hot water through coiled pipes. Between the floor levels, high speed lifts were installed operating at 430 feet per minute (probably the fastest in the world at that time). For consumers' information and internal training use, a luxurious lecture theatre and cinema was provided for audiences of up to 70 people. It was the first building to have electric vacuum cleaners plugged into wall sockets. The exterior of Carliol House was faced with Portland stone, a feature distinguishing itself from the city's traditional sandstone. The interior was designed with a combination of Art Deco, stripped classicism and Egyptian influence. Together with marble and mahogany this added to the grandeur which had become popular in commercial buildings of this period.

The development of the electricity board

From the beginning of the century industrial supplies grew together with demand for domestic electricity. For better and more enjoyable living, new household appliances were being introduced. The first to arrive were electric irons, heaters and fans, then electric cookers, washing machines and refrigerators. From the 1930s there was a continuous requirement for domestic electricity connections. NESCo promoted new consumer appliances through stylish shops and mobile showrooms. Through increasing demands both from the business and consumer sectors, new power stations were built. One of these built at Dunston for NESCo offered the advantages of having access to coal which provided a source of cheap fuel. With 2.25 million people living in Northumbria, as well as Dunston, other sources of power were from Carville, North Tees, Sunderland and Darlington power stations. The electricity generated from these power stations was produced from steam, which was obtained by heating water in coal fired boiler houses. The main power stations and all the chief electric lines were controlled from Carliol House, Newcastle. This was handled by control engineers who allowed so much electricity to be produced from each power station and meant they had to deal with thousands of switches. Following the Royal Agricultural Show at Newcastle in 1934, initiatives towards rural electricity supplies commenced. The electricity industry was nationalised in 1948. In this region, the North Eastern Electricity Board (NEEB) replaced NESCo and a variety of smaller private and municipal supply organisations. With lower distribution costs, rural electricity became more practical (with 80% of rural premises being supplied by 1952), although work continued into the 1960s to make connections to some of the more remote rural communities. The opportunity was also taken to re-brand the supply, distribution, appliance showrooms and service activities. Following the completion of the post war 275 kv supergrid (a spinal power line from Clydeside into central and southern England), new thermal power stations were commissioned at Stella on Tyne, Blyth and North Tees in the early 1960s. The first and only regional nuclear power station was constructed in 1968 at Hartlepool and commenced supplying electricity in 1972. This was seen to be an important stage in the development of alternative power stations. With the decline in the coal industry, coal fired power stations were not being replaced, whilst the smaller ones were phased out of commission.

Blyth Power Station breaks records

One of the North East's largest engineering projects from the 1950s to the mid 1960s, Blyth Power Station was designed by Mertz and McLennan, the consulting engineers responsible for the civil and structural engineering work. When commissioned it gained acclaim for its technical innovation and record breaking thermal efficiency and availability. This

Top: *Twin power stations, Stella North at Newburn, Stella South at Blaydon*

Turbine and boiler controls for 60 mw turbo generator at Stella, 1955

115

achieved a place in the Guinness Book of Records. In 1958 the power station installed the first 120 mw set. The arched roof structure of the turbine hall of the 'A' Station was innovatively designed utilising external pre-stressed pre-cast concrete beams, with a span of 180 feet. This was one of the last coal fired power stations to be de-commissioned in the 1990s. One of its last uses was as a film set in Sir Ridley Scott's film Alien. It was finally demolished in 2003.

Northern Electric created from NEEB in 1989

At its peak in 1965, NEEB employed over 9,000 people. However, with increased efficiency and the use of improved technology, employment was to fall to under 5,000 by the late 1980s, and to around 3,500 in the late 1990s. During 1989 Northern Electric was created from the previously nationalised North Eastern Electricity Board. Through privatisation it had inherited the prime monopoly of supplying electricity to commercial, industrial and domestic consumers. In the following year NEEB was floated on the

Blyth Power Station photographed the year before demolition in 2003

stock exchange. The rules then changed considerably under which the former Regional Electricity Companies (Recs) operated. A free market process was introduced where Northern Electric was able to sell electricity to consumers anywhere in the country. In 1996 American energy giants CAL Energy bought Northern Electric. From 1998 the domestic free market became open both for electricity and gas. This brought fierce competition between gas and electric companies for domestic and industrial supplies. As part of CAL Energy, Northern Electric was the first company in the UK to launch Dual Fuel to be cheaper than British Gas until 2002 with approximately two million electricity and gas customers. Northern Electric had become the third largest electricity supplier to medium and large businesses in the 100 kw plus sector. It had contracts with Marks and Spencer, Sainsbury, Granada, Allied Domecq, Northumbrian Water and Scottish and Newcastle. At that time the largest customers included the Post Office and NHS. Into the new millennium CAL Energy was interested in other acquisitions to become a global energy supplier.

From street lamps to domestic heating

A profile about the development of gas based on an account written in 1945. The Newcastle upon Tyne and Gateshead Gas Company. Providers of gas for public, industrial and domestic use. Offices: 30 Grainger Street, Newcastle upon Tyne.

The earliest experiments using gas for lighting were prior to 1691 when Doctor Clayton, of Kildare, filled bladders with coal gas to discover the potential use. However, it was William Murdock's application of this knowledge relative to the luminosity of the gas flame that led to the promise of a commercial future. He conducted many experiments in carbonising coal and in procuring a gas light. At this time the most common illuminants were oil and tallow. Murdock completed calculations comparing the cost of light from these against gas. In 1797, he successfully applied gas lighting in his home at Cumnock in Ayrshire. From this experience others followed. On the occasion of the Peace of Amiens in 1802, the engine works of Messrs. Bolton and Watts, in Birmingham was described as being spectacularly illuminated by gas lamps. In January 1807 part of Pall Mall, London had gas lamps installed. This greatly assisted the support required to found a gas company and obtain a charter. The result was the Chartered Gas Light and Coke Company, established in 1812. The following year Westminster Bridge, London had gas lamps installed. Interest in gas lighting soon spread to most provincial cities and large towns where gas lamps were being installed in streets and public buildings.

1817 – Public consumers offered gas lights

The first gas lamp installation in Newcastle was at a house owned by Mr Anthony Clapham at 141, Pilgrim Street. This was considered to be such a novelty that when the Grand Duke Nicholas of Russia visited Newcastle in 1816, he was taken by Mr Clapham to see the wondrous new illumination. Shortly after this the Newcastle Fire Office established gas works at Manors and Forth Street. Then on 15 November 1817 a general invitation for public consumers was issued. It was in Mosley Street that the first consumer premises were gas lit. As meters were non-existent, charging was organised by scale. It became the duty of inspectors to scour the town at nights to see that consumers kept

within their terms and only used lights during the agreed hours. Innkeepers were, in those days, free from restrictions and could remain open through the day and night which presented a special problem to gas suppliers.

North and South Shields oppose new gas lighting

Initially, there was resistance to the introduction of gas lighting in some areas. For example, North Shields produced its own champion, John Motley to oppose the change. The main concern was the local trade in whale oil used for lamps. During 1819, five whaling ships engaged in the Greenland and Davis Straits Fisheries fitted out in the seaport and spent some £5,000 on wages, provisions and gear. John Motley estimated that 500 masters, officers and men resided in North Shields and were engaged in whale fishing. Their average earnings of £25 a voyage would largely be spent in the district. Great emphasis was made about the National Bounty paid to each ship and the loss of profit derived from bringing whale oil into the country.

A typical gas appliance showroom, 1930s

Although his crusade was successful for a short time, the following year saw a speedy repentance of this resistance to gaslight, for the town discarded its oil lamps and adopted the new supply. South Shields took longer to overcome the resistance to change and its streets were not lit by gas until 1829. Gas supplies to Gateshead began in 1821 from a gas works in Pipewellgate built in 1819.

The beginning of an expanding gas industry

All over the country gas companies were being formed. There was free competition and often more than one supplier in a district. In October 1829, the Newcastle Subscription Gas Company was formed. It purchased the goodwill, works and plant of the Newcastle Fire Office and in 1831 established a gas works at Sandgate. By 1838 the name of the company was changed to the Newcastle upon Tyne and Gateshead Union Gas Light Company.

Gas company's offices, Grainger Street, Newcastle, Royal Jubilee, 1935

Although this was a joint undertaking there were disputes about gas charges and whilst Gateshead paid ten pence per lamp per week, Newcastle paid eight pence. Also, when mains were extended, Gateshead Council had to pay for the new lamp posts whereas these were free in Newcastle. This more favourable situation was probably due to Newcastle Corporation having the option to establish their own gas works, although this was not to happen. The Newcastle and Gateshead Union Gas Light Company extended its assets to include the purchase of the small gas works in Pipewellgate, Gateshead and all the specific interests of Richard Grainger. In particular, this covered the gas pipes and lamps which he was busy installing in Newcastle's new street network. It is worth noting that the headquarters of the company was situated in Grainger Street. During the successive years leading to the 1860s, Blaydon and District established a gas works through Messrs. John Cowen and Company. In 1859, the Elswick Gas Works was brought into use and the smaller works at Manors and Sandgate closed. By 1861 the Walker Gas Works was opened for gas supplies to Walker and Wallsend. This amalgamated with the Willington Gas Company formed in 1850 under the name of the Walker and St Anthony's Gas Light Company.

Coal tar causes problems for racing skiffs

Plans to supply natural gas were active in 1840 using the gas burnt off at the pit-head at Wallsend Colliery. For this purpose, The Spontaneous Gas Company was established but never pursued its objectives. Coal tar, a by-product of gas manufacture, was regarded as waste and allowed to drain into the river Tyne. As rowing was a popular pastime, the collection of tar globules on the sides of racing skiffs involved oarsmen and others using the waterway in great cleaning operations. This caused great annoyance and prompted recriminations against the Gas Company. During 1864, the first of a number of private acts was obtained and the Newcastle upon Tyne and Gateshead Union Gas Light Company was given an abbreviated name of the Newcastle upon Tyne and Gateshead Gas Company. The company was to purchase other local gas suppliers and extend its operations. The Redheugh Gas Works was opened in 1876 and inaugurated with an event which was stated to be 'befitting the extensive and costly character of the new works'. At a cost of £100,000 the Redheugh Gas Works was substantial. By the turn of the century the company's supply area included Newcastle and Gateshead, Walker, Wallsend, Willington, South Gosforth, Longbenton, Killingworth, Fawdon, Coxlodge, Callerton,

Ponteland, Dalton, Heddon, Prudhoe, Wylam, Ryton, Heworth, Lamesley, Chopwell, Byermoor and Usworth.

The introduction of slot meters

1901 saw the introduction of gas prepayment slot meters, and in 1905 the company started to hire out gas fires. In the first year there were 188 fires on hire purchase and 459 on simple hire. Whilst sales of gas continued to increase steadily, they were much affected by industrial unrest and a succession of disputes during the period 1908 to 1912. After 1913 sales recovered surpassing previous records. In 1916 the supply area was extended to include Cramlington, Horsley, Ovington, Mickley, Birtley and Ouston. Through a period to 1940 the Newcastle upon Tyne and Gateshead Gas Supply Company's supply area had been extended to a total of 284 square miles. Along the way acquisitions included the Walker and

Gas works like this one at South Shields were accepted landscape in towns

Wallsend Union Gas Company. This company also had dispensation to supply electricity in Wallsend and Willington Quay. However, the electrical side of the business had already been sold in 1903 to the Newcastle upon Tyne Electric Supply Company (predecessors of the North Eastern Electricity Supply Company). The Chester-le-Street Gas Company Ltd. also became an acquisition in the same year, 1924. Between 1924 and 1928 was a time of the most severe industrial depression, a prolonged stoppage in the coal industry and the General Strike of 1926. In 1927 the Tynemouth Gas Company was purchased and the company also completed arrangements with the Consett Iron Company for a substantial bulk supply of coke oven gas from their Derwenthaugh ovens. Gas interests were acquired at South Shields in 1937 and in 1940 when the Morpeth Gas Light Company was acquired.

1948 – Gas Companies nationalised

Coal tar was first commercially produced in 1917 through a distillation process in the By-Product Works situated at St Anthony's, Walker-on-Tyne. Following the Gas Regulation Act of 1920, a thermal based charging order replaced the previous volumetric charging system. Gas supplies were nationalised in 1948. A century earlier the annual sale of gas was 17 million cubic feet and through to nationalisation had grown threefold. It was an industry which established itself in lighting but developed in heating. North Eastern gas consumers accounted for over 23,000 fires; 186,000 cookers; and 270,000 meters. In turn the business employed between 2,500 and 3,000 people.

Powerful inventions made for worldwide use – 19th Century profile

Written in the style of the time.
Messrs. C A Parsons and Company. Electrical Engineers and Contractors. Heaton Works, Newcastle upon Tyne.

It could be stated that the progress made by electrical engineering during the last part of the nineteenth century was literally without parallel in the history of applied science. Its advances were to have an obvious effect on almost every department of industry, and almost every phase of civilised life. It may be noted that in this as in all other branches of mechanics, Tyneside had a distinctly leading position. Amongst the firms with a distinction in this part of industry was Messrs. C A Parsons and Co., whose works at Heaton could be classed as a thriving manufacturing centre with principle concerns in this country and abroad. The firm engaged in every part of electrical work, including

C A Parsons and Co.,
Heaton Works, Newcastle

supply and erection of complete electric plants, the execution of lighting contracts, manufacture of engines and dynamos, transformers, resistance coils, and electric locomotives, hoists, pumps and motors, search lights, Admiralty and Suez projectors and mirrors of several specifications, and general electrical accessories.

The condensing steam turbine and dynamo

As town lighting contractors from a central station, they achieved remarkably efficient results. For both Newcastle and District Electric Lighting Co. and the Cambridge Electric Supply Co., Messrs. Parsons supplied and installed the necessary plant, and superintended the undertakings. The total initial expenditure for these companies amounted to less than a mere £2. 7s. 6d. per lamp, and the entire cost of maintenance for a year amounted to 3.48 pence per unit of current generated. Parsons' condensing steam turbine and dynamo, being an invention of the principal the Hon. C A Parsons, formed the main part of their manufacturing. This plant would reduce the standard cost of generating electrical energy by a minimum of 15 per cent.

Improvements in efficiency and maintenance

Following capability trials in December, 1891, and again in August 1892, Professor Ewing stated, "The application of moderately superheated steam has put the performance of the turbine level with that of the best ordinary type of steam engines. A consumption of 27 or 28lbs of steam per electrical unit at full load and 30 or 32lbs, at half load, is a result not needing to have its significance emphasised. The efficiency under small fractions of the full load would probably be greater than in any steam engine, and is of special interest in relation

to the use of the turbine in electric lighting from central stations". Professor Ewing concluded: "Apart from other possible applications of a peculiarly light and efficient high speed motor, the turbine dynamo, is eminent for central station use, not only on account of its economy of steam under heavy and light loads, but also for being light and compact, small initial cost, independence of foundations, freedom from vibration, steady governing, simplicity, the ease with which it is handled, and the moderate outlay which it may be expected to require under the heads of maintenance, oil and attendance". Therefore, it could be deemed especially suited for electric lighting on board mercantile vessels, war ships, and torpedo boats, as well as for land installations – the light producing power ranging from 66 to 1,000 16 candle power (c-p) 60 Watt lamps. A type known as the steam Turbine Umpolar Dynamo had been constructed for low voltages and large current required in metallurgical and electrolytic processes, For central station work the firm would recommend the Steam Turbine Dynamo or

A turbine casing being moved at C A Parsons, Heaton Works

Alternator, which would produce up to 8,333 16 c-p. 60 Watt lamps capacity. Messrs. Parsons and Co., could also supply electric motors for use in combination with low lift pumps, fans and hoists respectively. Being compact each type of motor would require very little attention in working. In their efficiency, the electric hoist could lift 30 cwts., at 50 feet per minute being controlled by a reversing switch for lifting and lowering, and with an additional fast motion switch. Other products of note included several improved forms of Admiralty, coast defence and portable projectors, fitted with Parsons' patent automatic lamp, and Parsons or Magin's mirror. These generating plants and projectors were supplied to the English and other Navies, and being portable, simple and reliable rendered them equal to any others.

Extensive premises with offices and modern workshops

The Heaton works occupied a considerable area of ground flanked on one side by the North Eastern Railway, with a siding into the yard, and past the main shops entrances. There were adequate facilities for transport of material and machinery. The Walker Road frontage consisted mainly of offices, for the principals, corresponding and estimating, the drawing office, enquiries, cashier's and timekeeper's departments. To the rear of this block of buildings, and at right angles to it, were the stores, testing shop, boiler house, smiths' shop, and pattern shop, which, with three outbuildings used as a mirror factory and pattern store, extended from the entrance gates, almost to the railway side. The main fitting shop was in a building opposite these departments, and measured 170 feet long by 45 feet broad,

equipped throughout with the most modern machinery. Manufacturing was sub divided into sections for (a) engines, turbines, and condensers, (b) dynamos, (c) transformers and resistance coils, (d) electric motors, (e) mirror projectors, (f) switchboards, entrants, and electrical accessories.

Contracts for Corporations throughout the UK

At this time there was plant and machinery almost ready for the electric lighting of the town of Scarborough. This consisted of two steam turbine alternators, of 150 units capacity, with condensers, steam and exhaust pipes, switches, armites, transformers, and other parts. There was also, an alternator of 150 unit output for the Corporation of Portsmouth, complete with its condenser, a 750 unit alternator, equal to maintaining 12,000 16 c-p. lamps at one time. This plant considered the largest in England, and about the third largest in the world, was almost complete and ready to be worked by steam at 250 lbs pressure. Other alternators being manufactured were for the Newcastle and District Electric Company, besides many smaller units destined for the lighting of mills, country towns, ships, and other general lighting purposes. To this date the results of the firm ranks amongst the most economical in the production of direct drive dynamos by high speed engines.

A switch of lighting for collieries and ships

Messrs. Rowland Barnett and Co.
Electrical Engineers. Volt Works, Walker Gate and Dean Street, Newcastle upon Tyne.

A decade before the establishment of Messrs. Rowland Barnett and Co., electrical engineering was regarded rather in the light of its possibilities than of its actualities.

Certainly the firm made an enterprising bid for trade and within a short time their manufacturing demands outgrew premises both in Elswick and on the Quayside until they built special works at Walker Gate. In addition to the main works, a town office and showroom were situated in Dean Street, Newcastle. Dean Street was strategically chosen being the main approach to the Quayside, as well as to the strictly commercial quarter of the town. As Messrs. Rowland Barnett and Co., catered largely for shipping and industrial interests, a better situation could scarcely have been found. The advantages were fully utilised with one of the show windows affording a view of a miniature electric light installation, with engine, dynamo, switchboard and lamps in full working order. The other contained probably the most representative display of electric fittings and accessories to be seen in the city.

Electrical product manufacture

At their Walker Gate works Messrs. Barnett engaged in almost every branch of electrical manufacture from a dynamo to an indicator. The workshops contained every conceivable machine and plant conducive to productive and quality manufacture. Reflecting these high standards were extensive stores for materials, parts and finished goods. In particular, a large portion of production was taken with the manufacture of their own dynamos in a variety of patterns. They were also local agents for Norwich D Type dynamos, celebrated as being the best on the market for heavy duty work. Messrs. Barnett continuously introduced numerous improvements in electric lamps, instruments, and general fittings, particularly with respect to those used in collieries and on board ships. One item, a special portable lamp was in great demand by mariners on petroleum ships as it entirely eliminated the risk of fire. Complete bell sets, indicators, pushes of every description, commutators, transformers, electric batteries, speaking tubes, induction coils, switches, silk and cotton covered copper wire cables and in fact anything that could possibly be required by users of electrical plant, power or appliances, were provided in a great variety of make and price. The firm's electric signal bells for collieries and mines were specially

Rowland Barnett and Co:

Left: *Electrical Erecting Shop*

Right: *Corner of Machine Shop*

noted as being extremely reliable and singularly adapted to meet the demands of wear and tear of colliery use.

Installations throughout northern England and Scotland

In addition to being manufacturers and wholesale suppliers of electrical machinery and accessories, Messrs. Rowland Barnett and Co., conducted every branch of electrical engineering as applied not only to collieries and ships but also to private and public buildings and general places of business. The firm quickly gained a reputation throughout the northern counties of England and in the most northern highlands of Scotland for reliable electric light installations which gave the utmost satisfaction to clients.

Collieries fuel emerging power stations

An account based on a profile written in 1934. Wallsend and Hebburn Coal Company. Watergate Buildings, Newcastle upon Tyne.

Wallsend grew from a colliery village with a population of 4,000 in 1888 to a town of 23,000 people by 1913. The town became well known for coal of such outstanding quality that it was branded Wallsend for sales purposes. The winning of the famous Wallsend coal was at a period in the history of the northern coalfields when mining operations had been principally confined to comparatively shallow pits near the outcrops. Then it gradually began to extend eastwards along the banks of the Tyne where the famed High Main coal lay at great depths requiring increased capital and increased engineering skill for its winning and working. As well as being noted for domestic fuel, Wallsend coal was increasingly used for the emerging power stations.

The early days of coal mining at Wallsend

In 1756 the seams of coal in the Township of Wallsend were advertised to be let. The Chapman family took the Wallsend Royalty but had not sufficient money to complete the winning of the coal. William Russell, at that time a Bill Broker, came on the scene

Wallsend Colliery, C Pit

and shortly after made his fortune from Wallsend Coal from the High Main Seam. In 1778 the sinking of "A" Pit began close to the Roman Station of Segedunum and coal drawing began in 1781. Repeatedly from this date to 1815 serious explosions took place and the steel and flint mill which had been considered to be a safe means of lighting, was proved to be unsafe. Work continued with the greatest difficulty, sometimes in total darkness. An attempt was made to reflect sun light from the surface by means of mirrors, and experiments were made with the phosphorescent scales of fishes as a source of light.

Gas and ventilation present difficulties

For ventilation small underground furnaces fed by the single current of air passed round the entire pit and was often loaded with gas almost to firing point. It was a frequent occurrence for the sentry stationed near the furnace, candle in hand, to give the alarm for the hurried withdrawal of the men and ponies from the pit and the opening of the main separation doors to prevent an explosion at the furnace. So great was the quantity of gas given off at "C" Pit that it was piped to the surface and lit and burnt illuminating the district for many years. This is seen in the old print at the "C" Pit, taken from Hare's Sketches of Collieries. It was at one time seriously proposed to convey the gas by pipes to Newcastle and light the town, but the supply was found to be intermittent and the project was abandoned.

Developments through electricity providing new pumps, better winding, ventilation and cutting

The output at Wallsend in 1901 was 168,000 tons and the cost of pumping alone

was £16,000 a year. In one year over one thousand million gallons of water was pumped, or five million tons. In 1904, for every ton of coals raised to the surface, almost 9 tons of water were pumped 1,100 feet to the surface. After the water was drained from the old workings great quantities of gas had to be dealt with and was a source of great anxiety. The use of electricity was gradually extended to pumping, winding, ventilation fans, coal cutting, etc., until eventually all steam plant and boilers were replaced. The opening of the Rising Sun Pit gave a renewed era of prosperity to the colleries for a number of years. Eventually new difficulties were encountered, and the 1926 strike and a great fall in the selling price of coal and increased costs brought another period of depression.

1934 – New coal preparation plant opened

In 1934, arrangements were made by which the Bedlington Coal Company took over the controlling interest. The new coal preparation plant at the Rising Sun Colliery

View of the coal cleaning and grading plant, Wallsend

125

controlled the quality and graded coal for end use. It consisted of a plant encompassing screening, dry cleaning, washing, vacuum flotation, water clarification, drying, blending and mixing. Once coal arrived at the plant it was screened so that the smaller coal could be conveyed to two 250 ton capacity reinforced concrete bunkers. These acted as a reservoir taking peak loads from the screening plant to ensure an even supply to the preparation plant. Coal was discharged to the plant from the concrete coal bunkers by jig feeders. These delivered the coal to sizing screens so that it was divided into two sizes. The oversize was taken by conveyor to the washer, and the undersize to the dry cleaning plant by elevator. Through various stages of sizing by vibrating screens and separators, the coal would be divided into clean coal, middlings and shale. The clean coal was conveyed to dry screens; the middlings were re-circulated in the plant, while the shale went for disposal. The larger coal was conveyed through a washing plant and then to jigging screens for separation into sizes. By changing the screen plates, size variations could be made

A sectional view of coal preparation plant, Wallsend

to suit any special market requirements. The regular sizes were classed as cobbles, trebles, doubles and undersize. Hoppers with a capacity of twenty tons were situated beneath the screens to directly load the coal into trucks. With larger sizes, telescopic loading chutes were used to load trucks and provide blended coal as required.

The famous Wallsend brand quality coal

With quality coal mined at Wallsend combined with the preparation plant at the Rising Sun Colliery, this ensured a standard of excellence in coal supply for many years. Both the colliery and the plant operated successfully into the last half of the twentieth century supplying power stations when demands for alternative heating gradually replaced solid fuel.

The influence of electricity on Teesside's oldest established chemical company

The following profile describes a company that has adapted many times to market influences. It is certainly one of the oldest surviving companies on Teesside. The advent of electricity and less expensive power was to assist with the chemical processes that made the company world famous.

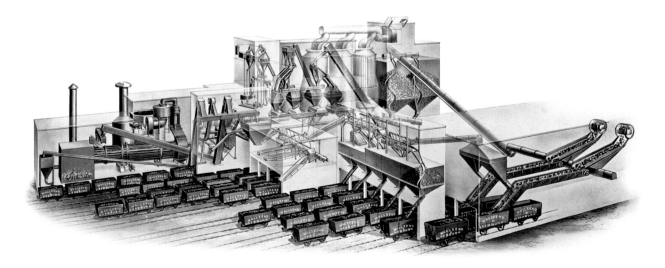

The first inland chemical company

Egglescliffe Chemical Company Ltd. Chemical Manufacturers. Urlay Nook, Yarm, County Durham.

Being established in 1833 by Mr Robert Wilson, this was one of the first firms to manufacture artificial manure. The works had a unique location, probably being one of the first inland businesses attracted by being adjacent to the Stockton to Darlington railway line. In 1825, this was the first public railway line to be opened in the world. It had an additional location advantage being only a few miles from the Port of Yarm for imports of raw materials. The works were basic and facilities consisted of acid chambers, grinding and mixing machinery, and sheds for the storage, both of the raw material and the manufactured article. The end product was simple superphoshate, or bones and acid or crop manures built up of nitrogenous, as well as phosphatic substances. The basic raw materials, phosphates, coprolites, and quantities of bones lay in heaps not far from the crushing operation. Several leaden chambers, continually used in the manufacture of sulphuric acid together with imported pyrites constituted the principle raw materials. A stone crusher reduced the rocky masses for subsequent treatment by which the whole was reduced to a powder or meal capable of passing through a sieve. This was drawn off and taken to the mixers and compounded with ground bones, fish guano, sulphate of ammonia and sulphuric acid, to become finished superphosphate. After a few revolutions of the mixing shaft it became a mass of hardened paste, then to be conveyed to storage heaps. These were finally quarried out to be disintegrated fine, dry and fit for the drill, sacked and sewn up, and dispatched by rail. Before electricity was available steam power for the process was supplied by a magnificent engine and steam boiler. In 1896, Tom Bell, a hand-furnace man was taken on, and was one of fourteen employees. He worked with the firm until his retirement in 1953.

Sulphuric acid for iron, coke and TNT

After the end of Robert Wilson's life in 1861, his son Robert Hutton-Wilson continued producing agricultural products. The first major development took place in

Main picture: *The works from Urlay Nook's railway crossing*

Inset: *Robert Wilson, founder of Egglescliffe Chemical Company*

1865 when linseed oil and cake mills were built to manufacture cattle feeds. He progressed with cattle feeds until 1890 when a process was installed for the manufacture of synthetic dyes (alzarine), a product of coal tar. During this time, there was a significant shift of the iron industry from the Tyne to the Tees area with significant new found iron ore deposits in the Cleveland Hills. The new iron and coke works increased the demand for sulphuric acid. The supply of sulphuric acid to local industry soon became the main part of the firm's business and for this purpose in 1906 the plant was extended. To supplement this in 1909 a process and plant was developed using cuprous pyrites fines. This produced a residue of iron and copper oxides. Once the copper was extracted the iron oxide residue (also known as purple ore) was made into briquettes for use in blast furnaces. Robert Hutton-Wilson's firm was beginning to expand and was incorporated as a limited company in March 1910.

A family business with a special kind of chemistry

Robert Hutton-Wilson had three sons who were all to become directors of the firm after Robert died in 1921. These were Cecil and Alec who became Joint Managing Directors, and the Colonel, Harry, who was appointed Chairman. Cecil was the most dedicated, although in the 1930s he began to develop new interests in coffee planting in Kenya. The Colonel lived in London and pursued his army career. My own grandfather knew them all very well. Henry Williams, having joined the firm in 1913 as an office boy, became Managing Director from 1937 until he died in 1949. They were an eccentric family and all had good brains for business. Both Cecil and Alec were very

The works locomotive and hands

keen on hunting and would leave my grandfather in charge of the business whilst they enjoyed their favoured pursuit. Henry was nicknamed 'Gunner' by them because during the 1914–18 war he served as a gunner with the Royal Garrison Artillery. It was very much a family business and had the kind of chemistry which bonded its employees. My uncle, Tommy Williams, became Commercial Director; my father Dr Donald Williams began his working life for the firm as a Research Chemist. In fact, the late Lawrence Grainge who helped me with details for this profile was another who dedicated his working life to the firm. Lawrence started as an office boy in 1931, learnt the business, became Works Manager in the 1950s and later, and until retirement, was Personnel Director.

Urlay Nook has its own community

Lawrence recounted "The business was growing so fast. If anyone was any good they were grabbed. Mr Alec tended to be very autocratic, Mr Cecil was the do'er with Mr Williams who was also a great disciplinarian but always very fair. He took me under his wing as an office boy. They were all good for the company in their own ways; played hell if they didn't think they were getting fair treatment." During the 1930s, Cecil and Alec took less of an active part in the business. After Cecil retired in 1936, a friend of the family, Mr H.E.J. Cory was appointed as Managing Director. Mr Cory left the business in 1937 and Mr Williams took over as Managing Director. It was a good working atmosphere. However, every Tuesday they made sulphuric acid, which wasn't very pleasant as there was always a smell of bad eggs. Cecil's son John came into the firm straight after leaving Sedburgh School to learn the business.

Lawrence Grainge recalled "For a time he lived in a caravan on the neighbouring farm to the works. John had to take night shift and got on well with everyone. His wife Joan was very supportive. When Mr Alec retired in 1945, everyone thought John got a directorship too soon; got it with the war, but he was a wonderful man and eventually went on to do a great deal for the business. He retired in 1980." The works became known locally as Urlay Nook. This was the name on the signal box at the railway crossing adjacent to the factory and offices. Urlay Nook in local dialect means sharp corner. Urlay Nook consisted of more than a chemical works, it had a small country community consisting of 18 terraced cottages. This was Wilson Terrace and belonged to the Hutton-Wilsons who rented the properties to loyal workers and their families. Serving the community and works was a small grocery shop which also supplied overtime teas for staff and a fair share of local and works gossip. This was everyone's business. During the First World War, together with supplying agriculture

Henry Williams, Managing Director, worked to perfect chrome production

129

Rotary kilns for chrome production

and the steel industry, business boomed due to the demand of sulphuric acid for the manufacture of TNT (Tri Nitro Toluene) explosive. The original core based business of fertiliser production had been steadily increasing. By 1925, to meet the demand, a new fertiliser plant was commissioned. It produced 100 tons per day of superphosphate compounded with murate of potash and ammonium sulphate to make balanced compound fertilisers.

A brave entry into the chrome industry

The company was soon to be faced with a problem of over-production in the sulphuric acid plant which became real in 1927. Following many executive discussions between the main board directors and Henry Williams and WH 'Billy' Morrow (who became Technical Director), chrome manufacture seemed to offer the best potential for diversification. There were growing demands for chrome used in tanning leather and other industries including chrome plating which was in vogue. Pioneering work had already been completed (apparently) successfully for full scale manufacture of chrome in Germany.

Based on this background, the executive team travelled to Berlin to buy a Zahn rotary kiln and learn about their methods of chrome production. It was the most forward-thinking yet almost the most disastrous decision the company was ever to take. Years later, John Hutton-Wilson recounted the difficulty it created for the family firm. "It nearly broke us, ... and had we in fact known what troubles were in store for us we would almost certainly never have started the venture." The new plant made the material all right but so wastefully that it was impossible to make any profit and led the firm into a huge loss making situation. At great expense, an expert from Germany was brought to Urlay Nook to solve the problems. He couldn't do it. Two people were left to correct the flaws in the German process. These were Henry Williams and Billy Morrow. Using every resource at their disposal, they worked day and night to make the rotary kiln produce material efficiently. Such were the troubles that at one stage the directors believed it had about a week before it would have to announce closure. However, at the same time two UK competitors increased the prices of their chrome products. This was the turning point. With new heart and enthusiasm, tremendous hard work and a final breakthrough, in 1928 the new rotary kiln process became viable. Within a year Egglescliffe Chemical Company Ltd., was recognised as the most advanced and technically competent firm in the chrome industry. It was a case of the tortoise and the hare with the competition, being a little complacent, finding themselves outmatched. The plant, using the Zahn furnace, produced two tons of bichromate of soda per day. The process used dolomite, sodium carbonate, chromite ore and sulphuric acid as its raw materials. It was the first firm in the UK to use a rotary kiln instead of the conventional hand burner reverberatory type. A second and larger Newell kiln was installed in 1932 to increase the production to 5 tons per day of bichromate of soda crystals.

A meteoric rise in chrome production

Another diversification in 1930 was the installation of a zinc oxide plant to supply paint, enamel, rubber and linoleum industries. This plant operated until 1935 when this part of the business was taken over by the Newcastle Zinc Oxide Company. A plant for producing high purity tin oxide commissioned in 1933 was longer lasting and had a capacity to output 20 tons per month. The product was used for ceramic enamel manufacture and was supplied until 1960 when unfortunately the plant was destroyed by fire. In 1938 the company celebrated its achievements by changing its name from Egglescliffe to Eaglescliffe, following local nomenclature, and going public. With the outbreak of war in 1939, expansion of chromium compound manufacture became paramount and a larger third rotary kiln was installed. The greater part of the increased output was used as a component of smoke screen mixtures for HM Ordinance. Still further expansion of the bichromate plant came in 1944 when a fourth and even larger kiln was commissioned. Also during the war there was a request to produce a pure chromic oxide required in the manufacture of engine nozzles for the newly developed jet aircraft. Production began in 1943 and by 1960 had expanded to an output capacity of 450 tons per month. After the war there was a great demand for chromic acid or chromic anhydride, and supplies were being flown to the UK from America. As a result of research and know-how gained by the directors whilst in Germany, a plant was built having an initial capacity of 30 tons per

Aerial perspective of chemical works, Urlay Nook

month. (By the 1960s this had increased to 180 tons per month). Between 1949 and 1951 further developments were incorporated into the fertiliser business. Until this time fertilizers had been produced in dry powder form but granular products were now being introduced. As well as two granulation plants a new continuous process was installed for superphosphate.

A series of amalgamations and mergers

From the 1950s John Hutton-Wilson led the company into a series of business amalgamations and mergers. The first of these involved an amalgamation with its two chrome producing competitors to become one business under the name of British Chrome and Chemicals Ltd. Then in 1957 a merger with the Brotherton Group resulted in another name change to Associated Chemical Companies Ltd., of which John Hutton-Wilson was Chairman. With factories in Clydeside, Lancashire, Merseyside, Yorkshire and Teesside, a new head office and technical complex was established at Harrogate. Through the 1950s almost ten years of research and work was

The works illuminated during nightshift

invested in converting chromic acid production into a safer 'no lime' process. The impetus for this initiative was principally for the health of employees. This was achieved by 1960 when all five kilns at Urlay Nook were converted. A further and larger kiln was installed in 1961. Within another year the process was totally mechanised and the facility had a capacity to produce 40,000 tons of sodium chromate per year. There were a number of rationalisations during the 1960s and 1970s. These included closing factories in Clydeside and Lancashire but also the fertiliser plant at Urlay Nook. This ended 167 years of fertiliser production in 1967. All fertiliser production was moved to a new facility at Barton on Humber. However, and most significantly before this in 1965, Associated Chemical Companies Ltd., joined the Albright and Wilson group of companies to become the Associated Chemicals Companies Division. Albright and Wilson was a respected and old established firm. It had a dominant position in some areas of the chemical industry, particularly in phosphorous manufacture. They initiated a major venture in Newfoundland that was a disaster for them. With years of phosphorous plant failures and pollution, the costs were so great that Albright and Wilson had to accept a takeover by an American company. By 1971, the Associated Chemicals Companies Division was disbanded and all the chromium business transferred to the Albright and Wilson Industrial Chemicals Division based at Oldbury, Birmingham. This involved the closure and disposal of the offices and technical departments at Harrogate. In 1973, the chrome business was sold to Harrisons and Crossfield Ltd., for £7.5 million. The Urlay Nook works reverted to their former name of British Chrome and Chemicals Ltd., and John Hutton-Wilson was appointed to the Board of Directors of a new parent company. The Hutton-Wilson connection was to end following his retirement in 1980.

Into the 21st Century – Elementis Chromium

During 1974 the parent company approved a £30 million plant replacement programme. Production capacity was substantially increased in 1982 with the completed installation of a very large (Number 7) kiln. At Corpus Christi, on the USA's coast in Texas, a chemical business was purchased in 1978 from the Pittsburgh Plate and Glass Inc. This was renamed American Chrome and Chemicals Ltd. Another link with Urlay Nook's early history was severed in April 1982 when the sulphuric acid plant was closed. By October 1988, British Chrome and Chemicals became part of the newly formed Harcros Chemical Group. Harcros was derived from an abbreviation of Harrisons and Crossfield. At Eaglescliffe, the next development was in 1990 when a further very large kiln (Number 8) was commissioned. This increased the potential site production of sodium chromate to 150,000 tons per annum. In addition, extensive use had been made of computer technology to improve reliability and to reduce costs. It is also noteworthy that in the last 20 years, the site cleanliness and environmental standards improved dramatically. Moving through the 1990s, a number of Harcros Chemical Group's businesses were sold. In 1998, their chromium specialities, pigments and speciality rubber interests were brought together in a new company, Elementis plc. The chrome business became known as Elementis Chromium. The global headquarters is based at Eaglescliffe and for this a new state of the art business complex was constructed and opened in 1999. During 2000, Elementis plc purchased from Occidental Inc., a chromium chemicals business at Castle Hayne, North Carolina in America. Elementis Chromium now controls all primary chromium chemicals production in the UK and USA and has become the world's largest producer. Throughout its history the facility at Urlay Nook has seen many changes and has progressed to supply many of the requirements of today's complex industrial society. It has survived world wars, depressions, recessions and the loss and transformation of connected industries. This is a truly remarkable achievement.

State of the art business complex for 21st century

Chapter Six

Landmarks of change and fame in Northumbria

Earlier in this account of Northumbria's commercial history, it was described that when the Roman legions came to this country their most difficult adversaries were northern based. It was a brilliant tactical general by the name of Julius Agricola who eventually broke the northern resistance before being recalled to Rome. Following this, and some time after AD 120, Emperor Hadrian came to Britain and ordered a wall to be built between the Tyne and Solway rivers. This was to maintain Roman occupation. It took about six years to construct and had permanent forts at approximately every five miles. Situated at the Tyne end of the wall the Romans built a bridge and fort known as Pons Aelius, after Hadrian who was a member of the Aelian family. The importance of this development was to give Newcastle the beginnings of a long and eventful history as a frontier station, a role which continued thirteen centuries after the fall of Rome.

Corstopium becomes a focal point and supply base for North, South, East and West Communications

Both Pons Aelius and the defence built at Segedunum (Wallsend) were only the subsidiary fringe of a great Roman defence network which spread from a great legionary base at York. The main northern artery for this was a great highway known as Dere Street stretching from Eburacum (York) through Corstopitum (Corbridge) to the wild lands north of Hadrian's wall. Corstopitum, a much larger centre than Pons Aelius, situated on Dere Street, was an important arsenal and supply base being only a mile or two south of the point where the Dere Street passed through the wall. Indeed it was the routes north–south and

east–west which formed the basis for early communications and subsequent 18th century developments. One of these was the construction of the military road in 1751, built on the foundations of the Roman wall between Newcastle and Carlisle. An improved road had been found necessary by General Wade, who during the Jacobite uprising had great difficulty in moving his artillery by the existing quagmire of a route across to Carlisle in an attempt to intercept the Young Pretender on his march south.

Newcastle's borough walls are bursting at the seams

By the middle of the 18th century, the signs for redevelopment within Newcastle's borough became more obvious. The increase in population, combined with commercial and industrial activity caused difficulties both for waggons and pedestrians. Newcastle's first major redevelopment was to begin in 1761 when a subscription opened with a plan for levelling several old houses and enclosing St Nicholas Church Yard. Dwellings known as the Hucksters Booths in the centre of Newgate Street were to be demolished, as

Opposite: *Hadrians Wall, Walltown Crags Turret 45A*

Top: *Corstopitum, a Roman supply base, Corbridge*

were ramshackle buildings called Alvey's Island, to allow the widening of the main part of Cowgate. Other property was pulled down at the foot of the Side where lines of merchants' carriers carts made the narrow turning into Sandhill hazardous. However, congestion within the confines of the borough walls, strongly built gates and narrow archways frequently caused waggons to be stuck. Pilgrim Street Gate where the arch was very low, often saw loads being dismantled to allow waggons passage.

1760s – The first city gates were demolished

Time gave way to the inevitable, something had to give. The sheer number of carriages using the Sand Gate and adjoining streets caused inconvenience and danger to pedestrians. In 1763, the walls and gates in this part of the town were the first to be dismantled, work continuing until after the end of the war with France. The role of the Corporation was increasing, and as well as being involved with jurisdiction, it promoted lighting in streets, a night patrol and by 1786, it obtained powers for refuse collection, monitoring areas for the sale of goods within recognised

The West Gate, Newcastle, 1788

markets, regulation of traffic and improvement of streets. Between 1795 and 1798 Pandon Gate, Close Gate and Sand Gate were pulled down, and from 1802 to 1811 Pilgrim Street Gate, the Postern Gate and West Gate followed, New Gate surviving until 1823. From September 1763 the streets within the walls were lit by public oil lamps and by 1812 this policy had been extended to the suburbs. During this time, with the increase in commerce, a new and more central Customs House was constructed in 1766, replacing the former premises situated at the west end of the quayside. 1814 saw the foundation of a Chamber of Commerce. There were also extensive alterations to the Guildhall and Exchange. Since the building had suffered serious damage in the riot of 1740 and again by fire in August 1791, the Common Council decided in 1796 to reconstruct the entire north front. These alterations were completed by 1823.

Sir Walter, the King of Newcastle

It is significant that during some difficult times during the early stages of the expansion of Newcastle, Sir Walter Calverley Blackett had been mayor five times. He had earned the title of the Patriot, Father of the Poor and King of Newcastle and had represented Newcastle as the sitting member of Parliament from 1734. However, even with the prohibitive costs of a contested parliamentary election there were three contests whilst Blackett was still representing Newcastle between 1774 through to 1780. Some of the town's freemen had become unhappy with Blackett, who had supported the justifiable claim of the Common Council to lease pasture land adjoining the Town Moor. A privilege of the freemen was the right to graze two cows on the moor. A number of freemen exercised their right over the leased land, which was already established with a crop of new corn. After inevitable litigation between the parties, the Common Council sought leave to regulate the issue by a private act of parliament. This act maintained the freemen's rights but allowed 100 acres to be enclosed at any time with rents going towards the poorer freemen and their widows.

The first waves of reconstruction – a new Tyne Bridge completed in 1781

In 1771 a devastating flood destroyed every major bridge on the rivers Tyne, Wear and Tees. The medieval Tyne Bridge was one of the main casualties. A new stone bridge with nine arches was constructed between 1773 and 1781, and one of the engineers consulted was John Smeaton. Although the third Eddystone Lighthouse was successfully built by Smeaton, the bridge which he completed at Hexham in 1780 was swept away through a problem with defective foundations. By 1801, builder David Stephenson was given the task of widening the new Tyne Bridge as it was then incapable of handling the traffic. In 1776, the Assembly Rooms were opened, the construction of which was through William Newton, who also planned the Charlotte Square development. Prior to 1789 the only way from the top of the town to the Quayside was by the steep and narrow Side or a route around by Manor Chare, Cowgate and Broad Chare. The way from the foot of Pilgrim Street to the Flesh Market was through an unsavoury maze of narrow dark and dirty alleys cut by the deep ravine of the Lort Burn.

1784 – Nathaniel Clayton and Alderman Mosley's contribution to re-development

The town had outgrown all of these early streets and badly needed a reshaped structure. The area of the Lort Burn was the key but the problem was the expanse of old property and alley ways on the sides of the dene. For many years the town's magistrates had discussed filling and levelling the Lort Burn dene. However, because of the enormity of the task nothing was done until 1784 when the town clerk Nathaniel Clayton and Alderman Mosley offered to advance a major part of the funding. Then architect and local builder David Stephenson was given the task of proposing

Medieval Tyne Bridge, 1760

137

The Side, Newcastle

Richard Grainger in developing the many landmarks which adorn the city today. Before this time shops were very much of an open type, until the introduction of the more fashionable shops with display windows. Formerly, the Side, Pilgrim Street and upper town were residential, but the Side was occupied by flax dressers and cheesemongers. The display window shops were to be found along the way from Pilgrim Street, Westgate and the lower part of Pudding Chare.

Richard Grainger makes a name for himself as a leading builder

Between 1820 and 1840 Richard Grainger (born 1797, the son of a Quayside porter), rose from poverty to fame by redeveloping Newcastle and becoming the North East's leading builder. With his solicitor and adviser John Clayton (also Town Clerk) he forged links with architects John Dobson, Thomas Oliver, John Wardle and George Walker to make whirlwind transformations to the street and buildings of the town. After an apprenticeship as a joiner, he started in business as a builder with his brother George, a bricklayer, as a partner. Unfortunately, George died soon afterwards and Richard continued with his first important contract which was to build a group of houses in Higham Place. Following this success and further developing his business through architect John Dobson, between 1824 and 1826 he built the greater part of Eldon Square and Blackett Street (named respectively after Lord Eldon, Lord Chancellor of England and John Blackett, Lord Mayor of Newcastle). Grainger lost no time with construction projects and his enterprise with Dobson extended to completing Leazes Terrace and Leazes Crescent in 1829, followed by the Royal

a suitably improved road link. After five years' work David Stephenson's scheme of two fine new streets and pavements was completed: one being Dean Street to give access to the Sandhill and the other Mosley Street adjoining Pilgrim Street and also the markets north of St Nicholas Square. The first Theatre Royal was built on Mosley Street and opened in January 1788, whilst in the following year a Post Office was founded at the east end of the street. Soon afterwards in 1801, two of the four town banks were based on Mosley Street.

1815 – Stephenson paves the way for Dobson and Grainger

After 1810 two more parts of the town were taken down, Wall Knoll to Sand Gate and from Pilgrim Street to Carliol Tower which made way for the construction of Newbridge Street across Pandon Dene. By 1815 there was considerable improvement where new streets had been constructed or old streets widened. Undoubtedly, it was Stephenson who achieved the first major steps forward in redevelopment and literally paved the way for John Dobson and

Arcade on Pilgrim Street in 1832. It is interesting to note that during the same year in 1832, the University of Durham was founded. (The privileges and revenues held by the Prince Bishops of Durham were abolished in 1836 when their castle was incorporated into the university).

A network of new and great streets

In 1834 Grainger commenced his greatest project, one which John Dobson had proposed ten years previously. This was to extend a number of streets from Blackett Street to Dean Street and Neville Street. It had previously been turned down due to cost but Richard Grainger himself spent £95,000 buying land and property to complete the project. This included the demolition of the Old Theatre Royal in Mosley Street and the new flesh market (which had been built in 1808) with an offer to build replacements. With the exception of the Theatre Royal's new portico (designed by Benjamin Green), John Dobson was the architect for the new buildings and streets. These included Grey Street, Grainger Street and Clayton Street, giving access to Hood Street, Market Street, Nun Street and Nelson Street. Richard Grainger was determined to progress quickly and within three hours of buying the

old Theatre Royal, its roof was demolished. By 1835 a new Grainger market was completed, then the largest in Britain. In total he employed two thousand workmen. By 1838 most of the work had been finished including nine streets, many public buildings, private houses and 320 shops.

Bainbridge – the woollen and linen drapers

In 1841, Emerson Bainbridge of Weardale took the opportunity to open a drapers store on Richard Grainger's recently developed Market Street. It began as a partnership and was among one of the very first traders to

The Grainger Market, Newcastle, completed in 1835

Bainbridge & Co., Market Street, Newcastle, opened 1841

died in 1861 whilst working in Clayton Street West.

Water for the dirty rich and poor

By the middle of the nineteenth century, Newcastle had grown to almost 100,000 in population. There was wealth centred around the Tyne and those with taste could buy the best goods and enjoy the finest life styles of the time. To illustrate this the Newcastle Assay Office passed approximately 12,500 ounces of silver in an average year around this period and almost eighty silversmiths were registered with their marks. However, the larger part of the working population was on the breadline. One amenity in short supply for both rich and poor was water, supplies of which had not developed with the increase in population. Water for Newcastle had been sourced from springs on the Town Moor and at Pandon was piped to public fountains with troughs for horses. By the end of the seventeenth century springs were tapped at Castle Leazes and spring water was piped from Gateshead Fell. The district in Gateshead known as Pipewellgate was so called because of the water it supplied. In North Shields, at New Quay, the Waterville reservoir supplied water but mainly for the local brewers providing ale for shipping needs. With poor water supplies and a lack of sanitation facilities, the conditions of the working class population were either taken for granted or unknown except to doctors and clergymen until 1831. Then it took an outbreak of cholera to awaken bureaucracy to the hazards of ignorance. There was substantial overcrowding in working class housing. Many families had to live in just one room, with water available only by standpipe or water cart and virtually no

adopt fixed price labelling to dispense with traditional haggling. The store led the way with the sale of ready made clothing and in 1849 departmentalisation. In 1855 Emerson became sole proprietor and the store continued to prosper and expand. (It remained at Market Street until the business was taken over by the John Lewis Partnership in 1952. Then, the store continued to trade under the Bainbridge name and later moved to Eldon Square, Newcastle).

1861 – Richard Grainger leaves lasting landmarks in Newcastle

Having developed Newcastle as a fashionable centre for shopping and living, Richard Grainger had both vision and energy. Unfortunately, he over-reached himself with the purchase of Elswick Hall for £114,000 and his ambition to turn it into an 800 acre business park. In 1842, he had lost everything and fled the area from creditors. Eventually, Grainger returned in a less dynamic role to finish his days when he

Top: *A Corporation fire brigade tender, 1868*

Above: *Drinking trough at Gallowgate, Newcastle*

sanitary conveniences. It took the Poor Law Commission to institute an inquiry (conducted by Dr D B Reid) into the causes of deaths amongst the destitute. This was to pave the way for the first Public Health Act in 1845. The main purpose of this Act was to enforce the provision of constant supplies of piped water, with proper sewage and sanitary facilities to prevent supply contamination. Any wastage or fouling of water was to become punishable by law.

The Newcastle and Gateshead Water Company established 1893

As a result of the Act and legislation, this was to be the catalyst for the formation of new water companies. One of the first in the country was the Newcastle and Gateshead Water Company established in 1893. This had been set up through the Newcastle Fire Office and the Subscription Water Company who had previously controlled water utilities. The first reservoir to be constructed was at Hallington. Through leakage this reservoir had a

continuous water loss of almost twenty per cent. This was highlighted after a serious fire could not be controlled due to insufficient supply from the new reservoir. Subsequently issues arose about ownership of both the fire brigade and the water utility itself. Although the water undertaking remained in private ownership, the local authority took responsibility for the fire brigade. Before the end of the century, to overcome local and national government criticisms, two new reservoirs were planned at Colt Crag and Swinburn. These reservoirs also suffered from water leaks. Once remedial work was completed, the Newcastle and Gateshead Water Company was able to provide up to 35 gallons of water a day to a total of 370,000 consumers. In 1888 a report had outlined that the demand for water on Tyneside would quickly grow from 12 million gallons a day serving a population of 320,000, to 20 million gallons a day. Although, the resources had been provided to cover the

Installation of a mains water feed pipe for Newcastle, 1900

141

existing demand, additional capacity would be required. The site was chosen at Catcleugh on the Rede in Northumberland. A 27 mile long pipeline was laid to make the connection to Newcastle. This was completed in 1895. A reservoir was subsequently constructed at Catcleugh, employing 600 people at its peak to become operational in 1906. By the middle of the twentieth century improved demands were met for rural communities. In 1944 the Rural Water Supply and Sewerage Act set aside £15 million for rural supplies. By 1950 a construction scheme was implemented to provide 64 service reservoirs and six treatment works for water supplies to rural areas.

1831 – Earl Grey gains greater regional representation

A movement towards parliamentary reform was gaining momentum. Meetings were held by leading dignitaries to advocate

1837-1838 Earl Grey's monument is erected in Newcastle

education issues, abolition of slavery, Catholic emancipation and free trade. Earl Grey (of Howick Hall near Craster, Northumberland) was the government minister who introduced a new reform bill in 1831 creating many new MPs for the region. In June 1832, the first Reform Act was passed and in December that year elections gave Gateshead, Tynemouth and South Shields representatives in parliament. It also increased the electorate from approximately 3,000 freemen to 5,000 householders. Important changes in local government soon followed and the Municipal Corporations Act of 1835 established modern town councils. Such was the importance of these electoral changes to the North East that a statue of Earl Grey was created and erected on top of a lofty column in the centre of Newcastle. In addition to this, one of Richard Grainger's streets was renamed from Upper Dean Street to Grey Street. Built at the head of Grey Street in 1837–38, the column houses a stairway and stands 135 feet high. Newcastle's council was based in a new Town Hall situated in a block between the Cloth Market and St Nicholas' Square. In the centre of the Town Hall complex was the Corn Market or Exchange, above which there was a large hall used for concerts and public meetings. It had capacity for a 3,000-member orchestra and seats for 3,000 in the auditorium. The council introduced a new rating system, replacing income from market tolls, stall rents and town property management. With proper accounts being kept, councillors were to be elected by rate payers and income was to be spent for the benefit of the borough. New responsibilities were taken by the councils which included police, transport, water and drainage. In

1836, the privileges of the Bishopric of Durham were transferred to the Crown after the death of Bishop William van Mildert. An act of 1832 then became effective, bringing an end to the Palatinate and giving future bishops a fixed income. The County Durham districts of Bedlingtonshire, Norhamshire and Islandshire became part of Northumberland in 1844.

1854 – The Great Fire causes devastation across the river

On 6 October 1854, the Tyne experienced a disastrous fire which affected lives of people and property on both banks of the river. It began at one o'clock in the morning in a worsted factory at Gateshead and quickly spread to an adjoining warehouse containing explosive chemical products, including 3,000 tons of brimstone. At quarter past three the building exploded and killed over fifty people, mostly spectators, when stones, bricks and blazing timbers were sent hurtling through the air and across the river. The explosion was heard over fifty miles away in Berwick and damaged houses at Shields. The glow from the fire could be seen at Smeaton, near Northallerton, whilst pitmen at Sunderland came to the surface in alarm. Flying debris set alight ships and caused other fires destroying medieval quayside buildings. As well as the death toll, almost 800 families were made homeless and most bodies were incinerated beyond recognition. The ruins were eventually replaced by new office blocks, examples being the Exchange Buildings and Princess Buildings built in the early 1860s and used as merchants' offices. In order to meet the demands from the new commercial buildings and the public, a General Post Office was opened in 1876 at St Nicholas Square. Its noble structure still stands today not as a post office, but as general office accommodation. The lower part of the building is in the Doric order, while the upper is mostly Corinthian. The building

Left: *Howick Hall, Earl Grey's country residence*

Below: *The Gateshead and Newcastle Great Fire of 1854*

Fenwick's first store
opened in Newcastle,
1882

was designed by J Williams and has a magnificent stone facade, beautifully ornamented.

1882 – Newcastle was given city status

Adjacent to the former General Post Office, St Nicholas' Church became a cathedral when Newcastle town became a city. It was also the same year when the original Fenwick's store opened in Newcastle's Northumberland Street. On 23 May 1882, the diocese of Newcastle was founded by an Order in Council to consist of Northumberland and the counties of the towns of Newcastle upon Tyne and Berwick-upon-Tweed, and the ancient civil parish of Alston, and its chapelries in Cumberland. The parish church of St Nicholas, Newcastle, became the Cathedral Church. By a charter, dated 13 June 1882, Newcastle was created a city. Until 1888, the Justices of the Peace were responsible for government in the counties. After this, elected county councils were established and followed in 1894 with urban and district councils which had similar powers to the borough councils.

The development of bridges across the Tyne

The increase of traffic and the development of the bridges across the Tyne underpinned the importance of Newcastle as a growing centre of communications. Until the middle of the nineteenth century there was only one river crossing which was by the Tyne Bridge. Now, through years of expansion, there are six road bridges covering seven miles of the Tyne between Newburn and Newcastle. Robert Stephenson built a dual purpose crossing in 1849, the High Level Bridge, which stands 120 ft above the river with a twin decked structure, carrying a railway on top with a road beneath. This was the earliest known bridge where wrought iron construction was used in conjunction with cast iron. The Swing Bridge was opened in 1876; designed and built by Lord Armstrong's company, its mechanism was designed to enable 10,000 ton coal ships to reach the staiths at Derwenthaugh. The double cantilevered 1,200 ton bridge was originally driven by steam but replaced by electric pumps in 1959. The hydraulic machinery pivoted the bridge through 180 degrees to give ships passage. The bridge took eight years to complete and replaced the stone bridge built in 1781.

Bridges at crossings between Scotswood and Newcastle

At Scotswood, road and rail crossings were constructed. A chain link suspension road bridge was opened in 1831 whilst a railway bridge was completed forty years later. The suspension bridge was replaced in 1967 and has a steel tied arched structure of 328 ft span with a height of 25 ft above high water. There were two original toll bridges, one being the Redheugh Bridge

Main Pic: *Reflections at night – Tyne Bridge*

Inset, left to right:
Transporter Bridge, Middlesbrough

Tyne Bridge under construction

The Wearmouth Bridge, Sunderland

Northumbria's famous river crossings

Clockwise from top left:

Yarm Bridge (built circa 1400), Teesside

Victoria Bridge, Stockton

Queen Alexandra Bridge, Sunderland

The Swing Bridge, Newcastle

*Newport Bridge,
Middlesbrough*

built in 1871 (replaced by a concrete bridge in 1984) and the Newburn Bridge. The Newburn Bridge was opened in 1893 and operated as a toll bridge until 1947, the original timber deck being replaced by concrete in 1965. The King Edward VII and Tyne Bridges were built early in the twentieth century; the King Edward being opened in 1906 and erected by the Cleveland Bridge Engineering Co., for the North Eastern Railway Company.

Teesside becomes famous for bridges

The oldest bridge in Teesside is the road bridge at Yarm which dates from about 1400. Yarm was the original port on the Tees but its trade was seriously affected with the opening of the Stockton Bridge in 1771 (replaced by the Victoria Bridge 1887). The Cleveland Bridge Engineering Company was established at Darlington in 1878 and became renown for erecting bridges throughout the world. In 1905, the Victoria Falls Bridge was constructed by this Darlington based firm. The twin foundation stones of the Transporter Bridge across the Tees were laid on 3 August 1910. The Transporter is the largest bridge of its kind

in the world, being 261 metres long, with a span of 75 metres and supporting towers 69 metres high. The Transporter Bridge was designed to carry 750 passengers and 600 vehicles across the river. It was the concept of Alderman McLaughlin with the advantage that it would not restrict shipping. Cleveland Bridge Engineering Company designed and built the bridge with the assistance of Sir William Arroll and Company of Glasgow. The transporter bridge at Middlesbrough was officially opened by Prince Arthur of Connaught in 1911 and cost £87,316 to build. The Newport Bridge was constructed by Dorman Long. This Middlesbrough bridge was opened by the Duke and Duchess of York in 1934. Designed by David Anderson, it is a vertical lift bridge, which means that the section which crosses the river raises to the height of the towers to allow ships passage. Two 325 hp electric motors took 1 minute and 30 seconds to raise or lower the central span. The Newport Bridge was the first of its kind to be built in this country; cost £430,000 and with 8,000 tons of steel used in its structure, this bridge was the heaviest in the world. Gradually, as the need for ships passage to Stockton declined, the last lifting ceremony took place in 1990.

Wear bridges were the largest and heaviest of their time

Until the end of the eighteenth century the Wear could only be crossed by ferry or by the bridge upstream at Chester-le-Street. The main difficulty of constructing a bridge across the river at Sunderland was its width 250 feet (75 metres) and height requirements for tall masted ships. An iron bridge was the least expensive option although the technology involved was relatively new. At Coalbrookdale in

Shropshire, the first iron bridge known as The Iron Bridge was built in 1779 but the river there was only half the width of the River Wear. Whilst the abutments were being constructed in 1792, the Walker Iron Works at Rotherham cast and tested the first iron rib. The construction consisted of six arched ribs made in 2ft 5in (75cm) pieces and held together by wrought iron bands. These six ribs were then connected by cast iron cross tubes. It was the largest single span iron bridge in the world when it was opened in August 1796. During the 1800s the bridge needed repairing and between 1927–29 was rebuilt with a new structure more capable of handling the volume of traffic. The other bridge, the Queen Alexandra, was designed to improve both the flow of general road traffic over the river and also provide a railway connection from the Annfield Plain collieries to Sunderland's South Docks. This bridge was officially opened on 10 June 1909. In order to accommodate the railway it was designed on two levels by Charles Harrison, the North Eastern Railway's Chief Engineer. With a high water clearance of 85 feet and a 300 foot width single arch span containing 2,600 tons of steel, this was the heaviest bridge span constructed in Britain. It was built by Sir William Arrol and Co Ltd., who also built the Forth Bridge. Initially about six million tons of coal were carried across the bridge annually. However, the upper deck rail line ceased to be used after 1921 as the volume of goods trains no longer justified maintaining the line. The bridge was also used by pedestrians and was adapted for gas and water mains, a pumped rising main for sewage and high voltage electricity cables.

1928 – The Tyne becomes a model for the Sydney Harbour Bridge

The Tyne Bridge was opened by George V

in 1928 and was built for Newcastle and Gateshead Corporations and the Ministry of Transport. It was the fourth successive Tyne Bridge and was constructed by Dorman, Long and Co., of Middlesbrough with a design by Mott, Hay and Anderson. The Tyne Bridge was also the prototype for the great Sydney Harbour Bridge in Australia (completed in 1832). The Tyne Bridge is a striking engineering achievement, the road being supported by a huge steel arch 170 ft high, with ends sunk deep in concrete below massive piers. Towards the end of the twentieth century the bridge was carrying 58,000 vehicles a day, whilst the combined volume of traffic on all six road bridges amounted to 140,000 vehicles daily.

Demand for better housing

It was the acute growth of Newcastle in the nineteenth century which quickly emphasised the need for improved standards in living conditions and amenities. In 1750, Newcastle had 3,433 houses, Sunderland 792, Darlington 444 and Stockton 431. A hundred years later, in Newcastle the population of Elswick alone was 3,539 and within forty years by 1891, Elswick had grown to a population of

Rows of terraced housing situated at Elswick near Armstrong's works

Jesmond Dene,
Newcastle upon Tyne

51,608. In this locality Lord Armstrong built many rows of houses which were occupied by the workers and families of those employed at Armstrong's works. Builders were not obliged to lay on services and most streets were without drains or sewers, and only 9% of houses had water. Bathrooms and toilets were rarely found in houses at this time. However, as a result of the work of the Health of Towns Commission (1845), town authorities had taken the initiative to provide public fountains and standpipes. Public baths and washhouses were also established. At Oakwellgate, Gateshead, public baths were built in 1855. Unfortunately, like others, initially the cost of use was prohibitive to the poorer classes. Gradually, through time, this improved and by 1906 around Newcastle there were public baths and washhouses situated on the Scotswood Road, Gallowgate, Pilgrim Street, Shipley Street, Gibson Street, Church Street and Northumberland Road.

Industrialists support local hospitals

With lack of sewage disposal and outbreaks of disease, health acts and the creation of new local government responsibilities were together the catalyst for improvements. In particular, the first priority was towards health and steps were taken to improve sewage collection and water facilities. Many industrialists turned their attention and support towards hospitals. Charles Mitchell, Sir George Hunter, Sir Charles Mark Palmer, helped to found hospitals in Walker, Wallsend and Jarrow, whilst in South Shields, The Ingram Infirmary was opened in 1873. More than half the total cost (£4,000) of The Ingram Infirmary was contributed by the Jarrow Chemical Company. The site was donated by the Dean and Chapter of Durham and the

income included weekly contributions (amounting to £1,200) from the workforces of local companies. This form of support was the main source of income until government reforms created health authorities. Tyneside became a centre for the study of industrial diseases including various forms of respiratory complaints and lead poisoning. There were opportunities for clinical studies in all aspects of medicine and surgery. In 1876 Newcastle's medical school proposed instituting degrees in Sanitary Science. By 1891 there were degrees of bachelor and doctor of hygiene, and in 1894 offered a Diploma of Public Health. In the following year Bacteriological Laboratories were opened and developed for testing milk for tuberculin infection and many other facets of public health interest. Clinical teaching became world renowned in Newcastle with many overseas students working in the study of epidemics, general practice and social medicine.

Basic infrastructure improvements

During the last thirty years of the 19th century there was a considerable improvement in street cleansing, lighting and town drainage and sewerage. Development in housing, where there was the worst overcrowding in Tyneside, was not to be addressed until after the First World War. One step towards providing additional land for workers' housing was in 1904 when Newcastle Corporation annexed Walker and Benwell urban district councils together with the rural areas of Fenham and part of Kenton. Newcastle then reconstituted its traditional subdivisions into electoral wards for the return of representatives on the city council. England's first all labour county council assembled in Durham City at Shire Hall under the leadership of Peter Lee in 1909.

Some of Newcastle's first town walks originated as a result of Dr D B Reid's recommendations through the Health of Towns Commission in 1845. In 1873 Leazes Park, and then Bull Park (opened in 1880 where the town bull had been kept) were developed into parts of the Town Moor. There were many park developments through the work of the Corporation and also the welfare of prominent industrialists. Brandling Park was established next to the Great North Road and Sir William Armstrong donated a park in Heaton (1880) and Jesmond Dene (1883). On the west side of Newcastle, the Corporation bought Elswick Hall, which less then forty years earlier had belonged to Richard Grainger, and laid out its grounds as a public park. In Tynemouth, Spittal Dene was donated as a park by the Duke of Northumberland in 1885, the construction of which gave work to the unemployed. On the other side of the river at South Shields, in 1867 the Corporation leased a derelict brickyard and made a recreation park with swings and a small lake

for model boats. Then between 1884 and 1899 it planned and constructed South and North Parks with unemployed labour. In Wallsend between 1901 and 1914 Sir George Hunter acquired a number of properties and land which he donated to the Borough. At Gateshead, Saltwell Park was created as a memorial to all those who lost their lives in the South African War (1899–1902). Clearly, with the growth of population it was an important time to be seen making environmental changes.

1887 – The new Exhibition Park, Newcastle

Some of the businesses described in various chapters of this book took part in The Royal Mining, Engineering and Industrial

Above: *Saltwell Park, Gateshead*

Below: *Royal Jubilee Exhibition, 1887*

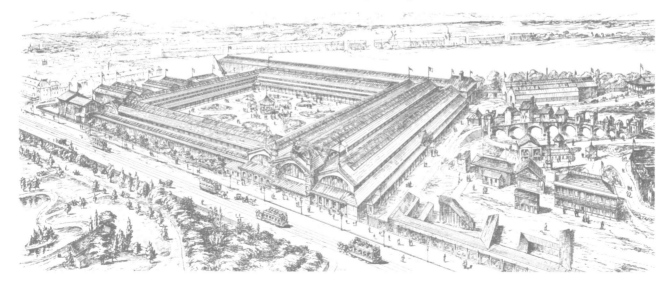

buildings at that exhibition, the Palace of Arts, was to become the Museum of Science and Engineering. From 1934 the collections grew until the renamed Discovery Museum was relocated in 1978 to the former CWS Northern Region Headquarters at Blandford Street, Newcastle. The original Palace of Arts continued in use as a military museum.

1936 – Team Valley Trading Estate established

After Black Thursday on 24 October 1929, when Wall Street crashed and the American economy spiralled into decline, it was not long before the effects reached the North East. Within five years, unemployment levels rose to nearly 22 per cent and the gap between north and south became very apparent. The Special Areas Act of 1934 led to the designation of part of Gateshead for light industry. The Team Valley Trading Estate was established in 1936 for this purpose and recognised the dangers of relying too heavily on a small number of manufacturing industries employing many people. One change for the better was easier home ownership for reasonably paid skilled or white collar workers. The 1930's saw a housing boom with the cost of a small terraced house averaging £250 with deposit requirements being reduced to 5 or 10%. With better streets and communications across the river, Newcastle grew steadily to the next period of planning reform. There was a reorganisation of Durham University in 1937. It was now recognised in two divisions; Durham and Newcastle with the Newcastle colleges grouped under the title King's College.

T Dan Smith's plans for re-developing Newcastle

From 1945 onwards local labour politician T Dan Smith developed his planning

Newcastle Town Hall (opposite St. Nicholas Cathedral), 1934

Exhibition held in May 1887 on the Town Moor, Newcastle (in the area which from that date became known as Exhibition Park). It was also known as the Royal Jubilee Exhibition and was a shop window to the world for Tyneside's commercial enterprise. There were great engineering displays from Lord Armstrong's Elswick works including a full size model of a 110 ton gun. There were large working models of coal and lead mines, model working bakeries and dairy, military engineering encampment, as well as an art gallery, royal state carriages, and a 360 ft. toboggan slide. One of the features was a reconstruction of the old Tyne Bridge as it existed before it was demolished by the great flood of 1771. This showed the bridge and its shops when it was the main access route between England and Scotland. Held in grounds covering 312 acres, the exhibition was enormous. There was music from two bands and a grand organ every day, all brilliantly illuminated by electric lighting. This was a magnificent show in its time, only rivalled by the North East Coast Exhibition of 1929. The 1929 exhibition was on a larger scale, lasting six months and attracting almost 42 million visitors. One of the

aspirations for Newcastle as the Brasilia of the North. Throughout the 1960s a number of urban redevelopments were carried out by the Northern Economic Planning Council under the leadership of T Dan Smith. During this time new concrete constructed landmarks appeared including a new Civic Centre and a central motorway. The former Town Hall built in 1858 was situated in a block of buildings between St Nicholas Square and Bigg Market. It was considered too small for the growing authority's needs. The new Civic Centre cost £4 million to complete with 12 storeys of purpose designed offices and an underground car park. Designed using teak on the staircases and marble walls, it offered courtyards with fountains, silver nickel bronze railings and Portland stone facing. The new Civic Centre was only the second in Britain to be completed since the war. Many of the depressed derelict post-war terraced rows of houses were also demolished. He also planned a two-tier concrete motorway with overhead walkways over the streets, a concept which was never developed. T Dan Smith's political career also paved the way for the Eldon Square retail development and the Kielder Reservoir scheme. The Eldon Square complex was developed with covered shopping malls, the first phase being opened in March 1975. At the time it gained acclaim for being one of the greatest in Europe with the largest recreation centre ever incorporated into such a complex. Eldon Square remains an integral part of the heart of Newcastle with restaurants, cafés, pubs, markets and main retail shopping outlets with frontages open to the malls. One great loss through T Dan Smith's twentieth century renewal was John Dobson's fine Royal Arcade on Pilgrim

Street, demolished in 1963 to make way for the concrete Swan House roundabout. 1963 was also noted for the University of Newcastle upon Tyne becoming independent without any ties to the University of Durham.

New town and county developments

During the 1960s new towns were developed at Killingworth (1962), Cramlington (1963), Washington (1964) and Peterlee (1968). These new towns were designed to soak up the increasing populations around Tyneside and Sunderland. In order to cope with increased road traffic, the Darlington bypass was the first section of the new A1(M) motorway to be opened in 1965. This was to become the main routeway through the North East. In April 1968, The County Borough of Teesside was created bringing into its boundaries the Old Durham towns of Stockton and Billingham, with the Yorkshire towns of Redcar, Thornaby and Middlesbrough. In 1974 local government reforms created new counties known as Tyne and Wear and Cleveland. Before this time Gateshead, Jarrow, Blaydon, South Shields and Sunderland were within the County

The Royal Arcade, Newcastle

until 1961 before construction began and six years to complete with a final cost of £8.5 million. At its deepest the tunnel was 50 feet below the river and ran for 5,500 feet. From the beginning the proposed tolls caused much controversy. When the Queen officially opened the tunnel in 1967 vehicles were charged between one shilling (5p) and four shillings (20p) dependent on type. At the beginning of the twenty first century the tunnel was handling an average of 38,000 vehicles a day compared to its original 24,000 vehicle design maximum.

Major reservoir schemes for Teesside and Northumberland

In the 1970s two major reservoir schemes were designed to provide water reserves sufficient to serve domestic and industrial demands for the North of England into the twenty first century. The first of these was the Cow Green reservoir opened in Teesdale in 1970, supplying Teesside. Kielder reservoir construction began in 1976 and was a development by Northumbria Water. It took seven years to complete and cost £167 million. The area of the reservoir covered 33,000 acres with a capacity of 44 million gallons of water. With a 27 mile shoreline, Kielder Water became the largest man made lake in Western Europe, set in the massive Kielder Forest Park of over 153,000 acres containing around 150 million trees. It remains a major tourist attraction in Northumbria with way marked walks and trails, picnic sites, visitor centres, ferry service, swimming pool, fishing, water sports and cycle hire. Opened at Falstone, Kielder Water there was the only reindeer farm in England, also with Cheviot goats, farm animals, fallow deer and rare birds.

Durham boundary. These towns then became part of Tyne and Wear together with most of the Tyneside area north of the Tyne (which was formerly part of Northumberland). The newly created County of Cleveland brought into its boundary the old borough of Teesside (created in 1867), including Hartlepool, plus areas of rural North Yorkshire including Guisborough. In 1996 Cleveland was abolished and Middlesbrough became a unitary authority although for ceremonial purposes it remained part of North Yorkshire.

A long awaited road tunnel opened in 1967

With a growing population and new towns being built both north and south of the Tyne, greater traffic was also becoming a concern. As early as 1946 the Labour Government approved a plan for the construction of a road tunnel under the River Tyne. Situated between Jarrow and Howdon, the new road and pedestrian tunnel would assist the traffic flow easing the burden on both the bridges and ferries. It was the largest civil engineering project of its kind for 30 years. Although the post war estimate for the work was £2 million, it took

Cow Green Reservoir (opened 1970), Teesdale

For over 150 years ownership of water resources had been locally retained. However, when Jerome Monod became president of Suez Lyonnaise des Eaux in 1980, all of this was to change. The French company was already active in the business of water and energy sources. In line with an ambitious international development programme, Jerome Monod formed a partnership with the Newcastle and Gateshead Water Company in 1988. North East Water was established as a result of this and an amalgamation with South Shields and Sunderland water companies in 1992. According to the National Rivers Authority, in 1990 Northumbria Water was reported to be of the best quality in England and Wales. Soon the scene was set for a merger between Lyonnaise company North East Water and Northumbrian Water. This happened in 1996, combining their resources to supply water and sewerage services to 2.6 million regional customers.

In 1981, work commenced on another great development in Northumbria, the MetroCentre. Europe's largest retail and entertainment complex was conceived by Sir John Hall. Born in Northumberland, Sir John started work as an apprentice surveyor with the Coal Board in 1949. After he spent time learning about land values and deals he left the NCB and became a partner in a Sunderland estate agency before establishing his own development business Cameron-Hall. The inspiration for the MetroCentre came from North America. The opportunity and time was right for the development of a former industrial site on the fringe of Gateshead. John Hall then successfully negotiated the use of the land which was owned by the Church Commission. The main construction of Europe's largest shopping complex took five years to complete and opened in 1986 as a role model for many other developments throughout the country. In 1987, two new agencies were established to regenerate the region. The Tyne and Wear Development Corporation, and The Teesside Development Corporation both invested millions of pounds developing major urban areas.

By the new millennium Newcastle's Quayside was subject to major redevelopment by Amec Developments, formerly in partnership with Tyne and Wear

The MetroCentre (before and after), Gateshead

North Shields Fish Quay Development Company Ltd. In 1973 the value of fish landed at North Shields reached a record of £4.3 million. However, after years of study and projections of future landings further project development was set aside. The decline in fishing in the last two decades of the century proved this to have been a wise decision. This assisted the Fish Quay to turn its fortune to profit after a number of loss-making years. Also at North Shields, a new Royal Quays development turned derelict dock land into a harbour village, with housing, a retail shopping outlet, water park leisure centre and commercial sites, all within an Enterprise Zone. The Royal Quays Marina was developed at the former Albert Edward Dock in 1998. With luxury yacht and club facilities, the marina would eventually have more than 400 berths. The Port of Tyne Authority constructed one of the finest ferry terminals in the world, secured through a Nissan car contract. On the site of the old Armstrong factory at Scotswood, a prestigious development known as the Newcastle Business Park attracted companies which brought employment to approximately 5,000 people.

Regional developments in Gateshead, Hartlepool and Stockton

On the south side of the Tyne many other twentieth century developments included business parks, leisure and sports centres. A National Garden Festival was held at

Top: *Hartlepool's Historic Quay*

Above: *Royal Quays, North Shields*

Right: *The Tees Barrage, Teesside*

Development Corporation, and with restoration and sympathetic construction brought new Law Courts, executive offices, hotels, cafés, restaurants and wine bars. Tyne and Wear Development Corporation directed millions of pounds in the reclamation of land and derelict property along the banks of the Tyne. At North Shields, the result of a successful partnership between the local fishing industry, North Tyneside Council, Tyne and Wear Development Corporation, Port of Tyne Authority and the European Community, saw a £1.6 million regeneration project with

154

Gateshead in 1990. It was designed to regenerate derelict industrial land for the future and covered an area from the river Tyne towards Dunston. In 1994, Hartlepool's Historic Quay was opened. The quay was developed by Teesside Development Corporation based on the reconstruction of an eighteenth century port. The following year in 1995, a £50 million project known as the Tees Barrage was completed at Stockton. It created ten miles of clean water between Worsall near Yarm and Stockton. The 70 metre wide barrage was constructed by Tarmac Construction and fitted with four mechanised steel gates to control the level of the river. As part of the project, a white water course for canoeists was specially constructed. Durham celebrated its 1,000 year anniversary in 1995. All of those years ago monks carried the coffin of St Cuthbert to his final resting place at Dun Holm where a settlement was established, to eventually be known as Durham. St Cuthbert became the Patron Saint of Northumbria and the construction of the cathedral commenced under the instruction of the Prince Bishop William St Carileph in 1093. Remarkably, it was completed within forty years.

Background of the Angel

Over 900 years later, in February 1998, the Angel of the North sculpture was unveiled and became the subject of many controversial discussions. One fact remains, it is now a highly prominent feature situated at Gateshead's Eighton Banks overlooking the 90,000 (per day) motorists who travel along the A1. With a structure 20 metres in height and a 54 metre wing span (almost the same as a jumbo jet), it symbolises the strength and great abilities of a region which has a history steeped in engineering and industry. The idea was first mooted by Peter

Davies, head of visual arts at Northern Arts (the regional arts development agency for the North of England) at the time of the Gateshead National Garden Festival, when he referred to the site as being perfect for a gateway sculpture. Gateshead Council conducted research for three years before short listing Antony Gormley and his concept, A Case For An Angel. In order to bring the project to fruition, there was a working relationship between the artist and engineers to solve the problem of aesthetics and the practical one of the sculpture having to withstand enormous wind pressures of up to 100 mph. Finally, a pledge from Gateshead Council was that it would not

The Angel of the North, Gateshead

155

plough any of the rate payers money into the project was also realised. The £800,000 cost of commissioning and making the work came from The National Lottery, the European Regional Development Fund, Northern Arts and business sponsorship. Mike White who joined the council in 1988 as assistant arts director, was the main driving force behind the project.

Spectacular developments for the new millennium

Gateshead's boldness and enterprise has been subsequently recognised through various funding bodies supporting the transformation project of the Baltic Flour Mills into an international centre for contemporary arts, and a futuristic building for The Sage, a new regional music centre situated between the Baltic and The Tyne Bridge. These projects together with the unique Gateshead Millennium Bridge and Newcastle's International Centre for Life were crowning developments for the beginning of the twenty first century. A world first for Newcastle was the construction of a spectacular £54 million educational leisure complex, the International Centre for Life. The Sage,

Left: *The Sage, Gateshead*

Right: *Millennium Bridge, Tyne*

supported by the Arts Council, provides a permanent home for the Northern Sinfonia orchestra with a state-of-the-art concert hall, music school and library, ranking among the top ten venues in the world for the performance of acoustic chamber music.

The Millennium Bridge – The blinking eye

The blinking eye as it has been described was voted for by the people of Gateshead to choose a bridge which would complement the existing six river bridges. Linking leisure developments on both sides of the Tyne, the bridge provides a stunning pedestrian and cycle crossing. Ships may pass through when the bridge opens, turning on pivots at each bank of the river to give 25 metre clearance access under the giant lid of the eye. Opening or closing, the procedure is completed in four minutes and, being highly energy efficient, costs only £3.06p each time the bridge is operated. It has a span of 126 metres and the elegant arch weighs 850 tonnes. The £22m cost included a £9.2m grant from the Millennium Commission. It was open for public use in September 2001 and at night features a dazzling light display which creates a stunning reflection on the river.

Written in the style of the time this profile is based on a visit to the works and yards in 1890. Armstrong, Addison and Co. Timber importers and preservers North Dock, Sunderland.

The works of Messrs. Armstrong, Addison and Co., at North Dock Sunderland was established in 1853 and became one of the most important industrial centres on the River Wear. Next to iron and steel, the timber trade grew to be our greatest national industry. The firm not only supplied many of the great railway companies, colliery proprietors, agricultural providers, and civil engineers throughout the kingdom and abroad with prepared and preserved timbers, but also made a special feature of supplying preserved telegraph poles to Her Majesty's Government. The timber business was founded on this site by the late Mr John Armstrong. He had helped to raise the Wear and the Tyne to their position of importance among the mercantile and industrial rivers of the world. Descended from an old border family, he took a prominent part in the development of the railway systems in the North East. His splendid business abilities were the subject of appreciative notices in all the leading northern newspapers following his death, in 1887. The firm then continued in the control of his son Mr W I Armstrong, Mr J G Addison, Town Councillor and River Wear Commissioner, and Mr R W Herbert.

Extensive works with every type of plant

The works at North Dock covered a considerable area. There were extensive steam powered saw mills, preserving works, and large yards stocked with innumerable piles of English and foreign timbers in the rough and prepared for a great variety of uses. In the steam saw mills there was every conceivable type of plant and machinery for converting wood including circular, band and other saws as well as planing and mortising machines. The workshops were constantly turning out palings, hurdles, fences, telegraph poles, gates, railway sleepers, pavement blocks, colliery timbers, wood for cattle sheds and other agricultural fixtures. The yards were intersected with a network of railway lines leading to the docks where along the great warf, timber from the Baltic, Canada, etc., would be received directly from the ships with minimal handling costs. Powerful cranes, together with other labour saving appliances and handling arrangements, enabled the firm to effect important economies whilst maintaining the highest standards of efficiency. Provision was made for the seasoning and drying of timber.

A choice of timber preservation

In the preserving works, carefully dried and prepared wood was taken into air tight tunnels, or huge cylinders. After the air was thoroughly exhausted, creosote would be forced into the wood's pores at a

Armstrong Addison and Co., Sunderland

Bridges over the River Wear, Sunderland

tremendous pressure, so that it would be impossible afterwards for air and moisture to lodge in the fibre of the wood to produce decay. Another process known as kyanising was also applied, and used a preparation of mercury as a preserving agent instead of creosote. Such were the demands for the company's timber, that immense reserves of both preserved and natural timber were stocked. There was timber prepared for all varieties of use and ready to be dispatched by rail or ship at the shortest notice.

Kit's Peth, a den for contrabrand

It was a somewhat odd coincidence that this, which became the seat of one of the industries on which the Government so largely depended for supplies, was at the beginning of the 1800s associated with smuggling. Long before the timber firm was founded here, there was on the incline above the creosoting works a ravine known as Kit's Peth where in the old times before the Revenue Officer asserted the supremacy of the law, many a goodly cargo of brandy, silk, and tobacco, was run in contrabrand style.

Pioneers of wood paving blocks

One of the greatest achievements of Messrs Armstrong, Addison and Co., was in

their successful experiments for the application of their timber preserving processes. In this context they were awarded a medal for this in the 1887 Newcastle Exhibition. As well as manufacturing telegraph poles and railway sleepers etc., the firm held a unique and distinctive position as pioneers of creosoted wood pavement block. Initially, by way of experiment, during 1867 the firm was permitted by the Sunderland Corporation to lay down preserved wood pavement over the roadway of the Wear Bridge. Two sections were laid and tested together, one of beech and the other of redwood. The severity of the test against the character of the traffic on the Wear Bridge was a great advantage as it conclusively demonstrated the superiority of the product. This brought them into such prominence that their wood pavement blocks were soon in demand by all of the major cities and great centres throughout the country.

Foundations built more than a century ago

Stephen Easten Ltd. Building contractors, specialists in restoration and conservation. Westgate Road, Newcastle upon Tyne.

The founder of this company, Stephen Easten was born in 1867 and served as an apprentice in the building trade close to his Lowick home in the borders. During his teenage years Newcastle had become an increasingly important centre of trade development. By 1882, it had been recognised with new city status. Having experienced some hard times, by the age of twenty one, the attraction of starting a business in Newcastle was irresistible. From small construction work Easten's firm grew to a notable size and by 1906 was incorporated as a limited company. During the same year Stephen Easten was elected as a member of Newcastle City Council. This was the start of his service in public office, being appointed Sheriff of Newcastle City in 1917 and serving twice as Lord Mayor.

Sir Stephen Easten, Lord Mayor promotes airport and bridge

It could be stated that following the death of Richard Grainger in 1866, there remained a gap before other important construction work was completed. Stephen Easten's enthusiasm and vision played a part in promoting the construction of an airport for Newcastle as well as a new Tyne Bridge. His business acumen and dedication towards high standards of workmanship within his firm had gained its rewards. A succession of Newcastle's famous buildings were constructed by Stephen Easten Limited. Eventually, for his enterprise, he was awarded an OBE and then was made a Knight of the Bath. As well as being Chairman of the Joint Bridge Committee, Sir Stephen Easten was Lord Mayor and welcomed King George and Queen Mary to open the Tyne Bridge on 10 October 1928.

Famous offices and headquarters constructed

During the first half of the twentieth century some of the notable buildings constructed by Stephen Easten Limited included Milburn House, Dean Street; Carliol House, New Market Street; and the University Union Building. There were many challenges for the company in the construction of Milburn House. Originally, Dean Street was completed by David Stephenson who began the task by infilling a ravine known as the Lort Burn. For Stephen Easten the Milburn House site was triangular with the narrowest point being

the lowest. Beyond the upper part of the site existing developments encompassed St Nicholas Cathedral and some of the city's oldest buildings in addition to many old walls of the city, castle and the Black Gate. The excavations needed great care to prevent any subsidence and to provide concrete foundations strong enough to support the new building. Although many traditional materials were used in the construction, a new steel frame structure formed the shell with concrete walls. The red granite plinth, stone and facing bricks were used for exterior cladding whilst oak was used for floors and panelled walls, and teak for staircase treads. Once completed Milburn House incorporated five hundred rooms used as offices by more than a hundred tenants. Between 1922 and 1927 Stephen Eastern built the new headquarters for the electricity company, NESCo. Designed by local architects L J Couves, it was the city's first office development in the modernised classical style of the inter war period. The 430 ft frontage to New Market Street was faced with Portland stone covering a reinforced steel structure.

Newcastle University, Union Building

159

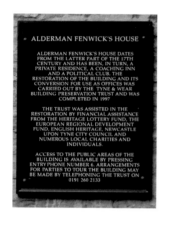

Alderman Fenwick's House, Pilgrim Street, Newcastle

Simple and dignified, the facade with domed corner, unbroken cornice, carefully proportioned windows together with refinement of detail were the expression of the architect's concept of quality. Internally, the main office walls were clad in marble and a bronze memorial was set to remember staff who lost their lives in the First World War. At the time Carliol House created immense interest and received visitors from all parts of the UK and abroad. The University Union building was also finished using Portland stone but combined with soft-toned sand faced bricks which complemented the effect both in texture and mellow features associated with good buildings. The architects planned the detail to be in harmony with the other college buildings and on the lines of one of the great houses of the Elizabethan period.

Listed buildings sympathetically restored

Stephen Easten gained a national reputation for sympathetically restoring listed buildings. Some of these included the former glassworks site at Lemington incorporating the original stone cone (used for molten glass). This site was converted into an award-winning garage and showroom complex for North Eastern Motors. Other restoration and refurbishment programmes included Alderman Fenwick's House, Pilgrim Street; Cross House, Westgate Road and Fenkle Street and many of the important buildings in Newcastle's Grainger Town. In particular, Cross House, a 1.2 million pound project required the replacement of a huge cross wall with a steel and concrete support. This new structure was critical in taking the weight load of the building and was constructed to the full height of the roof. During the restoration work, evidence was discovered of a disastrous fire which raged at Cross House in 1912 only six years after Stephen Easten Limited was incorporated. Over the years the company gained many awards for its construction, restoration and conservation work. With a tradition of craftsmanship, this has continued into another century, regular clients including banks, building societies, national retailers and local authorities. With over a hundred employees, the founders principle of retaining a nucleus of highly skilled trades people who can be relied upon to maintain the standards of services, has been supported by the testimony of time.

Ward Hadaway Solicitors. Sandgate House, 102 Quayside, Newcastle upon Tyne.

The commercial law firm Ward Hadaway was founded in 1988 by the merger of the city offices of long established Tyneside solicitors Hadaway and Hadaway, and Septimus G Ward & Rose. At that time, the firm comprised six partners and a turnover of about £¾ million. In 2004–05, the firm had a turnover of over £20 million, 53 partners and 340 employees, a success story of commercial life in the North East of England. The firm moved from their offices at Hood Street, Newcastle in 1998, to the newly developed East Quayside. The new Sandgate House premises had been constructed by the Tyne and Wear Development Corporation and Amec Developments Limited. It provided 29,000 square feet of space for the practice. At that time, with great foresight, the management of Ward Hadaway took an option on some land at the rear of Sandgate House. Three year's later the firm constructed another 27,000 square foot office building, Keel Row House. Ward Hadaway now occupies both buildings and has a flourishing commercial law practice servicing the major companies in the region. Some of these clients include Northern Rock, Northumbrian Water, Sage, HJ Banks, Alcan and TSG. In addition, the firm acts both for owner managed businesses and SME's, and has a particular specialism in looking after high tech companies such as Zytronic, Romag, and Bede Scientific. Ward Hadaway also provides services to the public sector undertaking legal work for, amongst others, North Yorkshire County Council, Newcastle City Council, many NHS Trusts and Foundations in the region, the Arts Council, One NorthEast and English Heritage. The firm is heavily involved in spinouts from the region's universities. The practice and partners have made it their business to become embedded in the North East business community. Former senior partner Peter Allen was National Chair of the CBI's SME Council, and Northern President to the IOD. A number of partners have roles as Chairmen of Employment Tribunals and other partners have held positions as Chairmen of the Mental Health Tribunal. In addition, a number of partners have held non-executive roles in NHS Trusts. At the time of publishing this book, Jamie Martin has the responsibility of being the firm's Managing Partner and the Regional Chairman of the CBI. Over the years in practice, Ward Hadaway has gained a remarkable reputation for progression and achievement.

Ward Hadaway offices, Quayside, Newcastle

Chapter Seven

Ships – empire trade origins from the three rivers

At first it was the Vikings who arrived in their long boats to impart their boat making skills. However, before the reign of Henry VIII comparatively few ships were built on Northumbria's rivers. It was only during the time of Elizabeth and James I that shipbuilding began to be an important business. Generally, the ships were small and built of good English oak, and they carried coal, as well as general cargo. During times of war with Holland and Spain, the owners of Northumbria's ships ensured they also carried plenty of guns and ammunition, and that they sailed together for mutual protection.

Privateers to tramp steamers

At the time of the Armada, merchants fitted out ships known as privateers which were private ships of war. The basis of the enterprise was usually that the subscribers to the privateer gained half the proceeds of all the prizes taken whilst the remaining half would be distributed evenly between the crew. It is recorded that during 1757 the Countess of Northumberland, with a company of ladies, invested in three privateers, and the guns for these ships were made near Chester le Street. Sailing ships continued to be built on the three rivers through to the middle of the nineteenth century when demand was superseded by the British tramp steamer. This new type of trading ship could be found in ports all over the globe exporting coal from the Tyne and bringing back raw materials for British industry. Boat building began on each of the three rivers, the Tyne, Wear and Tees several hundred years ago. As small boat yards grew, each of the rivers developed their own famous ship building identities.

Origins of shipyards on the Tees

Shipbuilding on the Tees was centred at Stockton, with the earliest recorded being a great ship constructed in 1470 for the Bishop of Durham. Although at this time there were merely a few hundred people living in the district, here were the beginnings of a trade which was to be synonymous with the Tees. Both Stockton and Yarm had an early shipbuilding history. In 1678 Stockton was building ships of 200 burthen, but the Tees saw no major expansion until the eighteenth century. Thomas Haw of Stockton built ships for the Napoleonic wars between 1790 and 1805. Middlesbrough began its transformation into a town and port from being a small farmstead in 1829. The first vessel to be built there was a wooden sailing ship called the *Middlesbro'* at Laing's shipyard in 1833. Before the 1850s and the beginning of the iron shipyards there were less than 200 men employed in shipbuilding on the Tees.

Development of Hartlepool into a port

During the 1830s on the coast north of the Tees estuary, Hartlepool's plans to convert

Opposite: *Sunrise to sunset Northumbria's rivers were the most industrious in the world*

Above: *River Tees, Stockton (18th Century)*

163

Iron screw schooner (1865)
M Pearse & Co, Stockton

the town and old fishing harbour into a port were developed. By 1835 the Hartlepool Dock was opened for coal shipments from a newly deepened harbour. The same year Thomas Richardson of Castle Eden and John Parkin of Sunderland founded a shipyard near the High Street in Old Hartlepool. The first ship to be built there was the *Castle Eden*. The port was to expand its shipbuilding facilities when William Gray established a yard in 1862. The yard was to become famous for regularly winning the Blue Riband prize for maximum output. In 1890 William Gray's yard had beaten the world shipbuilders with an output of 64,000 tons from eleven berths employing 4,000 men. Then in 1901 nearly 1 ton in every 5 built in the region came from Hartlepool. William Gray became one of Hartlepool's most influential people and became the town's first mayor in 1887.

Cleveland iron transforms traditional wooden shipbuilding

After iron ore was discovered in the Eston Hills near Middlesbrough in 1850, new blast furnaces were to influence production in the shipyards. The whole iron making process was to transform local shipbuilding from traditional wooden vessels to iron. A screw propellored steamer called *The Advance* was the first iron ship to be built and launched on the Tees. She was launched at the yard of the Iron Shipbuilding Company at South Stockton on 26 January 1854. In 1857, Rake, Kimber and Co. established a shipyard and a year later launched the first Middlesbrough built iron steamer named the *De Brus*. Steam tugs were built at this yard by J H Leach from 1862 until four years later, when the business was taken over by R Craggs (who had been building ships in Stockton since 1835). Raylton Dixon and Thomas Backhouse established The Cleveland Dockyard at Middlesbrough in 1862. The firm became well known for building fine vessels, both for passenger lines and the government. The first steel ship built on the river was the *Little Lucy* in 1858. The world's largest river steamer at the time was built by Pearse & Co., of Stockton. It was named the *Talpore*, was 377 feet long and was designed as a troop ship. Although there were the great Tees shipyards of Smiths Dock at South Bank, Middlesbrough (established in 1909) and the Furness Shipbuilding Co., at Haverton Hill (established in 1916), it was Pearse & Co., and Pearse Lockwood & Co., and the Ropner Shipbuilding and Repair Co., that were the first to expand the scale of their shipbuilding. Ropners built more than 528 vessels before being purchased by a syndicate of London and Cardiff shipowners in 1919. As well as Ropners, two other yards produced iron ships. These were Richardson, Duck & Co. which began as the Iron Shipbuilding Co., and Craig

Taylor & Co. As a comparative late-comer, the latter was founded by M.G.B. Craig in 1884 and traded into the late 1920s when the shipyards became part of Head Wrightson's business. In their time Craig Taylor's yard built ships for most nations of the world. At its peak the yard employed 1,000 hands and built bulk carriers, the largest of which had the capacity to take on board up to 4,000 tons of oil. On 26 February 1920 Ropners launched the *Great City* (weighing 10,000 tons), the largest vessel built up to that time on the higher reaches of the Tees. The Stockton shipyards closed in the late 1920s. It was only during the Second World War that Stockton was used again, but this time for building tank landing craft. Where ship building had grown so had other allied industries, providing everything from the iron and brass used in ship construction to the engines which powered them. These industries carried on supplying other shipbuilders and the Tees area continued to build ships at Wm Gray of Hartlepool, the Furness Shipbuilding Co., at Haverton Hill and Smiths Dock at Middlesbrough until the 1960s, 1970s and 1980s respectively.

Shipbuilding on the River Wear

It is difficult to ascertain when boats were first constructed on the Wear, but a primitive boat was discovered lying in the river bed at Hylton. Hewn out of oak in the shape of a canoe, this boat, which has been kept at Sunderland Museum is estimated to be some 4,000 years old. One of the first records of shipbuilding indicates that Thomas Menvill was building ships at Hendon from 1346. However, it took several hundred years before the larger shipbuilding yards were established. By 1750 shipyards were small and numerous.

The banks of the Wear to within a mile of Lambton Castle were studded with yards. Even pieces of waste land would be occupied by an enterprising shipwright, who would build a small ship in his spare time. Between Napoleonic Wars from 1801 to 1815 the number of main yards increased from nine to fifteen. Although there was a post Napoleonic War depression, a boom time between 1835–40 brought the number of ships built to a record 251 (64,446 tons). Iron construction and steam propulsion arrived almost simultaneously between 1845 and 1852, with the last wooden ship built in 1880 and the last sailing ship in 1893. During the Crimean War in 1853 there was another production peak when 153 wooden vessels were built with a combined record total of 68,479 tons. From the time of the Crimean War through to the Second World War Sunderland claimed to be the largest shipbuilding town in the world. In 1945 Sunderland's shipyards produced 48 ships of a total 218,175 gross tonnage. This compared with the Tyne and 37 ships of 122,635 tons; the Clyde 155,268 tons for Glasgow, and 103,061 tons for Greenock. In some years the Tyne and Clyde produced a greater gross tonnage

Wooden ships built in small yards on the Wear, 1870

from their shipyards, but no single town along these rivers ever returned higher figures than Sunderland. In 1938, the production of ships built in the USA amounted to 201,251 tons. These are some of the facts substantiated in later years by the returns of Lloyds Register of Shipping which support Sunderland's claim.

Great shipbuilding firms established on the Wear

Between 1750 and 1850 revolutionary changes were to take place in the development of shipbuilding. The coal trade continued to provide an increasing stimulus to shipbuilding. As time went by vessels increased in size, and barques, schooners, brigs and brigantines left the building berths to engage in commerce and trade with all parts of the world. By 1790 Sunderland was building around nineteen ships per year. Many of the great firms of shipbuilders were founded during these hundred years. The oldest of all, Sir James Laing and Sons, was established at Sunderland in 1793, building Sunderland's first East Indiaman in 1815. William Pile and Thomas Havelock were two other renowned shipbuilders of this time. Havelock's great achievement was the building of the *Lord Duncan* in 1798, a vessel of 925 tons. Surtees, the historian of Durham, describing her launching, writes:

'Thousands of spectators covered the borders of the river, many of whom were engulfed to the middle by the rising of the water on receiving this ponderous body.' In the early 1800s, John Storey had a shipyard. He operated this for 23 years although he was first in business with a rope works and sail making loft. Robert Thompson, who later made a great name as a shipbuilder, was manager for John Storey and his sons Joseph and John were apprentices at the same yard. Other famous firms were soon to be established, S.P. Austin and Son, 1826; Bartram and Sons, 1838; William Doxford and Sons, 1840; Joseph L. Thompson, 1846; Short Bros, 1850; and William Pickersgill in 1851. In 1840, the Wear had become the most important shipbuilding centre in the country and had 65 shipyards. Among these, Doxford's were believed to be the world's most productive shipbuilder. In 1878 they expanded their interests, developing into a wide range of steam, turbine and later diesel main engine manufacture. Between 1893 and 1911 Doxford's launched no less than 178 turret deck steamers, representing 1 million tons of shipping. In 1906 they were building an average of one ship every two weeks. Wooden shipbuilding practically ceased after 1876. The first iron ships began to be built from 1852. There were 2,025

Robert Thompson's Shipyard, Southwick, Sunderland

shipwrights employed in the Wear shipyards in 1850 when more than 150 wooden vessels were built.

Tyne's harbour is a crowning glory

The earliest record of shipbuilding on the Tyne was a galley built for Edward I in 1294. It was constructed of oak which was probably cut from woodland on Newcastle's Town Moor. Although William Rowe's shipyard at St Peters had origins to 1756, most of the well known Tyne based yards were established after 1846. The Tyne was well placed for the steam ship revolution with a ready made infrastructure. At Howdon, there was a dry dock as well as a shipbuilding yard. Several frigates were launched from there during the American Civil War. One of these was the *Argo*, mounting forty four guns and when launched in 1781 was the largest vessel built on the Tyne. By 1809 based on the Tyne at both North and South Shields there were twelve shipbuilding yards, an even larger number of docks and six roperies, two of which were worked by steam. Particular achievement in 1790 at South Shields was the construction of *The Original*, the world's first dedicated lifeboat

designed by William Wouldhave and Henry Greathead. The crowning glory of North and South Shields was the harbour, nearly a mile and a half in length, in which 2,000 ships might ride at anchor, and in spring tides had water sufficient for vessels of 500 tons burden.

1814 – First steam vessel launched on the Tyne

The advances from sailing ships to vessels powered by steam began in 1802 when William Symington built the first steamboat. It was a tugboat called the *Charlotte Dundas* and was originally designed for towing barges along the Forth-Clyde canal. The tug was never fully commissioned due to the damage it caused to the banks of the canal from the heavy

Top Left: *Laing's, La Hogue was the largest ship built in the North East in 1855*

Top Right: *Brotherly Love being towed into the Tyne by a steam tugboat*

Left: *Wouldhave Memorial and lifeboat, South Shields*

167

throughout the year and coal shipments were more regular during the winter months. There were many tugs built and used on the three main rivers, at first propelled by paddles and then in the 1930s by screw propellers. The *Friends Adventure*, a low laden sailing ship was the first to be towed on the Tyne by a steam tug in 1818. By 1815, a regular steamboat service ran between Liverpool and Glasgow, followed in 1819 by a Holyhead to Dublin service. In 1824 a Tyne boat, the *Rapid*, gained fame by steaming from Newcastle to London in a record of 56 hours. A summer service to London by the *Hylton Joliffe* commenced from 1827.

1842 – The Prince Albert is first Tyne built iron ship

wash following its wake. From 1814, the sight of the new type of ships became more frequent at northern ports. Churning through the water by means of paddles, at first the new vessels were no match either in size or grace for the tall masted East Indiamen. During 1814, the *Tyne Steam Packet*, later re-named the *Perseverance* was the first steam ship to be built on the Tyne. She was used both to ferry passengers between Newcastle and Shields and also for towing sailing ships out over the bar into the open sea. Adverse winds had in the past prevented ships sailing for weeks. Now sailings could be made

Birkenhead shipyards claimed to build the first British iron steam ship but it was not until six years later in 1840 that the Tyne saw the first iron ship arrival, the *John Garrow* of Liverpool. Two years before this in 1838, the London-owned Sirius made the first successful British crossing of the North Atlantic from Cork to New York in 17 days. In 1842, the *Prince Albert* was the first Tyne-built iron steam ship launched from Coutt's Yard at Walker. Soon afterwards Samuel Cunard founded the world famous trans-Atlantic line, a fleet of four similar steamships making regular passenger and

Above: *The John Bowes, being repaired afloat*

Below: *Sir Charles Palmer's Shipyard, Jarrow*

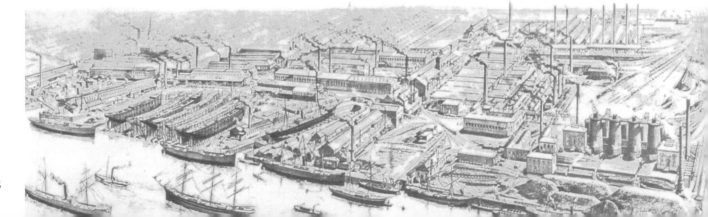

mail shipments to Halifax and Boston in America from Liverpool.

1852 – Palmer's launches the first Tyne vessel with a screw propeller

One of the most important progressions with the steam ship was the 1836 invention of the screw propeller. The *John Bowes*, an iron-built collier vessel launched in 1852 was the first on the Tyne using the new propeller. From the Jarrow shipyard established by Charles Mark Palmer in 1851, it was built for John Bowes of Barnard Castle for shipping coal to London. With a capacity of 650 tons and steaming at nine miles per hour, the *John Bowes* could voyage to London in five days, a trip which would previously average a month. The success of the *John Bowes* laid the platform of a great steam ship trade. After the start of the Crimean War in 1854, there was a demand for armour plated warships. One of the first of these, the *Terror*, an ironclad made with rolled armour plates instead of forged iron plates, was built by Palmers in a record of three months. From this time, Jarrow yards gained a national reputation for building merchant vessels, frigates, torpedo boats, destroyers, cruisers and first class battleships. The first of many tankers to come from the Tyne was the *Vaterland*, built by Palmers. They built ships through to 1933 when the depression witnessed the near collapse of the Tyne's shipbuilding industry and resulted in mass unemployment. The main casualty was the closure of Palmers Yard at Jarrow and Hebburn. This caused great economic strife and shocked the nation. The last ship launched at Palmer's Jarrow shipyard was the *HMS Duchess*, on 19 June 1932. One of the largest warships ever built by Palmers was the battle cruiser *HMS Queen Mary*,

sunk during the first world war at Jutland in 1916.

Tyne shipyards built ships for every purpose

All the well-known Tyne-based shipbuilding and repair companies were founded after 1846, although Smith's Dock Co., with origins through William Rowe's shipyard at St Peters could claim to be established in 1756. It was the largest yard on the river Tyne during the Napoleonic wars. Here, a young man named William Smith, serving his apprenticeship, in 1808, witnessed the launching of the largest war ship ever seen on the Tyne. This was the *HMS Bucephalus*, of 970 tons and pierced for 52 guns. William's father, Thomas Smith, once Mayor of Newcastle, purchased Rowe's shipyard in 1810 and with his sons as partners, refounded the firm as William Smith & Co. The yard specialised in building East Indiamen like the *Duke of Roxburgh*, 417 tons, the *Hotspur*, 523 tons

French sailing ships, Smith's Dock (1901), North Shields

Above: *HMS Victoria being towed from the Elswick shipyard for sea trials, 1888*

Below: *Armstrong's Elswick shipyard on the Tyne*

and the *Ellenborough*, 926 tons. Finest of all in 1846 came the *Marlborough*, 1,300 tons. Then the 1,600 ton *Blenheim* was launched in 1848. Together, these were acclaimed as the finest vessels in the British Mercantile Marine at the Great Exhibition of London in 1851. Through expansion the firm eventually relocated to a larger yard at North Shields and in 1899 became Smith Docks Co Ltd. In 1910, the firm established a yard at South Bank, Middlesbrough following a decision in 1909 to use North Shields as a ship repair yard. Other early shipbuilders who made their names famous around the Tyne were the North East Marine Engineering Co., James Wigham and Richardson (Walker), the Wallsend Slipway Co., John Redheads (South Shields) and

Blyth Shipbuilding Co. At these yards there were ships being built to suit every purpose for passenger, merchant and naval requirements. Specialist vessels were also built, one of these was launched in 1873 from Newcastle's Low Walker Yard. The *Hooper*, built in just three months, was a 5,000 ton cable laying vessel for the Transatlantic telegraph service. The *Hooper* went on to lay cables between Britain and Bermuda and from Sydney to Auckland.

Warships a speciality for C W Mitchell's yard

Scotsman Charles W. Mitchell began shipbuilding on the Tyne at Walker in 1852. When his yard had excess orders he extended his interests and in 1873 purchased a 6.5 acre site at Wallsend. When Mitchell's Wallsend yard had financial difficulties he handed it over to his brother-in-law, Charles Sheridan Swan. Mitchell was still successful both at his Walker shipyard and with the repair yard, the Wallsend Slipway Company which he established in 1871. Both Charles Sheridan Swan and his brother Henry Swan were directors of the Wallsend Slipway Company. Charles Mitchell was also working closely with Armstrong's. Following the launch of the first gunboat for the Admiralty in 1868, a vessel built to Armstrong's order in C W Mitchell's Walker yard, there were orders for a succession of warships. Working together, these companies merged in 1882 to form Armstrong, Mitchell and Co., building warships at Elswick and commercial and merchant ships at the Walker yard. Their nationally famed steelworks was opened in 1884. Three years later, the armaments business of Sir Joseph Whitworth at Openshaw, Manchester combined with Armstrong, Mitchell and Co., to become Armstrong

Whitworth and Co. The company developed to an enormous size and when Armstrong died in 1900, his business stretched over 230 acres and employed twenty five thousand people.

From warships to oil tankers

From the beginning of the twentieth century Armstrong Whitworth's reputation was gained through the combined expertise of the company's key executives. Sir Andrew Noble was responsible for a series of important developments in ordnance, Colonel Swan for the modern oil tanker, and George Rendel for the evolution of the cruiser type of warship for the protection of commerce. Many famous warships were built in the Elswick yard for British and foreign governments, including the bulk of the Japanese navy which annihilated the Russian fleet at Tsushima. By 1911, the increasing size of battleships made it necessary to establish a larger shipyard below the Tyne bridge, so a naval yard was laid down at High Walker and the Elswick yard eventually closed in 1921. In the inter-war period building warships in the North East reduced to about twelve per cent of the rearmament years between 1907–13. However, there was an increasing demand for oil tankers also involving simpler types of construction. During six years from 1924–30 almost 1 million tons of tankers, representing 159 ships, were built in the region. This was one third of the world tanker output and two thirds of those built in the UK. After the fortunes of war, prosperity declined for Armstrong Whitworth and in 1927, an interest with Vickers of Sheffield was formalised. The new Vickers Armstrong's retained the Elswick works and the naval yard at Walker, whilst Armstrong Whitworth kept the Scotswood works, the Close works in Gateshead and the Walker shipyard. Armstrong Whitworth then concentrated its operations on commercial shipbuilding and marine engines until business declined and it ceased trading fifteen years later.

Charles Parsons launches The Turbinia

In 1894, ten years after Charles Parsons had invented a working turbo-dynamo, he decided to apply the new power source to marine work. For this purpose he established the Marine Steam Turbine Co. Ltd. As a result a steam boat, the *Turbinia*, was born, an experimental vessel 100 feet long, of 44.5 tons displacement and fitted with a 2,300 h.p. turbine. Its three years of development was crowned in glory when at the 1897 Naval Review (held off Spithead in commemoration of Queen Victoria's Diamond Jubilee), the *Turbinia* stole the show by steaming at speeds of up to 34.5 knots through an array of naval vessels. Today, the *Turbinia* is in the care of Tyne and Wear Museums Service and may be

The Turbinia, CA Parsons experimental steam turbine vessel, 1897

seen on display at the Discovery Museum in Newcastle. After this sensational performance, it was almost certain that the marine turbine would be widely adopted, justifying the formation in 1898 of the Parsons Marine Steam Turbine Co. Ltd., Wallsend. The first order for a turbine fitted vessel was from the Admiralty. It was for the destroyer *Viper* launched in 1900, a ship to be tragically lost in bad weather off the Channel Islands. Trials of the turbine in warships were so successful that in 1904 the Admiralty decided to use it for the new *Dreadnought* battleship built at Portsmouth. Its sister ship cruiser the *Invincible* was built on the Tyne by Armstrong Whitworth in 1908. Other ships were fitted with Parsons

Above: *HMS Viper, turbine destroyer*

Below: *HMS Triumph, the largest warship in 1945, launched by Hawthorn Leslie*

turbine propulsion. In 1901 the *King Edward* was the first of the commercial steamers and by 1907 the 26 knot Cunard liners *Mauretania* and *Lusitania* had been launched and fitted with the new turbines. So, less than ten years after demonstrating the *Turbinia*, Parsons' turbines were gaining fame through their use in some of the largest ships in the world.

Robert Hawthorn moves into marine engines

One of the finest shipbuilding and engineering amalgamations was with R and W Hawthorn Leslie and Co., in 1885. This consisted of Hawthorn's locomotive works at Forth Banks and engineering works at St. Peter's, with Leslie's shipbuilding business at Hebburn. Andrew Leslie, a Scottish shipbuilder, founded the Hebburn yard in 1853 initially working alongside men he employed as ordinary craftsmen. The Forth Banks works was founded in 1817 by Robert Hawthorn, who began business with four men, and with machinery worked by hand. In 1819, Hawthorn bought an adjoining piece of land and with a work force of twenty he built a much larger shop with steam power, which was then managed in partnership with his brother William. The Hawthorn brothers manufactured steam engines and machinery for saw mills, corn mills, collieries and general industry. After they introduced steam power into the works, they made small marine engines. In 1829 they built a 6 h.p. road traction engine and in 1831 their first railway locomotive. Over the next forty years Hawthorn's produced over a thousand locomotives before developing a niche in the manufacture of marine engines. Robert Hawthorn died in 1867 and in 1870 after William's retirement, the business was restructured and bought T

& W Smith's St. Peter's shipyard, converting it into an engineering works for the manufacture of marine engines.

From engines to naval destroyers

Hawthorn's amalgamation with Leslie's was to provide valuable engineering and shipbuilding achievements. First, the company pioneered the transition from sails to steam and half a century later in the change from the reciprocating engine to the turbine. Hawthorn's was to manufacture the engine for the Tyne built iron ship *Q.E.D.*, one of the earliest sailing colliers to use auxiliary steam and the first to be fitted with a double iron skin hull for water ballast. In 1899, Hawthorn Leslie made the hull and boilers for the turbine destroyer *Viper*, contracted through Parsons' Marine Steam Turbine Co. By the First World War the firm's locomotives, marine engines and ships were world famous. Hawthorn Leslie made cranes, boilers and machinery for naval vessels, high speed destroyers, and commercial liners, oil tankers, exploration vessels, troop ships, tug boats, ore vessels, salt ships and passenger steamers. The firm employed over 1,250 people in 1831 but reduced its workforce by about a fifth in the following two years during the depression. By 1937 Hawthorn Leslie amalgamated their locomotive business with Stephenson's, to become known as Robert Stephenson and Hawthorn's Ltd of Darlington, later disposing of their interests in 1943. Hawthorn Leslie continued to trade for another thirty years. Difficulties in the industry had brought competitors together in the interests of survival. In 1979 Hawthorn Leslie and Geo. Clark NEM merged to become Clark Hawthorn. Another merger with Kincaid of Greenock in 1984 kept the Clark Kincaid engine

building works at Wallsend in business until it finally closed in 1986. Hawthorn Leslie's shipyard was most famous for building naval destroyers including the *HMS Kelly* of the Second World War. A number of early makers of ships engines emerged from general engineering firms. George Clark on the Wear concentrated on marine work from 1854. Other firms which grew through marine engineering were Clarke Chapman at Gateshead, White's Marine Engineering at Hebburn, North Eastern Marine Engineering at Sunderland, and the Wallsend Slipway and Engineering Co., which made the engines and boilers for the *Mauretania*. Two of these firms, George Clark and North Eastern Marine Engineering, amalgamated with Richardson Westgarth, Hartlepool in 1938. Until the Second World War, shipbuilding faced recurrent crises. The firms and yards hardest hit were those producing tramp steamers or those attempting to build too wide a variety of once off ships.

Tyne commissioners work on the river

From 1850, through the River Tyne Improvement Act, Newcastle Corporation

The Swing Bridge opened in 1876 for a better access to Elswick

was relinquished of its responsibility for the maintenance of the river. New powers of conservancy were given to the Tyne Improvement Commission, otherwise known as The Tyne Commissioners. Their first task was to deepen the shipping channel to aid greater river traffic and continue maintenance of the river's lighting from Trinity House, Newcastle. Before the First World War, the Tyne had become almost as famous for ship repairing as for shipbuilding and once steel became universally used, local yards were turning out nearly half a million tons gross of shipping a year. The enormous expansion of shipbuilding, engineering and coal export was aided and accelerated through the work of the Tyne Commissioners continuously dredging the river between 1861 and 1914. Without deepening the river above the bridges, warships could not have been built at Elswick, nor coal shipped from the staiths at Dunston and Derwent Haugh. At Shields where the river was dangerously narrow, the channel was widened to 670 feet, and the river through to Derwent Haugh was dredged to a depth of between 25–30 feet. Two great piers were built at the mouth of the river forming a protective harbour, a task which took over fifty years, finally being opened to the public in 1910. In order to reach the upper parts of the river in 1876 the Swing Bridge replaced the low-spanned eighteenth century stone bridge at Newcastle. Then the upper river channel was dredged, cutting a new channel and shortening the distance from Scotswood to Newburn by three quarters of a mile.

Expansion of dock facilities

Unfortunately, the dredging of the river weakened the Newcastle Quay's foundations and between 1866 and 1884 it had to be rebuilt. Once completed, the new quay extended from the Swing Bridge to the Ouseburn. Passenger steamers regularly departed from the quay for London, the continent and other parts of the world. Cargo boats were loaded or unloaded by cranes using long lines of goods waggons, while regular passenger steamboat services shuttled frequently between Newcastle, Shields and Elswick. The growing volume of shipping made enclosed docks a necessity. The Tyne Commissioners built the Northumberland Dock at Howdon which was opened in 1857, and at North Shields, the Albert Edward Dock in 1884. In addition to these docks, the North Eastern Railway constructed the Tyne Dock on fifty acres of Jarrow Slake. The work of the Tyne Commissioners was succeeded by the establishment of The Port of Tyne Authority in 1968. This gave conformity with other authorities throughout the United Kingdom. The Tees and Hartlepool Port Authority replaced the Tees Conservancy Commission in 1967 to become responsible for managing the whole port area. The importance of the Port of Tyne Authority

The Broadhurst at Tyne Dock (owned by local shipping agents), 1950

progressed into the twenty first century with continuous developments along the river and maintenance of regular Scandinavian passenger and cargo services from their quay at Whitehall Point, North Shields. A regular ferry service to Bergen and Oslo in Norway was first established in 1937.

By the beginning of the twentieth century the gross tonnage of ships being built on Tyneside was approximately half a million compared with 900,000 tons only a quarter of a century before. Shipyard closures in the twentieth century were inevitable, triggered by economic depression and recession. The problems endemic to British shipbuilding were slow to reveal themselves after the Second World War. Shipyards had been working near to capacity through the war and there had been little time for reorganisation and modernisation. Immediately after the war a phenomenal demand for tanker tonnage ensured steady order books and there was little overseas competition. Scandinavian owners were prominent in ordering tankers averaging 10,000 to 15,000 tons. Tanker size grew with a striking speed after 1959. Until then the largest tankers launched were 15,000 tons (Furness – 1949), 22,000 tons (Furness – 1953) and 27,585 tons (Swan Hunter – 1959). During the 1950s orders from foreign owners diminished. There were problems in the steel industry, difficulty with supply, rising material costs and particularly in 1956 and 1957 serious labour stoppages. In 1957 steel shortages, especially in sections, were said to be keeping shipbuilding some ten per cent below its possible output. However, in 1956 a post-war record for the North East was reached of 646,000 tons launched. The years 1958–64 were the most difficult since the 1930s. A depression in world shipping coincided with falling demand in the steel industry. Order books declined and in 1962 only five bulk carriers, twenty six cargo vessels and six tankers were launched in the North East. Like the 1930s the financial effects were severe on some yards and led to closures. The government shipbuilding credit scheme of 1964 greatly assisted local shipyards and this led to some recovery. It is believed that on the Wear only 100,000 tons would have been launched instead of an

Below: *Furness Shipyard, Haverton Hill, River Tees, 1960*

Bottom: *Launching of The Brittany at Austin and Pickersgill's, Sunderland*

175

actual figure of 234,000 tons. The Wear yards were estimated to be working only at two thirds capacity. However, in 1964 almost half of Britain's total ship building was under construction in the North East. Large oil tankers continued to be built and escalated in size. By 1968 the first 100,000 ton tankers were under construction and 200,000 ton tankers were being planned on the Tyne.

Shipbuilding restructured for survival

In 1969, with the near closure of the Furness shipbuilding yard at Haverton Hill on the Tees, 3,000 employees jobs were saved when the firm was taken into a new Tyne-based consortium. With a highly successful tradition of building tankers and having been acquired by Charles Clore in the 1950s, the Furness shipyard had been extensively modernised and equipped. Despite this, profitability had fallen and the yard was scheduled for closure early in

1969. In 1968 all Tyne shipyards had merged into a new consortium, Swan Hunter and Tyne Shipbuilders Ltd. This process began two years earlier when Swan Hunter and Wigham Richardson merged with Smiths Dock Co. There was also rationalisation on the Wear, Doxford's yard to build specialised vessels, Sir John Laing's to concentrate on bulk carriers up to 46,000 tons and J L Thompson to build bulk carriers and tankers. In August 1968 Austin and Pickersgill (who had themselves merged in 1955) amalgamated with Bartrams. They had already been successfully working together in the building of the SD14, a 14,200 ton standard cargo ship. The industry had been reshaped and restructured for survival but not without many casualties. Between 1909–37, there were twenty eight shipyard closures of which six were on the Tees, and fourteen on the Tyne, culminating with Palmer's shipyards in 1933. In the 1960s and 1970s

The SS Mauretania built by Swan Hunters and launched in 1906

176

eleven more shipyards closed their gates. These included W Gray, Hartlepool in 1962; a specialised builder of tugs and barges, T Mitchison, Gateshead in 1963; Short Brothers, Sunderland in 1964; The Blyth Shipbuilding Company in 1966; and the Furness Yard, Haverton Hill in 1979. This almost totally wiped out Tyneside's shipbuilding industry leaving nine remaining yards. At around this time and having been scheduled for redevelopment, the Tees and Hartlepool Port Authority closed Middlesbrough dock. Despite problems in shipbuilding the Tees remained strategically important for the chemical industry. In 1986 the Tees was rated as having the third largest port in the UK in terms of tonnage shipped. However, the real story in the shipyards was that they were being affected by competition from low cost yards in Japan. The closure of Smiths Dock Co. shipyard at Middlesbrough in 1987 saw the end of shipbuilding on the Tees. The last ship launched on the Tees at Smiths Dock was the 15,000 tonne *North Islands* on 15 October 1986. Through the closure of Smiths Dock 1,295 people lost their jobs. The following year on the Wear, the Doxford Pallion, and Austin and Pickersgill yards closed completing yet another era. Employment in Tyneside shipyards had fallen from 21,000 in 1978 to about 16,000 in 1984 and 4,000 in 1987.

Swan Hunter a legend born in shipbuilding

The story of Tyneside's shipping would not be complete without remembering the names of famous North East owners including Common Brothers, Runciman's Moor Line, Ropner, Stag Line, Hall Brothers and Burnett, with ships built by Redhead's, Wood, Skinner, Palmer's and Short Brothers

of Pallion in Sunderland. However, the longest lasting name in shipbuilding is that of Swan Hunter. A Tyneside shipbuilding legend which was started by Sir George Burton Hunter. George Hunter began his career as an apprentice at the firm of Thomas Meek, the river commissioners engineers, and from there he moved to W Pile, Hay and Co., where he became head of the drawing office at the age of 26 years. After a short move to Scotland, George returned as company manager with S P Austin, the Sunderland based shipbuilders, to become a junior partner of a renamed Austin Hunter yard. The involvement with Swan came when Charles Sheridan Swan, owner of C S Swan, Wallsend shipyard died. A partnership had been planned between George Hunter and Charles Swan in 1878. Unfortunately, before plans reached a working stage, Charles had a tragic accident at sea. He died in 1879 when he fell overboard from a channel steamer whilst returning from the continent with his wife. George Hunter continued with his

HMS Ark Royal Aircraft Carrier launched by Swan Hunters in 1985

plans and joined C S Swan's shipyard in 1880 to become the firm's new managing partner. The business was then known as C S Swan and Hunter. They built their first oil tanker in 1889. George Hunter led the firm through a number of acquisitions and partnerships whilst building a reputation for making fine ships. In 1903 there was an historic amalgamation with John Wigham Richardson of Walker, Newcastle and the purchase of a controlling interest in the Wallsend Slipway and Engineering Co. This extended the shipyards to an area of more than 80 acres. By the beginning of the twentieth century ships were being built on 17 slipways with output averaging 93,000 tons a year. After the Swan Hunter yard had built its first ocean liner, The *Ultonia* in 1898, a further 21 liners were built during the following five years. One of the greatest landmarks for Swan Hunter's came in 1906 when the Cunard liner, the *Mauretania* was launched, a ship 790 feet long, a beam of 88 feet, and a gross 1,938 tons. It was designed to carry 2,335 passengers and 812 crew. On its maiden voyage on 16 November 1907 it carried 2,000 passengers and gained The Blue Ribband for the fastest Atlantic crossing, a record held for twenty two years.

Swan's 12,000 workforce at its peak

In 1912, Swan Hunter moved into a national ship building league with the acquisition of Barclay Curle and Co., of Clydeside. The company gained a reputation for building naval vessels through the world wars whilst also developing merchant vessels and super tankers. In 1969, the largest super tanker ever to be built up to that time was launched on the Tyne. The *Esso Northumbria* at 253,000 tons, was built at

Swan's Walker yard and the first of several which were to become an embarrassment as OPEC price rises, rationing and Middle East conflicts cut world oil demand. At its peak Swan Hunters employed approximately 12,000 men. By the late 1960's, Swan's owned three yards on the north banks of the Tyne and two on the south side, formerly Hawthorn Leslie and John Redhead's yards. Being earmarked for nationalisation, in 1977 Swan Hunter Shipbuilders Ltd., passed into public ownership and became a member of British Shipbuilders. With a general decline in the industry in 1986 the government decided to re-privatise shipbuilding and the company was bought by four directors for £5 million. It continued to pursue Naval contracts and employed 3,600 people until the end of the cold war when the demand for contracts virtually finished. Two of the finest ships built for the Royal Navy were the *HMS Illustrious* and *HMS Ark Royal* aircraft carriers. *HMS Illustrious* was completed twelve weeks early in order to be used in the Falkland Islands conflict in 1982. The *HMS Ark Royal* was launched in 1985. Swan Hunter gained a number of alternative ship building contracts which included the technically complex British Atlantic Survey Ship, the *James Clark Ross*. However, without enough new business the company eventually went into receivership in May 1995. The last ship to be built by Swan Hunters before receivership was *HMS Richmond* completed in 1993.

Swan Hunters name lives on into the new millennium

The Swan family connection ended in 1994 when Charles' great grandson David was one of the hundreds who lost their jobs during this time. However, the name Swan

Hunter lived on after receivership, when in 1995 the Dutch based firm THC Fabricators bought the yard in a deal believed to be around £5 million. Its first major contract was for the multi-million conversion of the *Solitaire* bulk carrier into the largest pipelaying vessel in the world. This £150 million order for the 50,000 tonne vessel provided 20 months work for 3,000 workers. This contract was completed in 1997, firmly establishing Swan Hunter (Tyneside) Ltd., in the offshore industry business. Shipbuilding was brought back to the Tyne in 1999 with a £140m Ministry of Defence order to build two identical 16,160 tonne naval landing ships, the *Largs Bay* and the *Lyme Bay*. This was estimated to provide four years work for 2,000 people. Swan Hunter chairman Jaap Kroese remained confident about Swan Hunter's future. Negotiations for the construction of two 50,000 tonne Royal Navy aircraft carriers were Jaap Kroese's main focus for the beginning of the twenty first century. During a 130-year existence Swan Hunter built over 1,600 ships including more than 400 naval vessels. The Tyne, the Wear and Tees rivers have a heritage from which Northumbria can truly be proud, retaining a wealth of experience and facilities re-shaped for the twenty first century.

Steering a course for shipping and general industry – 19th Century Profile

Written in the style of the time.
The Dunston Engine Works Co. Marine and General Engineers, Steam Ship Repairers, etc. Gateshead.

Amongst the important houses which assisted in the commercial developments of Tyneside, the Dunston Engine Works Co. occupied a prominent position. The site on which the premises were built possessed considerable possibilities. The two comparatively small sheds which sufficed at the beginning expanded into a splendid line of works extending along the river nearly 350 yards. These were supplemented by one of the finest ship engineering and repairing jetties on the south side of the Tyne. Here, with the far famed Elswick establishment of Sir W G Armstrong, Mitchell and Co., directly opposite them, the Company, under the co-direction of Mr Mark Archer and Mr R W Armstrong, carried on extensive operations in almost all branches of engineering.

Archer patent ships steering is world renown

The Archer Patent Hand-steering Gear stood in great repute for sea and river purposes and rapidly replaced other steering gear on vessels up to 400 tons. As it was absolutely self holding, the wheel would remain in position without any exertion on the part of the steersman, and without being affected by the pressure on the rudder, even in the heaviest seas, and could be worked with certainty in any weather. Over 1,000 of these gears were supplied to the Chinese Government for torpedo boats, the Portuguese Government for passenger boats, the Tyne Improvement

The Dunston Engine Works, Gateshead

Commissioners, The Tyne General Ferry Co., Sir W G Armstrong, Mitchell and Co., Palmer's Shipbuilding and Iron Co., Swan and Hunter, and numerous other important bodies, both at home and abroad. They were also in great demand for gentlemen's yachts and for fishing trawlers. The gear was awarded Silver Medals at the "Fisheries," "Inventions," and "Liverpool" Exhibitions.

Diverse manufacturing interests

In addition to the manufacture of marine engines and boilers, and the repair of iron ships, the firm were makers of colliery plant, including pit heapsteads, iron roofs and girders, winding, pumping and hauling engines, pit cages, keps, kick-ups, coal tubs, pulleys, coal cleaning and screening apparatus, coal crushing machinery, and every description of colliery castings. They also turned out high-speed engines for electric lighting and other works, iron and steel boilers, tank locomotives, mortar mills, contractors and chemical works plant, and brick-making and saw-mill machinery. A feature was made of the solely-owned Archer patents, embracing Archer's Improved Stone Breaker and Ore Crusher, and Archer's Patent Self-holding Hand-steering Gear. Other specialities, included patent wrought iron reels, winches, and nippers for gripping and holding wire hawsers. The stone breaking and ore crushing machinery was specially adapted for dealing with gold, quartz, silver, copper, zinc, tin, lead, ganister, phosphate, rocks, slag, emery stone, pyrites, coprolites, gas coke and the like. It was supplied to mine and quarry owners abroad, as well as to Lord Armstrong, Lord Hindlip, and many other landowners, giving the most efficient results. At Newcastle's Royal Mining and

Industrial Exhibition of 1887, it received the Bronze Medal, which was the highest and only award offered.

Famous shipyards on two rivers

Smiths Dock Co. Ltd. Shipbuilders, ship repairers and engine builders. North Shields and South Bank, Middlesbrough.

Based on a 1949 profile, this is an account of a shipbuilding and ship repairing organisation at work and how by drawing on a vast storehouse of experience, it adapted its methods to the changing pattern of marine requirements. The history of Smith's Dock can be traced back to the 18th century. The Smith family launched their enterprise in 1756 at St. Peter's, Newcastle upon Tyne. Not long after in 1768, a similar business was founded by the Edwards' family at High Docks, South Shields. Not only did these two families repair and build ships, but for a time they were also owners.

Docks established at North Shields and Middlesbrough

The St. Peter's establishment became famous for building such East Indiamen as the *Blenheim, Marlborough, Hotspur, Tudor, Ellenborough* and when this yard became inadequate for the growing amount of business, a move was made to North Shields. Meanwhile, the High Docks establishment of the Edwards' family was expanding their ship repairing business, as well as building ships and running them as owners. In 1893, the business was transferred to North Shields on a site next to that occupied by Smith's, thus facilitating the amalgamation of the two firms which took place in 1899. The firm's activities were then centred at North Shields and at South Bank, Middlesbrough. The industrial development on the Tees was quite a modern affair compared with that of the Tyne and up to the year 1909 there was only one graving dock on the Tees capable of docking large ships. Two years earlier, a large site situated about two miles nearer the river mouth than Middlesbrough, had been purchased by Smith's Dock. A shipyard with four berths, each of which could take a vessel of approximately 300 ft. in length was laid out. Two dry-docks were initially established and an engine building works was built and equipped. Later two more dry docks were completed.

Facilities at the North Shields yard

The North Shields yard was situated about two miles from the mouth of the river. By acquiring property in the vicinity of the yard, the perimeter enclosed a site of 20 acres. At the head of the dry docks was the platers' shed. In this large and well equipped building, heavy steel repairs and reconstruction work could be handled. The extensive fitting shop was equipped with all the necessary plant, including two overhead travelling cranes lifting 50 and 20 tons respectively. This enabled the most extensive overhauls to machinery including steam reciprocating, diesel and turbines. In the erecting shop complete engines could be dismantled and rebuilt under cover. Their experience in boiler overhauls and repairs was unrivalled, and particularly in the use of electric welding. Portable welding plants were provided for expert welders to carry out both hull and boiler repairs. Underground tanks with pumping and heating equipment and with a capacity of 4,000 tons, provided another facility for the temporary storage of oil bunkers whilst vessels were undergoing repairs. High class joinery work, including

complete reconstruction of accommodation, was another part of the works. All classes of plumbing work could be undertaken, with Heating Coil Installations and Oil Burning Conversions being a special feature. All docks and quays were fitted with electric cranes having lifts varying from 3 tons to 50 tons, with special jibs giving the greatest possible outreach. In addition, there were also a number of steam locomotive cranes for dealing with the lighter lifts.

Repairs to large tankers and smaller ships

Repairs to oil tankers had been a specialisation for many years. All docks were equipped with steam, fresh and salt water services so that oil compartments could be steamed, washed down with hot water, cleaned and afterwards tested. A unique facility available in the shape of a barge was equipped with plant for dealing ballast water from tankers and cargo vessels carrying oil in the double bottoms. Situated at the eastern end of the main docks was Baird's Dock, equipped to carry out all repairs to small vessels such as tugs and trawlers.

Smith's Dock, North Shields

The Yard at South Bank, Middlesbrough

Above: *Whale catchers at Smith's Dock, River Tees, 1929*

Below: *Smith's Dock, South Bank, Middlesbrough. One of four dry docks for ship repairs and conversions*

Situated at South Bank, Middlesbrough Smith's Dock activities included shipbuilding, engine building and repairing and ship repairing. This combination increased scope as well as helping with labour. The yard was well equipped with four berths, capable of building ships up to 500 ft. in length, and serviced by four 10-ton mobile luffing cranes. These operated on concrete runways between berths, and were supplemented by four 10-ton fixed Butters' cranes. An outstanding feature was the provision of modern plate and bar storage accommodation from where six overhead cranes had access directly into the platers' shed.

Marine engines to power the ships

The engine works consisted of a machine bay 200 ft. x 108 ft, and 30 ft. high to crane rails and a similar size erecting bay, 50 ft. high. Overhead cranes with 10 and 30-ton lifts serviced the works, whose main manufacture was reciprocating engines and also of engines under license from Messrs. Fredriksstad of Norway. Diesel engines were purchased outside. As well as manufacturing, there were repairs to all kinds of machinery and at the yard's quays constructed engines could be fitted to ships built at other yards. Engines for the war time Corvette were designed at the South Bank Works. All types of repair work to oil tankers, cargo liners and cargo boats could be carried out including lengthening and shortening ships and conversions.

Smith's Dock Company played a leading part, in the last two great wars, in designing and building specialised types of craft. The "Zed" Whalers and "Kil" Tyne Patrol Gunboats were produced during the 1914–18 and the last war, the "Flower" Class Corvette became one of the most successful types of vessel. Intended primarily for dealing with the larger and faster types of submarine, the design was based on the large type whale catchers that had been produced by Smith's Dock for the whaling industry. These vessels were exceptionally quick manoeuvring, with a good turn of speed and excellent sea-going qualities. In fact, in the early stages they were known as "Patrol Vessels, Whaler Type," later changed to Corvettes, the series being named after well known flowers. The first of the Corvettes was completed in five and a half months from the laying of the keel, and successive vessels were completed at the rate of one every three and a half weeks. Smith's Dock built nineteen of this type and large numbers were turned out, from plans supplied by them, by various yards in the United Kingdom, in Canada and elsewhere. A further development of the Corvette was the "River" Class Frigate, designed for increased speed and longer endurance at sea. These vessels had an overall length of just over 300 feet with twin engines of Corvette type and two water tube boilers giving a speed of about 20 knots. Towards the end of the war, these vessels were produced *en mass*, sections being prefabricated by various constructional firms and assembled at shipbuilding yards around the coast. The same Corvette engine was also used in Frigates and the later models of Tank Ferries; in the two latter classes twin engines were installed. Some 1,250 sets of engines were built during the war from the original designs and plans of Smith's Dock Company.

Restoring the war casualties

The war at sea during 1939–45 was particularly fierce. Ships with broken backs, ships with torpedo damage, ships whose superstructure had been bombed out of recognition and even ships in two separate pieces, filled Smith's yards. Repairs were made under the threat of air attack and the

Below: *A Royal Naval Ship HMS Glenearn before conversion*

Bottom: *HMS Glenearn after conversion for peacetime shipping*

handicap of blackout; but these were only some of the difficulties. Shortages of materials and the peculiar dissimilarity of war damage repair jobs stretched Smith's Docks to the limit.

Full ahead on peace production

Smith's Dock's contribution to the development of the shipbuilding industry was immense. This consisted of repair work and building of new tonnage on a large scale for the British and Foreign Merchant Navies, as well as pioneer work in connection with oil separating barges and Smith's Patent Oil Burning Installation for land and marine use. Despite difficulties in the pre-war years and even during the war, extensive technical development plans resulted in an organisation capable of carrying out all kinds of work speedily and efficiently. Some of the later vessels under construction included oil tankers from 6,000 tons up to 14,500 tons, and cargo vessels with passenger accommodation from 4,000 tons to 8,500 tons. Other orders included Norwegian timber carriers of 3,500 tons to 4,200 tons and numerous British and Norwegian Whale-catchers and trawlers.

Barbour's headquarters and factory, Simonside, South Shields

A company that has weathered the years into the 21st century

J Barbour and Sons Ltd., Simonside, South Shields, Tyne and Wear.

From a modest beginning, the name Barbour has become known internationally for manufacturing garments that will withstand the rigours of the worst weather conditions. The founder, John Barbour, was born in 1849 at the family's farm situated in Galloway, Scotland. Whist he was raised there, part of John's duties included those of being a shepherd. With plenty of experience in attempting to keep dry and warm in extreme weather on the hills, eventually, John was to use this to his advantage. By the time he was 20 years old, John had made a decision to make a new life for himself over the border in Northumbria.

The beginnings of a trade in the drapery business

After a year of working as a travelling draper, he married his childhood sweetheart Margaret Haining. The couple settled in Newcastle where they started their own family and began to raise ten children. Margaret encouraged John to expand his enterprise and in 1890 the firm of J Barbour and Sons was established. It produced practical clothing that was hard wearing and also fashionable. After four years of trading and at the insistence of his wife, who was then suffering though invalidity, a decision was taken to move to a workshop and office at 5, Market Place, South Shields. With newly acquired premises there was greater scope for expansion. There was a ready market for oilskins and durable garments to protect sailors, fishermen and port workers from the severest coastal weather conditions. At that time Barbour was only one of many clothing manufacturers geared towards heavy use commercial markets and field sports. However, John Barbour believed in providing quality clothing with a unique after care service. This gained the firm a reputation that became the envy of their competitors. Beacon oilskins soon became an established brand with the Barbour reputation spreading inland to farmers and country folk, and abroad to patriots in British Empire colonies.

In order to meet overseas demand, the first catalogue of 16 pages was published in 1908. The size of the catalogue increased progressively and by 1912 it was being posted to customers in Argentina, Australia, Brazil, East Africa, Canada, Chile, Holland, Hong Kong, Jamaica, Newfoundland, New Zealand, Rhodesia and Spain. By 1926, the catalogue had increased to 120 pages with 100,000 copies being distributed in the UK and 20,000 overseas. Mail order grew to be a substantial part of the Barbour business. Applications for the use of Barbour all weather durable clothing became extensive. In 1937, special waterproof suits were manufactured for the personnel of British U-Class submarines. Barbour motorcycle wear became famous and was to be worn by almost every British international motorcycle team for over forty years from 1936. After 1956, Barbour moved from their premises at the Market Place to a factory and offices on an industrial estate at Simonside on the outskirts of the town.

A name made by generations of weavers, tailors and seamstresses

Today, with eight hundred staff based at the South Shields factory, despite the modern equipment, much of the operation

would still be recognised by previous generations. A great part of the detailed work on each garment is completed by hand as it was done over 100 years ago. Each jacket is made from long staple Egyptian cotton which is machine sewn together with an average of 15,000 stitches. The thread itself is also treated with the same secret formula to ensure complete waterproofing. There are up to two hundred components including solid brass studs and large tooth metal zips, and for the purpose of the after care service every Barbour jacket is given a reference file. Some jackets are still returned to Barbour for refurbishment after three generations of wear. A worldwide network of outlets has been established over the years to provide sales and service. This is backed by Barbour's operations at South Shields and their web site that provides details of the garment range, locations of their preferred suppliers and own shop outlets. Many of the firm's competitors are no longer in existence, but it was the long-term philosophy of John Barbour that has ensured the continuity of this world famous brand name from Northumbria.

From John Barbour's roots, a landscape for extreme weather

Chapter Eight

A time of transformation – the twentieth century

During the last quarter of the nineteenth century and to the First World War, coal, shipbuilding and traditional heavy engineering industries were at their peak. Between 1861 and 1901 the population had more than doubled to two million. The population of Newcastle was over 215,328, Sunderland 146,077 and 91,302 people were living in Middlesbrough. Northumbria was the most prosperous region in Great Britain. This had been stimulated by the dramatic growth of Teesside; the result of being able to combine the resource of iron ore mined in Cleveland and coking coal from south west Durham for Teesside's smelting furnaces and expanding industries. The shipyards along the Tyne, Wear and Tees were building forty per cent of the national shipping tonnage. Passenger liners and warships were built on the Tyne, whilst the Wear and Tees produced cargo liners and tramp steamers. Specialisation also developed along the Tyne and Wear for marine, heavy electrical and general engineering, whilst around the Tees, construction engineering, bridge building, iron and steel founding and metal trades were prominent. Based at Darlington, famed for being one end of George Stephenson's first public railway line, there was a huge industry manufacturing locomotives and railway repair work. In particular, it was the building of railways which stimulated the demand for iron bridges and viaducts and encouraged the growth of construction engineering.

Newcastle becomes the world's coal exchange

At the beginning of the twentieth century there were hundreds of collieries throughout Northumberland and Durham. Annual coal shipments from the Tyne had reached 15 million tons in 1900. Whilst the older mines of west Durham had been depleted, some of the largest collieries were still being opened in the south eastern part of the east Durham plateau. Similarly, new mines were also being opened in the Blyth hinterland. As a reflection of coal mining from the peak of production between 1884–88, a Durham miner's annual output fell from 371 tons to 258 tons in the years between 1909–13. The mine workings in Durham required increased distances from the face along underground haulage ways to raise coal to the surface. However, the volume of overall production increased due to more than double the number of miners being employed. The

Opposite: *Teesside petrochemicals works with conservation*

Below: *Ellington Combine Colliery, Northumberland*

coal which had become the greatest source of world energy. However, British coal no longer had the monopoly of the overseas markets and competition was intense. It became clear that greater volumes of coal would be required for the industrial home markets. Mining in the North East, like shipbuilding and other core industries had been hit badly during the slump years from the 1920s into the late 1930s. There had been many casualties with pit closures and others operating with losses. With less available manpower, new initiatives were directed towards the more accessible coal seams. Following a policy of supplying coal at any price, the mining industry badly needed re-organisation and re-equipping. The government believed salvation would be in the form of nationalisation when the National Coal Board was established in 1947.

New coal seams located offshore

Traditionally markets for north east coal were for the domestic fuel market, iron and steel foundries, the gas industry, steam power in transport and industry, and coal fired power stations. Following nationalisation there was an increasing demand for high quality coking and gas coals. The Coal Board's priority was to invest heavily in improving efficiency and for the next twenty years £100 million was spent on major schemes. Despite enormous capital expenditure mechanising production at the coal faces, there was no spectacular mining transformation. Each mechanised face incorporated new cutting machines, supports, and conveyors which cost upwards of £150,000. However, many of the collieries were unsuited to the new installations and modifications and experiments were necessary for the most

Durham coalfield produced 27,483,000 tons of coal between 1878–1884 and employed 72,500 miners. The Northumberland and Durham coalfields reached peak output in 1911 with production of 56,000,000 tons. Before the First World War, shipments from the Tyne had reached 20,000,000 tons with 15,000,000 tons being destined for export markets. Newcastle had become the foremost coal exchange in the world and was the hub of the North East's major industrial operations.

1947 – Nationalisation of the coal industry

The Tyne, Wear and Tees ports were built on the coal trade which had become the greatest asset both to shipping and rail transport. Up to the time of the Second World War, Britain was a major supplier of

Top: *ALCAN coal fired power station*

Above: *Ellington, the last deep mine colliery*

adaptable collieries. The dwindling coal reserves at some of the older pits increased the need to locate new workable sources. To achieve this the NCB commenced an offshore boring programme in 1958. This proved to be hugely successful when some 18 boreholes off the Durham coast located at least 550 million tons of coal. The discovery of these seams beneath the sea were close and accessible for collieries already operating along the coast. At the time the national assets were estimated to have increased by approximately £2,500 million with these coal reserves.

NCB increases coke production

However, during 1957–1959 recessionary conditions had not helped industry and more than this, imports of cheap oil particularly affected the demand for coal. During the 1960s the fuel requirements for the steel industry changed. Blast furnace efficiency improved and reduced the consumption of coke from 20 cwt to 12 cwt per ton of iron produced. This reduction in demand was partly offset by increases in the domestic market. The introduction of smokeless zones and more extensive domestic central heating provided an impetus for the NCB to install additional facilities for the production of Sunbrite domestic coke. The number of miners in the whole of the region fell from 140,000 in 1958 to just 63,000 in 1969. In Northumberland, towns like Amble, Ashington and Bedlington saw increasing mining unemployment, although a number of pits in the area were designated as long life pits by the N.C.B.

Dorman Long becomes a giant in the steel industry

The years 1902–04 saw a depression in

shipbuilding and the iron and steel industry. Closures of pig iron based firms had been numerous particularly around the Tyne from the 1860s to the turn of the century. Although the status of the North East remained high within the national industry, it was now the turn of steelworks and rolling mills to face difficulties. Further recessions in steel followed in 1907. The advent of the First World War hastened a process of amalgamation and rationalisation which had gained momentum since the late 1880s and which culminated in the years after 1919. Two giants emerged from this regrouping, the Dorman Long Company and South Durham Steel and Iron Company. Arthur Dorman worked for Richardson Johnson's Yorkshire Ironworks at South Stockton in about 1870. Albert de Land Long worked for Whitewell and Company when together they bought the West Marsh Iron Company (1875) where Arthur Dorman had become managing director in 1874. From a small Middlesbrough-based wrought iron and engineering business (only one of fifteen in the town), Dorman Long embarked on a series of acquisitions to increase their

Dorman Long's Universal Plate Mill Redcar, 1920s

189

iron and steel capacity and product specialisations. Initially, these included the Britannia works of Bernard Samuelson (in 1880), the Cleveland Wire Works (in 1899), the North East Steel Co. (in 1890), and Bell Brothers at Port Clarence in 1902. During the First World War, Dorman Long acquired the Redcar steelworks, constructing new melting shops and rolling mills to develop plate manufacturing, and they also took over the Ironmasters' district site of Samuelson and Co., at Newport, Middlesbrough. The interests of Bolckow and Vaughan's business had grown more through expanding their own works rather than through acquisitions, although they bought several firms before being the subject of a takeover themselves. Prior to this they had taken over a sheet and galvanising mill at Eston (Clay Lane Iron Co.), the Darlington Rolling Mills and Redpath Brown, construction engineers. The economic crisis of 1920 led to further closures and amalgamations, the most outstanding of these being the takeover of Bolckow and Vaughan by Dorman Long in 1929. Eventually, in 1967, and in line with many others in the industry, Dorman Long became part of the British Steel Corporation. At Hartlepool, the shipbuilder Furness Withy was the firm behind the formation of the South Durham Steel and Iron Company. It was established in 1898 to purchase works at Stockton and Hartlepool (the Moor Iron and Steelworks and Stockton Malleable Ironworks). The following year they bought the Weardale Steel, Coal and Coke Co., and when in 1901 the Tudhoe steelworks of the Weardale Co. was closed, Cargo Fleet Iron Co., was acquired. Then through a reverse takeover Cargo Fleet Iron Co., took control of South

Durham to co-ordinate plate manufacture north of the Tees with rail production at Cargo Fleet. Between 1907–10, steel production was developed at outlying Skinningrove works. In 1918 and 1919, the Middlesbrough cast iron pipe manufacturer Cockrane & Co., and Seaton Carew Iron Co., were acquired.

1919 – A third of British Steel produced at Middlesbrough

Despite economic difficulties, the fortunes of Northumbria's industries continued through to the 1920s. Although the region's coal industry had lost its monopoly of the London trade to the Midlands (which had become more accessible by railway), exports assumed increasing importance. As a result in 1913 the Durham coalfield, with an average labour force of 165,800, achieved a peak output of 41.5 million tons, while coal and coke shipments from the Tyne alone

Iron Masters District, Teesside, 1912

190

totalled 20.3 million tons. At the same time the manufacture of pig iron on Teesside had risen to a peak output of 3,869,000 tons, almost thirty nine per cent of national production. The output of steel ingots and castings amounted to 2,031,000 tons, approximately twenty seven per cent of the nation's total. By 1919, Great Britain's steel production had reached ten million tons, of which one third came from Middlesbrough. The industry suffered badly during the depression and probably marked just the beginning of the difficulties which were to follow. In a regional economy which had become very narrowly based with shipbuilding and armament manufacture featuring strongly, there was a dependence on sustaining demands in overseas markets. Trade for the North East was stimulated by the war and coal shipments in particular achieved incredible price premiums. However, the lead in new twentieth century industries, motor cars, aircraft, electric lighting and light consumer industries was already being taken by southern England. Steelworks were nationalised in 1967 to become the British Steel Corporation and on Teesside the resources were centred around one blast furnace situated at Redcar. However, it was not long before competition from the US and Japan brought the inevitable redundancies. The corporation became British Steel in 1988 and eleven years later in 1999 it merged with a Dutch company Hoogevans to become rebranded as Corus. From employing more than 40,000 people at its peak, hundreds of workers took voluntary redundancy or early retirement. By the year 2000 the great steel industry of Teesside was employing about ten per cent of its peak employment figure.

The centre of the fishing industry – North Shields

Particularly during the first thirty years of the twentieth century, there were great developments in the facilities and industry centred around the Corporation Fish Quay at North Shields. Before the First World War, North Shields was landing fish to the value of over half a million pounds annually. It had become recognised as one of the most important fishing ports in Britain. The port's industry supplied several large smoke houses and Shields Spring Kipper became increasingly popular with each successive herring season. Other subsidiary industries developed in box-making, ice-making, canning, fish-oil and guano works, net and rope making, repair yards and coaling facilities. Nothing was wasted. The oil from the livers of cod was used for tanning and making soap. Fertiliser and feeding meal for animals was obtained from the bones, skin and waste parts of the fish. Canning was established in 1904 with Shields Ice & Cold Storage Company Limited (established in 1901). Commencing in a small way with canned fish products (Tyne Brand Herrings canned during the herring season), the

Herring fleet under sail, North Shields

SOON PASSING THE HALF CENTURY **1901-1949**

Tyne Brand
PRODUCTS LTD

From these three Tyne Brand factories, Tynemouth despatches quality food products all over the world.

Now one of the leading canners of food products — the name TYNE BRAND has become a household word for quality foods. Sold everywhere throughout the British Isles and distributed throughout the world. During the late war the Company supplied no less than 130 million cans of various foods to H.M. Services.

The Tyne Brand Range Herrings In Tomato Sauce. Fresh
Herrings. Kippers. Herring Roes.
Cod Roes. Haddocks. Etc., etc. Fish and Meat Pastes (in glasses and tins).
Tomato Ketchup. Chutney. French Mustard. Horseradish Sauces, etc. Mint Sauce.
"So-Taist-Ee" Extract. Canned Fruit and Vegetables. Soups. Puddings. Meat Roll,
and a large variety of prepared canned meats and ready meals.

FOR PEOPLE OF GOOD TASTE

business expanded to produce a range of foods with worldwide distribution. By 1942, the name was changed to Tyne Brand Products Ltd., and by 1950 they were employing 750 people in their canning process operations. In addition, Tyne Brand had cold storage facilities and an ice manufacturing capacity of 200 tons per day. In 1933, a total of 22,445 tons of fish were landed at North Shields and only four other ports in England and Wales landed more. During the Second World War, the greater part of the North Shields fishing fleet was requisitioned for active service. Trawling had become the most important part of the North Shields fishing industry since it could be practiced throughout the year and resulted in the greatest bulk catch. Before the war in 1938 there were 58 trawlers operating from North Shields with an

annual total landing of 325,000 cwts of white fish. In 1948 although the fleet of trawlers had diminished to 43, the annual whitefish landing total had increased by 14% against the 1938 figure. Until the second half of the twentieth century the most prolific grounds in the North Sea fished from North Shields consisted of the Barnacle, North East and Aberdeen Banks. Cod would be caught from January to April and in September, whilst haddock and soles could be caught all year. Other fish taken included skate, halibut, turbot and plaice. Prior to 1939, all fish was sold by auction and most trawler companies had their own salesmen. Much of the fish would be taken by road to London, Glasgow, Liverpool, Birmingham and Manchester. By 1970 North Shields had maintained the status of being the most important fishing port between Aberdeen and Hull. The local industry employed 1,500 fishermen in 500 vessels and landings during this year amounted to about 1,000,000 cwt which was worth £3,500,000.

A time of consolidation and mergers

By the mid 1920s the North East was already feeling the economic bite through lower demand both at home and abroad. Shipbuilding and coal mining were experiencing a forty per cent unemployment rate. Many local communities were so badly affected that eventually substantial proportions of their populations were lost through migration to other parts of Britain and to Australia, New Zealand and Canada. Heavy engineering, iron and steel, marine engineering, construction and locomotive industries were facing a severe depression which forced many companies into liquidation and others into mergers. One of the largest of these was in 1927 with the amalgamation between Armstrong Whitworth of Elswick, Newcastle, with Vickers of Sheffield to become Armstrong Vickers. In addition there were some new growth industries which were to become increasingly prominent. In particular, heavy electrical engineering was established by Charles Parsons following the development of his turbo dynamo invention. On Teesside the chemical industry was on the verge of major expansion and the heavy organic chemical industry was established from 1928 at Billingham.

1833, Robert Wilson begins the first chemical company

The first chemical company on Teesside began by Robert Wilson manufacturing fertiliser at Urlay Nook near Yarm (1833). By the beginning of the 1900s, this firm had already increased its product base with industrial chemical production. At the time of the First World War, it was one of several companies manufacturing explosive products, although nitrate used in the processes had to be imported from Chile. During 1917 this supply was threatened by a German submarine blockade. Shortly before this, plans had been made to establish a site at Billingham for a process of the synthetic fixation of atmospheric nitrogen. The site at Billingham was favoured by a Government inquiry for the accessibility of coal, coke, electricity from the new NESCO-B power station, and the river frontage. After the end of the First World War, the government's scheme was abandoned but the undeveloped site was taken by Synthetic Ammonia and Nitrate Ltd, a private venture established in 1920 by Brunner Mond and Company Ltd. Their objective was to make fertiliser using the

same synthetic nitrogen fixation process. In 1923, ammonia was manufactured for the first time in the country at Billingham.

1926, ICI Limited is established

By 1926 the interests of four firms including Brunner Mond merged to create ICI Ltd, and research began into a process to extract oil from coal. The government requested coal oil production in 1930. From 1928, Anhydrite, also known as dry gypsum, used in fertiliser manufacture began to be mined 700 feet below Billingham in miles of networked subterranean streets. Production of perspex commenced in 1934 and the coal oil plant was officially opened in 1935. This was an operation for making oil and petrol from creosote and coal through a process called hydrogenation. With almost 7,000 employees by 1931 ICI had become firmly established as a major regional employer. This figure had grown to 12,500 people by 1939.

Anhydrite (Gypsum) Mine, Billingham

193

Aluminium and aluminium alloy ingots from the Lynemouth smelter of Alcan (UK) Limited are converted into sheet, strip, plate, sections, wire, castings and forgings, for use in a countless variety of applications—from the Spacelab to knitting needles; from Concorde to costume jewellery; from ships' superstructures to pie plates.

It all starts here at Alcan !

ALCAN (UK) LIMITED
P.O. Box 6, Ashington
Northumberland
Telephone:
Lynemouth Works: Ashington 813811
Commercial Division: Ashington 816501
Telex: 53381

140

Trade advertisement for Alcan

1936 – The Jarrow March

However quickly the new industries grew, there was an underlying instability during the 1930s and the stage was set for mass unemployment. Signs of this were already apparent. In 1926 the General Strike brought industry to a halt throughout the country. Among those on strike were coal miners demanding better wages and working hours, but they were striking whilst unemployment was already high in the region. The national average was 14%, Middlesbrough was 45%. The situation became worse in Jarrow where the unemployment rate reached a massive 80% in 1936. In desperation and in an attempt to gain assistance from the government, two hundred unemployed men of the town set out on a 274-mile hunger journey to London and the House of Commons. This was the well chronicled Jarrow march.

The Second World War boosts industrial demand

As the North East emerged from the recession, the chemical industry continued unabated to expand across Teesside's skyline. The last period of high demand in the region's traditional industries was triggered by the Second World War and extended beyond post war reconstruction continuing through to the late 1950s. During this time unemployment rarely exceeded three per cent. By 1952, there were six industrial estates in Tyneside managed by North East Trading Estates for the Board of Trade. With 145 tenants these organisations provided approximately 17,000 jobs. However, the newer industries tended to employ female labour rather than the unemployed men. It was a time when the region needed new industry and in 1968, with government assistance, a new Alcan aluminium smelter, costing £50 million, was built at Lynemouth, north of Ashington. At the time this development also looked likely to ensure 1,000 miners jobs at local pits. In its heyday during the 1980s from its main UK smelting plant and power station in Lynemouth, Alcan had annual production levels of 130,000 tons. By 1991 the aluminium market was deluged with cheap supplies from former Soviet states. As a

result Alcan almost halved its 800 strong Lynemouth workforce. However, after four years of improvements in the plant, plus the rising popularity of light, recyclable aluminium required by packaging and vehicle manufacturers, the company was prepared for growth into the new millennium.

ICI spreads its Teesside interests

During the Second World War ICI manufactured high performance aviation fuel and plastics. It also had a top secret research team which worked on atomic bombs. Throughout the war ICI was targeted by German bombers and around 100 bombs fell on the site but the plant was only completely out of action for three days. The ICI Wilton Works was established in 1946 on the southern side of the Tees. This site was developed by ICI to complement their extensive operations at Billingham where approximately 11,000 people were employed. The extent of ICI's land acquisitions were increased further in 1962 when an area reclaimed from the sea at Seal Sands was purchased for the site of a new chemical plant. During the 1960s,

Teesside saw new developments in petro-chemicals. Coke ovens used in the production of chemicals at Billingham were replaced by new plants operating with the steam naptha process which facilitated the use of crude oil. This was a much less expensive process for manufacturing ammonia. Between 1964 and 1969, Phillips Petroleum, Shell and ICI constructed oil refineries at the Tees estuary. The prime purpose of these refineries was to supply the chemical industry at Billingham. The scale of the industry also warranted laying down a pipeline for conveying ethylene 138 miles between Teesside and chemical plants at Runcorn. Seal Sands was chosen by Monsanto for the site of a new plant (in 1970), for the production of acylonite for making acrylic fibre. In the last quarter of the twentieth century many of ICI's interests were broken up and sold. However, the chemical industry was still thriving into the next millennium with new tenants in ICI's Teesside plants. One of these, Frutarom manufactures flavours and fragrances and another, Oxy-Wax specialises in coatings and corrosion

Top Left: *ICI Billingham, 1960s*

Top Right: *Teesside's industrial landscape*

inhibitors. In 1999 another giant in chemicals, the American Corporation, Huntsman almost doubled in size with the acquisition of ICI's polyurethanes, titanium dioxide, aromatics and petrochemical global businesses.

NEI is largest private employer

By the mid-1980s the largest private sector employer with headquarters based on Tyneside was NEI (Northern Engineering Industries plc). It employed a total of 20,000 throughout the group's UK and overseas operations. Approximately 7,000 people were employed within the region. The group business was formed in 1977 and incorporated both Parsons and Reyrolle interests. Encompassing both power engineering and heavy marine engineering,

Seal Sands, petrochemicals, Teesside

associated activities included electronics production, project management and research and development. A deepening recession after 1977 impacted most severely in manufacturing. By 1986 there had been a progression of redundancies and closures of whole plants reducing a regional workforce by half. Despite a substantial investment in new technology to maintain profitability in highly competitive markets, with severe fluctuations in demand, NEI Parsons at Heaton had cut its workforce to 3,000 by 1987. Previously, it had a successful record in winning export orders for its turbine generators for power stations in Singapore, China and India. However, in the home market plans for both coal fired and nuclear power stations had been deferred. This had not been helped by the Russian nuclear

power station disaster at Chernobyl in 1986. At Gateshead, NEI Nuclear Systems plant, which was one of the leading boiler making factories in the world, was another casualty. Although in 1982, £8 million had been invested in state of the art plant, orders diminished and a business which employed 2,000 people in the early 1980s finally closed its production facilities in 1986.

The National Grid boosts demand for electrical switchgear

At Hebburn, Reyrolle reached a peak during the 1960s when its electrical switchgear for power stations and power distribution systems were in high demand for the construction of the National Grid. At that time the company had a workforce of 7,000. Under NEI, the company was reorganised and by the late 1980s employed 1,500 people. It gained a large order for substations in Saudi Arabia in 1987, securing work into the 1990s. Another long established company which had become part of NEI was Clarke Chapman. Traditionally, the business had developed in marine engineering, building deck cranes for ships. With a decline in this market, by 1982 there was a workforce of 500 people. Through a joint venture with an Australian company, the business diversified into the construction of ship lifts for dockyards. New markets were also exploited for the fabrication of jib cranes for the offshore oil and gas industries. Through the 1990s other markets for Clarke Chapman's engineering were actively sought with work being completed for rail and mining industries.

NEI Parsons, Newcastle

A period of rapid technological change

It has become a cliche to say that we are in a second industrial revolution. Progressing into the twenty first century is in every sense greater and more important than the industrial revolution. During the space of a lifetime there have been more technological changes than in many life times before. It is only in this period that such dramatic changes occurred in all accepted forms of communications. One of the first of these began in 1922 with the opening of the British radio station 2LO at Marconi House, The Strand, London and was soon followed in 1925 by John Logie Baird's invention of working television. More recently, before the 1970s, very few people had heard of a fax; before the 1980s mobile phones and before the 1990s, the internet and virtual reality. To illustrate by increases in energy consumption; in the mid-nineteenth century this would have been equivalent to burning 160 million tons of coal. During the nineteenth century the total consumption of energy was as much as was used in the previous 2,000 years. In 1996 the General Household Survey revealed an outline of the average British family. It showed that from 1972 to 1995 families with access to a car or van rose from 52 to 71 per cent. In 1971 less than half of households were privately owned by those living in them. This was partly reflected by the average weekly wage which had risen from £124.90 to £384.50 between 1981 and 1997. Retail prices had risen by 57 per cent between 1987 and 1997. From 1981 telephone ownership had gone up from 76 to 94 per cent; homes with central heating had risen from just over 60 to 89 per cent; washing machines from 81 to 91 per cent and video use from 77 per cent in 1994 to 84 per cent in 1998. The context of all of this serves to show a rate of progression which underlined a basic need for transformation towards a new commercial base capable of adapting and moving a regional economy into the future. The first signs for action were demonstrated some years ago. Due to a recession between 1978 and 1984, Tyneside lost 38% of its manufacturing employment. Jobs had fallen from 415,000 to 282,000 while also in the primary sector there was a reduction from 93,000 to 49,000. Local unemployment was the highest in the country and by then nearly 70% of employment was in the service sector.

Mine, shipyard and steel closures

As a result of coal mine closures during the 1970s, this became a major political issue of the 1980s and led to the 1984 miners' strike. The last colliery to close on the north bank of the Tyne was the Rising Sun Colliery at Wallsend in 1969. At the end of 1980 there were only six remaining collieries between the Tyne and Tees. During last decade of the twentieth century Northumberland's remaining deep pit Ellington Colliery was being considered as uneconomical. The colliery operators, UK Coal, were employing more surface workers in opencast at a massive site at Stobswood, Northumberland. There, UK Coal's opencast output was averaging more than 1 million tons a year. With 850 surface and deep mine workers in Northumberland, UK Coal's rich coal reserves near the surface offered a cheaper source of energy. Ellington Colliery's future into the new millennium remained uncertain. The stage was also set at Consett in a traditional steel industry. Consett had become economically unviable and was closed on

12 September, 1980, as 3,000 steel workers clocked off for the last time. Steel from the town helped the construction of the first nuclear power station in Britain, the Sydney Harbour Bridge, the Queen Mary ocean liner and the Blackpool Tower. The cost of closing the Consett Steel Works was approximately £30 million, but British Steel estimated saving £40 million a year by closure.

The regeneration of Consett

Since the closure, the 700-acre steel works site was a focal point for potential re-development. Plans were for an extensive parkland with business and residential areas landscaped into woodlands. Under the banner of the Genesis Project, led by Dysart Developments, Jack Fawcett, chairman, described it as 'probably the largest urban regeneration scheme to be taking place anywhere in Europe'. However, the main impetus came with almost £200 million of public and private sector funding to dismantle the works,

develop industrial estates and improve the town's road infrastructure and access to the A1. Derwentside Industrial Development Agency, one of the key taskforce players was successful in attracting a list of 181 new employers. These included Derwent Valley Foods, International Cuisine, Union Snacks, Aerospace Systems and Technologies, Integrated Micro Products, and Bio-Processing. Twenty years after the end of an era of steel making, Derwentside helped to create 6,700 new jobs, an achievement which many people thought would be impossible. Consett, a town which once had a landscape of slag heaps and red dust had become an attractive area with incredible views.

Traditional brewery businesses diminished

From the earliest trading times, brewing has always taken a place in our regional economy. In the new millennium following the closure of Vaux Breweries Sunderland, there remained some small independent brewers. Vaux Brewery, Sunderland was

Consett Iron and Steel Works

THE TYNE BREWERY, NEWCASTLE UPON TYNE
Home of Newcastle Blue Star Beers

Top: *Old Tyne Brewery*

Above: *Tyne Brewery into 21st Century*

familiar sight on the streets of Sunderland were Vaux Brewery horse drays. They were colourful and impressive and were never totally replaced by lorries and trams for deliveries throughout 162 years of business. Moving into the new millennium, Scottish and Newcastle was the UK's top brewer employing 600 people in Newcastle. The history of this great business began more than 250 years ago when William Younger left the family farm to begin brewing at Leith, near Edinburgh. At the same time and also from a farming family at Whickham near Newcastle, John Barras began brewing. The other brewery which was to eventually become part of this famous dynasty was established at Edinburgh in 1856 by William McEwan. The two Scottish firms merged in 1831. Newcastle Breweries of the Tyne Brewery was floated in 1890 and were an amalgamation of Barras & Co., Carr Bros & Carr, JJ & WH Allison, and Swinburne & Co. These were local breweries with bases at North Shields and Gateshead. The combined force of the Scottish and Newcastle breweries took place in 1960. In the early 1990s Scottish and Newcastle diversified into holiday sites Centre Parks and Pontins. At the turn of the century Scottish and Newcastle was concentrating on international brewing interests and also developing pubs with food outlets. As well as being top UK brewer, Scottish and Newcastle remained as one of Europe's largest brewers with brands like Becks, Miller Pilsner, John Smith's, McEwans and Newcastle Brown Ale. During 1999 the brewer invested in a £16.50 million Newcastle bottling plant having a capability of producing 600 bottles of brown ale an hour.

founded in 1837. It was one of the largest regional breweries in the country and became famous for such tipples as its Highly Nourishing Stout, Indian Pale Ale and Double Maxim. In July 1999, the brewery closed its doors following an unsuccessful attempt to find a buyer. Vaux's parent company, The Swallow Group, had decided to axe their brewery interests to concentrate on developing their hotel and restaurant chains. A

The development of an offshore industry

The complex difficulties of bringing ashore North Sea oil and gas stimulated northern industry to adapt its world famous shipyard skills to this new marine development. By the 1970s it was estimated that expenditure on UK continental shelf activities would reach £4,000 million within ten years. The North East's geographical location in relation to the oil and gas fields made the region particularly suitable. The Tyne established two yards to design, fabricate, erect and equip modules for the offshore oil and gas industry. The first yard was established by William Press in 1972 on a seven hectare site at Howdon, formerly used by the Port of Tyne Authority as their marine repair yard. The yard was reconstructed to house an assembly pad specially equipped for sliding large structures across the assembly area as required during construction. The completed structures were jacked up so that heavy bogies could be driven underneath and rolled on to specially designed barges for towage. On arrival at their final location, the structures were lifted into position by floating cranes. In the first five years more than fifty modules (some in excess of 2,000 tonnes) were completed for the Leaman Gasfield and the Auk, Claymore, Forties, Thistle, Cormorant and Ninian Oilfields. The heaviest unit handled in the Tyne was a little over 11,000 tonnes, including lifting gear and fastenings, a world record. Charlton Leslie Offshore Ltd., entered the module building industry in 1974 when they took over a Wallsend shipyard. A quay of 259 metres was built for loading out modules and the 6.9 hectare site included enclosed fabrication buildings, materials storage space and over two hectares of hard surface erection area designed for flexible operations and movement of offshore structures. The fabrication capability included the construction of very large steel structures including auto fab beams, deck sections,

Offshore oil industry module construction

heli-decks, flare booms, nodes and modules in excess of 2,000 tonnes. This type of work was completed for Shell, Esso, Texaco and Chevron. In addition, shipyards became substantially involved in the conversion of vessels for offshore operations. North East Coast Shiprepairers Ltd., also saw the potential of North Sea Oil. At an early stage they diversified to become one of the most successful companies specialising in the conversion of bulk carriers to drill ships, the manufacture of oilfield equipment and the repair and maintenance of supply vessels.

Regeneration and new industries

The decline of traditional industries followed by the early 1980s recession with the loss of some large employers, created a need for regeneration. One of Northumbria's home-grown successes began in 1985 with the founding of Sage, a computer software company specialising in accountancy packages. The business originated from a printing company, Campbell Graphics owned by David Goldman and Phil Lever. They had an idea of diversifying into user-friendly estimating and accountancy systems. Together with a Californian scientist Paul Muller they set up a fledgling company. At the same time Graham Wylie created the first piece of Sage software whilst completing

his degree in computing and statistics at Newcastle University. David Goldman had been awarded a government grant for Wylie to modify the software so that it worked for his printing company. Then Goldman and Wylie toured the UK promoting their Sage software to printing companies. The major break came in 1984 when Sir Alan Sugar launched Amstrad low cost computing systems. At this point sales soared from 30 to 300 a month. As UK Managing Director, Graham Wylie worked with David Goldman building the business until Goldman retired and Wylie floated the Sage Group on the stock market in 1989. From being established in 1981, within those first eighteen years Sage had a turnover of £400 million and was employing 4,000 people worldwide. By 2005, particularly through Sage's global acquisitions, the number of employees had increased to almost 8,000 with 1,000 of these being based in the North East. Then, also in the early 1980s, Sunderland secured the initial investment for Nissan's European vehicle manufacturing base. The Nissan car plant was opened in September 1986 and was the first Japanese company to establish a factory in this country. Within two years it employed 1,300 people and subsequently became the fastest-growing automotive centre in the UK. It provided a stimulus for over thirty companies supplying direct to

Headquarters of The Sage Group plc, Newcastle

Clockwise from top left:

- *Call centre, Sunderland*
- *Computer data recovery facility*
- *Commodities warehousing*
- *Port of Tyne container handling quay*
- *Telecommunications mast*

Main picture: *Wind turbines, Blyth*

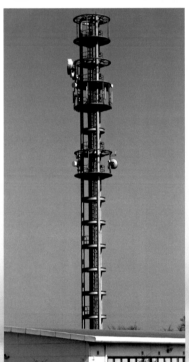

Nissan with a further two hundred second and third tier component and sub contract firms. Nissan's arrival helped to place Sunderland on the map and following this attracted other industrial companies such as Reydel, Calsonic, Mi King, Hashimoto, Lucas SEI and TRW. As a result Sunderland council gained more than 11,000 jobs and secured billions of pounds of investment. A great accolade was given to the town of Sunderland when it gained city status in 1992. During the last decade of the century, political parties, local authorities, development corporations and agencies joined forces to make the necessary transformation of fortune. The result was a staggering £7 billion international investment, with more than 60,000 jobs retained. The manufacturing base was exporting more per head of population than any other in the United Kingdom. Fine examples of inward investment were demonstrated with over 400 companies throughout the world having operations in the North East aiding the regeneration of the economy.

Headquarters of One NorthEast, Newburn

A switch from manufacturers to service industries

By the end of the century, history was once again being repeated. This time the high price of the pound against the euro (making British products more expensive in their main European export markets), increased global competition, lower demand and new technology meant fewer people were required to do the work. In December 1997 approximately 20% of the regions workforce (191,000), was based in manufacturing. Three years later, this figure had plummeted by 17,000, 9% of the sector's workforce. With an accelerating decline in manufacturing, many skilled jobs were being lost. Although many replacement jobs had been created in the service industry, many of these situations eg., in retail and call centres, could not provide equivalent levels of pay. By 1999, nearly 75% of employment was represented by the service sector, with half of those employed being women. During the period between 1981–95 the greatest growth regionally (73.5%) was in the financial and business sector.

A new role for a regional development agency

In 1986, the Northern Development Company (NDC) was established with the support of the business community, trade unions and local authorities. It was a region wide agency which incorporated the long established North of England Development Council. One of the most significant steps towards the prosperity of the North East in the new millennium would be the resulting work of the Regional Development Agency. Known as One NorthEast, this agency began its operation in April 1999 with twelve members all appointed by the Deputy Prime

Minister John Prescott. Six of the members including the Chairman, Dr John Bridge, were drawn from the business sector, with four from local authorities, one from the trade unions and one from the voluntary sector. The RDA was set up to cover the four North East counties of Northumberland, Durham, Cleveland and Tyne and Wear. Its brief was to develop regional economic strategies with councils and Tec's; to manage the Single Regeneration Budget Challenge Fund; to advise ministers about grants to inward investors; to spearhead the formulation of new EU regional and financial packages; develop and monitor the workings of Business Links and Tec's; to buy and prepare land sites for reclamation and development (replacing the role of English Partnerships and the urban development corporations); to market the region for business investment, and to develop a regional skills strategy. This was the development of a much more powerful agency than the North East ever had before.

Changing the fortunes of North East England

The headquarters of One NorthEast is situated in a purpose built complex constructed on a redeveloped and historic site at Newburn. The site had been used for a coal-fired power station, Stella North, but previously it was a colliery. In 1640, it was the scene of a bloody battle, the Battle of Newburn when the Scots defeated the army of King Charles I. During 2003, Dr John Bridge saw One NorthEast's move to the new headquarters at Stella House before handing over his position to Margaret Fay on his retirement later that year. Margaret received an accolade from Prince Charles in 2005, being named His Royal Highness's Ambassador for The North of England. For the first six years of its operations, One

NorthEast has taken a strategic lead in urban and rural regeneration, business support, tourism, research and development, skills and education, and ICT and new technologies. It has worked to accelerate the renaissance of North East England, creating and safeguarding 86,607 jobs, assisting with 17,029 business projects, and providing thousands of learning opportunities (25,821 in 2005). At Gateshead Quays, One NorthEast's investment of £22 million contributed greatly to the development of the Millennium Bridge, the Baltic a centre for contemporary art and the Sage Gateshead, a centre for music.

For business, a great investment in time and money

Together with its regional partners, there have been many initiatives by the agency to influence business growth. One NorthEast worked to influence USA microchip giant Atmel to establish both a production and research and development facility at the former Siemens factory, North Tyneside. This resulted in the confirmation of a £550 million investment and the creation of 1,500 new jobs. Together with investments by companies Filtronics and Senstronics, this has re-established the region firmly on the microchip world market. With a total of £3.8 million funding provided mainly by One NorthEast but also English Partnerships, business complexes were created at Dabble Duck Industrial Estate, Shildon and Villa Real, Consett. These developments were designed to provide hi-spec accommodation for SME's. On Teesside at Morton Palms, Darlington a £22 million scheme is in place to develop redundant land for leisure and light industrial use. At Hartlepool, Queen's Meadow Business Park has attracted major investment. Whilst national developers have been constructing industrial units, UK Steel Enterprise has invested in a multi million pound Hartlepool Innovation Centre for new and expanding businesses. Working with local partners in the Tees Valley, regeneration projects of both South Bank of the Tees, and particularly North Shore, Stockton, development could ultimately create 2,500 new jobs and bring £300 million to the town's economy. There are other multi million pound flagship schemes at Newburn, Newcastle and Middleshaven, Teesside. All of these and an involvement with over 3,000 other projects underpin the leading role and enterprise of One NorthEast's initiatives to re-vitalise business in the region.

Excellence counts first for North East England

In its achievements for the region, One NorthEast has gained a series of national firsts. One of these was the launch of a regional internet portal, n-e-life.com. This has created a virtual regional entity acting as an electronic gateway to economic, educational and administrative data. At the same time the portal provides businesses and organisations with a springboard into the digital age. In 2004, the Government made a decision to designate Newcastle as a Science City. In response, One NorthEast together with Newcastle City Council and Newcastle University pledged a multi million pound investment to turn Newcastle into a world-beating Science City. By building on the region's existing strengths in pioneering research it is estimated that 5,000 jobs could be created within five years. Other leading initiatives include plans to become the UK's centre for bio-fuels production. In 2005, at the world's largest production facility at Teesside, the first year's output capability was planned for 250,000 tonnes. In total, 30

'One Green Routes', have been planned across rural parts of the region. The first of these, a garage in Witton-le-Wear was opened in 2004 to sell only environmentally friendly bio-diesel fuel. Rural areas have also benefited by One North East's £10 million investment to bring broadband connectivity to all 87 of the region's exchanges. Completed in 2004 and bringing 95 per cent coverage across the whole of the region, this was an achievement not matched by any other RDA outside London.

Raising the profile of North East England

At the beginning of 2005, a multi million pound strategy was launched to raise the profile and improve the image of North East England. For this purpose, the region was re-branded: from being known as Northumbria it was now to have the more expansive-sounding name of North East England. With a series of themed advertisements, assistance towards the overall achievement has been planned with a new network of tourism partnerships. Specially targeted promotions will be aimed at the region's natural, cultural and heritage assets, and the development of themed experiences. The region's cities, towns, former mining areas and rural communities continue to be the focus of One NorthEast's attention. In February 2004, the three northern regional development agencies, One NorthEast, Yorkshire Forward and the North West Development Agency launched the Northern Way Growth Strategy. The heart of this is an ambitious target to bridge a £30 billion productivity gap between the North and the average of the other regions of England. All of this is a good indication that One NorthEast is on track to greatly improve the well-being of Northumbria, or as it is now to be known, North East England.

Moving into the twenty first century the North East continued to improve transport links through road, rail, air and telecommunication systems. Through the country's first teleport (earth satellite station) outside London, this would link 90% of the world, 24 hours a day to the North East, opening the door to global markets and information next to the capitals of New York, Tokyo and Paris. This achievement was designed through Technology and Communication International who were to project manage the development in conjunction with Orion Network Systems (a major satellite company) and Zephyr Communications Inc, (Internet Service Provider). For those organisations with regular international links, at the Earth Centre, Doxford, Sunderland, potential communication savings of up to fifty per cent were predicted. At the start of the new millennium the region possessed the foremost communications infrastructure in the UK with an investment of over £268 million in five years. The North East demonstrated a track record for being a particularly attractive area for the development of call centres due to the region's ability to supply flexible, skilled staff with low operational costs.

Industry into the twenty first century

Some pockets of manufacturing had seen something of a renaissance, winning contracts to build oil rigs and Royal Navy ships. They had begun to embrace new working practices and were looking further afield and forming clusters with other companies to win orders. The North East's largest employer (5,000 people) Nissan,

heralded as the most efficient car plant in Europe, was destined to build a new Micra car to secure the factory's future. Some economic experts wished to develop the region as a manufacturing centre of excellence, generating up to 20,000 jobs within a few years. This would follow the shipyards' lead by moving manufacturing practices into the twenty first century. With 5,000 manufacturing companies in Northumbria contributing £5 billion per annum to the regional economy, and a further £6 billion being exported, the figures were highly significant. In conclusion, Napoleon once said of our country that we were a nation of shopkeepers. At the beginning of a new century our profile greatly resembled a nation of small businesses. In a report revealed in October 1997, out of 3.7 million businesses in the previous year, 2.5 million were operated by the self employed and a balance with those who employed less than fifty workers. Therefore, our future prosperity could be held in the balance between inward investment and the attraction of larger businesses (as demonstrated by Nissan), and the ingenuity and entrepreneurial spirit of regional business people.

Hartlepool Innovation Centre, Queen's Meadow Business Park development

Canford Audio's big blue mail order catalogues

A company whose success is built on broadcasting

Canford Audio plc. Crowther Road, Crowther Industrial Estate, Washington, Tyne and Wear.

Founded in 1976, Canford Audio plc has grown to be the UK's largest manufacturer and distributor of pro-audio components and accessories. The company has a range of more than 14,000 products that are purchased by the broadcasting industry, studios, hospitals, schools and colleges. The business began by Iain Elliot and Hugh Morgan Williams sharing an interest in broadcasting. This went back to student days but progressed when Iain was to obtain work as a broadcast engineer at a commercial radio station and Hugh as a broadcast journalist. It was a time when commercial radio was in its infancy and operational speed was vital. Broadcast engineers needed a single source to obtain advice and essential low cost components. With a belief that Iain and Hugh could provide this, their business was set up with £500 each and a bank loan of £3000.

For the first few years the company traded from offices at a disused colliery. The directors believed they could expand the business through the enterprise of mail order. In 1982, the first catalogue produced consisted of 24 pages and took a full year to publish. The results were positive but it was not until 1985 that the company showed any profit and Hugh Morgan Williams could join Iain Elliot in the business on a full time basis. The Canford catalogue has since made a name for being the industry's most comprehensive reference tool for engineers. By 1986 they had outgrown the colliery premises and the directors made a decision to transfer operations to Crowther Road, Washington. Then, the company employed about 20 people and was turning over around £1.5 million. Now, Canford employs 225 people with a turnover of £20 million. The catalogue has grown substantially to editions of almost 1,000 pages, and with French and German translations. The distribution list consists of 30,000 names, costs over £10 per copy to produce and contributes to approximately 85 per cent of Canford's business.

Manufacturing and exporting from Washington

At Washington, the headquarters encompass two buildings that have been expanded to provide 6625 square metres of floor space. One houses an extensive warehouse in which £2.5 million of stock is held (covering the majority of the catalogue range), to make orders available for same day despatch. As well as Canford's own products, other top industry brands are stocked including Audio-Technica, Beyer, Electro-Voice, HHB, Neutrik, Panasonic,

Roland, Shure, Sony and Warfedale. Between 200–300 orders are processed every day. Exporting over 30 per cent of annual turnover, the company can invoice customers in all European currencies and the US dollar, and in most cases with local banking arrangements. Freephone numbers have been set up in most European countries and link to a multi-lingual export sales team, technical support, and administration staff also housed in the same building. Manufacturing together with the design and quality assurance staff are based in a factory across the road. This was purchased in 1996, and in this facility Canford, NEAL, EMO, ASC, Totalsystems and Techpro products are made. The range of NEAL audio and audio-video interview recorders are used by every UK police force, and Scottish courts record proceedings on multi-channel NEAL recorders. In the South West of England, Canford has another manufacturing operation at Portland, Dorset. This has extensive metalworking and assembly resources for the production of video connectors and panel products.

An investment for future business growth

With more than 16,000 customers,

Canford's sales extend from Europe to the Far and Middle East, the UAE, Kuwait Bahrain and Jordan, bringing almost 120 countries within its customer base. Complementing the set up in Washington there are Canford sales offices in Dublin and Strasbourg that have real time access to stock, technical, accounts and other information. One of the company's major contracts in the UK is with the BBC to supply almost all of their broadcast studio requirements. For the future and new products the company is looking at new technologies such as digital and internet broadcasting. In the meantime a major investment in the company's IT infrastructure will provide everything needed for the next stages of company development. This is based on Microsoft's Great Plains business application software that will enable Canford to maintain an enormous system for thousands of products with reports and analyses. This will assist in building client profiles, looking at buying patterns, improving workflow and exploiting e-commerce. More than this Canford people are themselves a major asset to the business being genuinely interested in customers and their requirements.

Canford Audio plc.,
Headquarters,
Washington,
Tyne and Wear

Authentic flavours of the world

Blendex Food Ingredients Ltd.
Hetton Lyons Industrial Estate, Hetton-Le-Hole,
Tyne and Wear.

Originally known as Blendex Spice Company, the business was established in 1959 to supply seasoning blends to the North East's butchery trade. It was based in a 2,000 square foot factory in the centre of Newcastle and provided blends for use in sausage, black pudding, pies and beefburgers. Whilst situated in Newcastle, Oris Limited purchased the company. Blendex was then relocated to its present site at Hetton-le-Hole, operating adjacent to

the parent company. Although the business was growing, the two operational profiles were more individually suited. It was for this reason Blendex was sold in 1989 to three partners and became Blendex Food Ingredients Ltd. Norman Robinson became Managing Director and after fifteen years of developing the business, bought the interests of the other partners in 2005. Norman can be justifiably proud of his company's achievements which have extended the flavours it supplies to suit a wide variety of commercial food applications. From a very modest turnover and a handful of employees in 1989, the business has grown into a multi million turnover organisation employing around 80 people.

Flavours that reach all parts of the UK and abroad

Norman began working at Blendex in 1980 and knows the business inside out. As Managing Director, Norman has always maintained a philosophy which strives for continuous improvements and developing new areas of business and products. Quality has become a watchword at Blendex, where everyone takes pride in their work producing specialised products for food

Blendex factory,
Hetton-Le-Hole,
Tyne and Wear

manufacturing industries both in the UK and abroad. During Norman's management of the business, he has introduced a catering division, cooked meats and bakery divisions, liquid blending, speciality product blending and the latest addition in 2005 is sauce production. The turn of the century saw Blendex embark on an ambitious expansion plan. An investment of £2.5 million has provided a 4,650 square metre purpose built production unit. This consists of a state of the art blending factory, warehouse, technical and administration centres. The production facility utilises a range of blending equipment to accommodate food manufacturers' individual product requirements from fine powders and granules to bulk liquids.

Technical department at Blendex factory

Blendex has a recipe for success time after time

The market trends in food production are dictated by an ever increasing cosmopolitan palate, discerning taste and fast pace of modern day living. In meeting these demands, food producers require high quality blends for both innovative and traditional flavours. It is in the production of these that Blendex has gained its expertise and reputation over the years. Each customer's recipe profiles are produced to meet the same rigorous commercial standards, time after time. This ensures that when manufacturers food products arrive on supermarket shelves, the flavours provided are consistent. Within Blendex's technical department, there is the equivalent of an artist's palette of spices, herbs and flavourings. Blendex is able to meet new market demands. Working closely with food manufacturers, every existing and new product development complies with current legislation, and is kept secure and confidential. With over 12,000 current formulations Blendex is committed to retaining much loved traditional flavours, and for the future, creating new and exciting taste sensations.

Chapter Nine

A capital of sport, entertainment and arts

Before the latter half of the nineteenth century when life had become a little easier for the working man, there were few leisure activities. However, there were several long established and barbarous practices. Two of these, bull-baiting and cock-fighting continued into Victorian times. Bull-baiting was the practice of testing the bravery of dogs by setting them on a bull. The dogs were specially bred and the bulldog and bull mastiff can be traced to these times. Bull-baiting was practiced at Sandhill, Newcastle until 1768. It survived later in Sunderland and Alnwick to eventually be banned in 1835. In 1745, the Newcastle Courant advertised cock-fights at John Dawson's pit, Newgate and at a new covered pit near the Black Bull, Gateshead. There were other regular cock-fighting haunts at the Bull and Crown in the Flesh Market and the Turk's Head in the Bigg Market. Almost all the large inns in the main towns had cock pits. Heavysides, the Stockton historian is quoted: "In the beginning of the present century (19th), when I resided at Darlington, there were two cock pits at that place, one at The-Hole-In-The Wall Inn, and the other at the Talbot, then the head hotel." Most of the cocks were bred by pitmen and were brought into town well before the fights so they could be fed up to tip-top condition. When they fought they usually wore silver spurs. The season for cock fighting was between Christmas and Easter. Events which also drew great crowds were public executions, the last of these being held on the Town Moor in 1844. Other attractions developed and from 1830 a Cumberland and Westmoorland Wrestling Ground was established at Spital Field, Newcastle with

prizes amounting to £140 in some later competitions. Tyneside's pitmen were eventually to become keen on bowling, foot-racing and quoits as well as being supporters of horse racing, rowing and prize fighting. Cycling was also to become popular and the North East's own George Waller became a national sporting hero in 1879, when on a penny farthing, he won the world long distance cycling championship.

Prize fighting ends in tragedy

All of these activities played an important role in the early days of the industrial revolution's workers' playtime. The carnival atmosphere and crowds, sometimes with as many as 200,000 spectators attending sporting events, gambling, drinking and cheering would have been a sight to behold. Tyneside was developing with a huge working class population and sport created a wonderful opportunity for people to socialise. Although there was a certain magnetism towards arenas of blood and gore, there was a gradual swing away to other pursuits. Prize fighting continued and had no particular rules until the Marquis of Queensberry introduced a set of regulations in 1866. Before this, in one fight in 1846 between William Gleghorn and Michael Reilley, held on Blyth Links, after two and a half hours Reilley suffered so badly that he died soon afterwards. The last local big prize fight spectacular was held in 1860 between Sayers and Heenan, but with a new set of rules, boxing continued in a more civilised way to be part of the sporting scene. In his day, the most famous of the new style boxers was Jack Palmer. A Benwell-born heavyweight, Palmer made his name locally and then turned professional in 1898, to go on to win the British heavyweight crown in 1903, a title he

Above: *Newcastle Races as seen from the Grandstand, Town Moor*

Below: *Town Moor Grandstand 1867*

kept until 1906. He retired after being knocked out by Tommy Burns in a World Championship fight in 1909 and is recognised as being Tyneside's greatest heavyweight. Another of these heroes was Seaman Tommy Watson from Byker, whose boxing career was at its height between the wars. In 1932 he rose to be the British featherweight champion, a title which he held until July 1934, when he was beaten by the great Nel Tarlton. Between these years he fought for the world title against Kid Chocolate in New York, but after 15 rounds, he was narrowly defeated on points. There was Jack Casey too, a middleweight from Sunderland with a reputation for being the toughest on the British boxing scene. Others included Micky Maguire, Billy Charlton and Benny Sharkey, each having a tremendous following on Tyneside. Other champions came on the scene in the late 1980s and 1990s when Billy Hardy, John Davison and Glenn McCrory brought glory to the area. Glen fought Lennox Lewis in 1991 to win by a knockout in the 2nd round. Between June 1989 and March 1990, Glen McCrory was World Cruiserweight boxing champion. Hardy and Davison were featherweights. John Davison was British featherweight champion. Twice he took the European Champion Fabrice Benichon to points decisions in France, but failed to become World Champion only through the agony of a split decision. Billy Hardy, from Sunderland's Hylton Castle Town End Farm Boys Club, became European Featherweight Champion in 1992.

A day at the races brings out the crowds

Horse racing was an event which gained great popularity in the social calendar. Early horse races were recorded at Woodham, near Aycliffe in 1613, and also at a course on Newcastle's Killingworth Moor. There is a record in the municipal accounts that the corporation presented prizes of two silver pots at Killingworth Moor races in 1632. In Georgian times horse races were held at Barnard Castle, Bishop Auckland, Blaydon, Chester le Street, Darlington, Durham, Gateshead, Hebburn, Heighington, Lanchester, Ryton, Sedgefield, South

Shields, Stockton, Sunderland, Tanfield, Whickham and Witton Gilbert. Smaller race meetings were banned by an Act of 1740, although others, including Durham continued into the early part of the twentieth century. The races at Newcastle's Killingworth Moor were relocated to Newcastle Town Moor in 1721. The first Pitman's Derby, also known as the Northumberland Plate, was held on 25 June 1838. This became such an attraction that gentry from the countryside would stream into Newcastle for the races with their carriages, which packed Northumberland Street and Percy Street. The ladies wore long dresses with tight waists and poke bonnets and a day at the races was one of the most exciting events of the time. Some race meetings recorded crowds in excess of 50,000 spectators. During race week there were concerts and organised public assemblies for dancing and card playing.

Gannin along the Scotswood Road

The Blaydon Races was established in 1861 and immortalised by the ballad which has become Tyneside's Anthem. The song became the most famous of George Ridley's songs. George Ridley was born in Gateshead in 1835 and worked in the coal mines when he was eight years old. Some ten years later he worked as a waggon rider for the Gateshead iron works of Messrs. Hawks, Crawshay and Sons. Then at the age of twenty one he was involved in a near fatal accident when his train of waggons ran out of control. He was unable to continue his work but fortunately he was quite an accomplished singer of comic songs and quickly gained popularity. His first professional appearance was in the Grainger Music Hall. Of all his songs the most well known today are Blaydon Races

and Cushy Butterfield. There is no particular reason why the Blaydon Races was to become the most famous of his songs. However, it was closely associated with a Tyneside comedian and singer J.C. Scatter, and was also used on posters advertising the races at the turn of the century. The chorus of the song is as follows:

"Oh! lads ye shud a' seen us gannin,

passin' the folks upon the road just as they were stannin,

Thor wis lots o lads and lasses there all wi smilin faces

Gannin alang the Scotswood Road to see the Blaydon Races".

The song originated in 1862, at an event at Balmbra's Music Hall which took place four days before the races. This was a concert in aid of a testimonial to Harry Clasper, one of a family of famous Tyneside oarsmen. The race course ran from Balmbra's Music Hall near St. Nicholas Cathedral, through Newcastle and along the Scotswood Road

The Wheat Sheaf Inn became known as Balmbra's

to the Robin Adair public house (which was at Benwell near the Scotswood Bridge). Originally Balmbra's was the Wheat Sheaf Inn, Cloth Market and then popularly named after John Balmbra, who was the landlord for nearly 25 years from 1840. It was also known as the Oxford Music Hall and later the Carlton Hotel. The last of the Blaydon Races came in 1916, when over four thousand spectators gathered in brilliant weather and in good humour, certainly on the first day. The second day was different, as a disputed decision upset the crowd and then there was complete disorder. It concerned controversy about a horse named Anxious Moments and claims that the trainers and jockeys were dishonest. The final straw was when the angry mob smashed up the weighing house and threw equipment into the river.

The Town Moor – a venue for fairs and skaters

The Exhibition Hall, St Mary's Place

In 1882, Town Moor race meetings were transferred to Gosforth Park whilst The North of England Temperance League established a counter attraction during race week. This festival was to completely change in character to become known as the Hoppings, the Town Moor Fair. The gathering of fair people during race week is still regarded as the largest of its kind in the country. The Town Moor race meeting grandstand was eventually dismantled leaving buildings which were converted to an industrial school for boys, the Bishop Chadwick Memorial School. Later between 1910 and 1912 these buildings were used as a skating rink until Armstrong Whitworth and Co. occupied it for aircraft manufacture. From 1908, roller skating became a craze and whilst popular many large halls were converted to accommodate skaters. The Exhibition Hall, St Mary's Place, built in 1907, was turned into a roller skating rink until enthusiasm dwindled. By 1914 the Hall reverted to its original purpose.

Keelmen become famous oarsmen

Rowing was a sport which had working class origins, but also became very acceptable to the upper classes. It evolved through the competitiveness of keelmen, the oarsmen who ferried coal in keels from various staiths along the river. Some of these became particularly famous rowing personalities. The sport had an enormous following before football ever gained popularity and the best oarsmen could gain prizes of up to £1,000 in a single race. They drew immense crowds and were followed by masses of screaming female fans. It became such an attraction that songwriters (particularly, Joe Wilson) wrote lyrics around many of the great names of the day. When one sculler died, his funeral procession was followed by 15,000 mourners and watched by another 60,000. There were several local

heroes, one being Harry Clasper, who with two brothers and his uncle won the world team championship in 1845. Following this success, by 1850 Harry decided to go solo and won two Scottish championships. Harry Clasper was acclaimed for his boat building and designs, particularly the scull, a boat which is still used competitively every year at the Henley Regatta. Rowing was also a great tradition in Durham where a regatta was established in 1834 (before the Henley Regatta), and has continued to be an annual event. Harry Clasper also invented outriggers, the hooks which retain a boat's oars. Harry trained many of the sports celebrities during the 1860s and 1870s. The picture shows the team which went to Canada in 1871 to row against a team from St John, New Brunswick. During the race James Renforth tragically expired. Many believed the circumstances were mysterious, although the inquest's verdict was death from natural causes. He was buried in Gateshead cemetery with an estimated crowd of 150,000 at his funeral. One of these was Robert "Honest Bob" Chambers who won the World Championship in 1863. Although the Tyne's oarsmen had gained international recognition, the fans' passion was gradually moving over to football. However, rowing continued to grow as a participating sport through to the 1950s even though there were no longer any great prizes at the annual Tyne Regatta events.

Olympic sailing and record breaking voyages

Building prize-winning racing boats is a tradition on the Tyne which has been re-established by Tyneside boatbuilder Dave Ovington. Over a period of 30 years he has built a reputation for constructing some of the finest competition sailing dinghys in the

world. Employing twenty people at a complex of boat building sheds in North Shields, he made more than half the fleet which sailed in the 49er class at the 2004 Olympic regatta in Greece. Dave Ovington celebrated a triple medal win, gold, silver and bronze with boats which had been built at North Shields. The 49ers were first raced in the Sydney Olympics where Ovington boats won two medals. However, the story of Tynesiders and famed sailing adventurers would not be complete without David Scott Cowper. From 1980, the Newcastle-born (1942) chartered surveyor began to embark on some record-breaking ocean voyages. Single-handed, he is credited for a number of firsts; circumnavigating the world west-to-east and east-to-west via Cape Horn; completing three true circumnavigations;

Five famous oarsmen, 1871. From left: Robert Chambers, James Percy, Harry Kelly, James Renforth and John Bright (reclining)

single-handedly completing a transit of the Northwest Passage (which had challenged sailors for four hundred years); he was the first to navigate into the Pacific from the Atlantic or vice versa; and first to circumnavigate the world via the Northwest passage. The definition of true circumnavigation is the result of passing through two antipodal points which are at least 12,429 statute miles apart. David Scott Cowper navigated around the Cape of Good Hope, Leeuwin, South East Cape

Tasmania, South West Cape at Stewart Island New Zealand, and Cape Horn. His epic voyages were completed in both his 40 foot Bermudan sloop, *Ocean Bound* and a 42 foot converted RNLI lifeboat originally built in 1957, but refitted at Smiths Dock, North Shields in 1983. Powered by two 48hp Gardner Diesel engines, he set off in the *Mabel E Holland* on 14 July 1986, heading towards the ice-filled mouth of the Northwest Passage. Although it was to be a successful voyage, it was one from which the *Mabel* could not return for four years. There were two winters when the *Mabel* was completely iced in and on each occasion David Scott Cowper had to leave his boat until she was free from the ice. David Scott Cowper is one of those unique individuals with a single-minded conviction to succeed against incredible odds. His courage in facing continual danger with months alone at sea has been rewarded only by the satisfaction of personal achievement and firmly placing the name of David Scott Cowper in the record books. During the 1980s another explorer, Robert Charles Swan, born at Neasham in County Durham, courageously walked to both poles. He was awarded the Polar medal in 1985 and an OBE in 1995. Only a short time before publishing this book, Conrad and Hilary Dickinson, explorers from Hexham, entered the record books. After 70 days on ice in the freezing conditions of Antarctica, on 23 December 2004, they became the first married couple to trek unsupported to the South Pole. Hilary also became the oldest British woman (at 51) to trek 600 miles to the Amundsen-Scott base. Single-handed they completed their journey skiing with the assistance of wind powered kites.

Brendan Foster, 1976 Olympics 10,000 m (bronze medal)

From the 1850s to 1860s, Jack White, the Gateshead Clipper, was one of the first whose achievements in running put the North East on the road racing map. It was not until 1970, nearly a century later, that Brendan Foster, a Hebburn school teacher, began an amazing eleven years at the top of British track events. He excelled in distances over 5,000 and 10,000 metres. His achievements included one Olympic bronze medal (10,000m, 1976), one gold and one bronze in the European Championships, three Europa Victories, five AAA titles and one gold, one silver and two bronze in the Commonwealth Games, as well as setting two world records. He was awarded the MBE in 1976. Under Brendan Foster's influence Gateshead became an international athletics centre, bringing world famous athletes to the Tyne. It was Brendan Foster who established Europe's largest half marathon on Tyneside in 1981. Elswick Harrier Mike McLeod won the first Great North Run in 63 mins 23 secs. (Mike won an Olympic silver medal for 10,000m in 1984) Comprising of world class athletes and fun runners together, the Great North Run attracts around 40,000 competitors every year. The 1980's was also a great success for the Geordie running scene, with Steve Cram following Brendan Foster in the athletics hall of fame. In 1983 Steve was world champion 1,500 metres, 1982 and 1986 European and Commonwealth gold medallist 1,500 metres, 1984 Olympic silver medallist 1,500 metres and 1986 Commonwealth Champion 800 metres. During 1985 he broke three world records for the mile, 2,000 metres and 1,500 metres. He was awarded the MBE in 1985. During the same era Kirsty Wade of Blaydon

Harriers gained commonwealth 800 metres and 1,500 metres gold medals in 1984. It was the athletic stamina of individuals like these who brought Tyneside into the limelight to give a new enthusiasm to the local running scene. During the 1990s, a Gateshead Harrier, Jonathan Edwards made athletics history with a record breaking long jump. On 25 June 1995 he achieved a massive jump distance of 18.43m (invalid for a record through being wind assisted). The following month he became the triple jump world record holder with a jump distance of 17.98m. This record was achieved in Salamanca, Spain in July 1995, but at the World Athletics

Jonathan Edwards, 2002 World Cup, Madrid

Championships in Gothenburg later that year he gained a double world record on the same day. With two consecutive jumps, his first measured 18.16m (beating his own world record) and his second attempt at a distance of 18.29m (60ft ¼ in) made Jonathan the first triple jumper in history to legally better 60ft. For his championship performance he gained a silver medal in 1996 and a gold in 2000 at the Olympics; at World Championships, a bronze in 1993, gold in 1995, silver in 1997, bronze in 1999 and gold in 2001; at European, a gold in 1998 and bronze in 2002; at Commonwealth, a silver in 1990 and 1994 and gold in 2002. Jonathan was awarded the MBE in 1996. Joanne Conway was also a lady to remember in the 1980s and 1990s. Wallsend born Joanne made a name for herself by becoming British Figure Skating Champion 1985–88 and 1990–91.

1827 – Cricket matches on the Town Moor

Team-based sports of football and cricket were comparatively late in becoming popular pastimes. A rudimentary form of football had been played since the middle ages with early cricket matches taking place on Newcastle's Town Moor around 1827. In 1846 an All England XI was formed and this team toured the country playing three day matches against local sides. Some of these visiting matches were played at Darlington, Stockton, Sunderland, Durham and Newcastle. Even though the All England team won every game up to 1850, with the exception of a match with Newcastle, which was drawn, they did improve the interest and popularity of the sport. There are few records of early cricket, but it is known that from 1877 the Newcastle Cricket Club played on a ground which later became the site for the Fleming

Memorial Hospital. Other clubs were gradually established, including the South Northumberland Cricket Club, the Gosforth Cricket Club and the Northumberland County Club (which had its ground on Northumberland Road, Newcastle until 1882 when the site was sold for property development, part of which was for Dame Allan's School). Durham County Cricket Club was established in 1882. It was not until 1890 that the cricket counties were officially organised and six years later when the existing Northumberland County Club ground in Osborne Avenue, Jesmond was purchased. The best regional first class cricket facilities are those that were completed virtually a century later by Durham County Cricket Club at the Riverside Stadium, Chester-le-Street. After many years of success in the Minor Counties Championship, Durham joined Yorkshire in the Senior Counties Championship in 1990. Two years later the club joined the first class cricket league.

1599 – A deadly medieval game of football

The region's main sporting obsession is football, and strangely enough Chester-le-Street is one of a few places (Alnwick and Sedgefield are others), that on Shrove Tuesday ritually continue to play an ancient form of rough-and-tumble football. A form of football was played in medieval times and matches between border reivers were recorded. Coincidentally, Charlton, Milburn and Robson were family names associated with border reivers. One deadly match in 1599 involving the Armstrongs at Bewcastle (Cumbria) was interrupted by enemies when someone from the Robsons was killed and another from the Ridley clan had his throat cut. At Kielder Castle in 1790 a great football game was played between players from Redesdale and Tynedale resulting in a 2–3 final score.

1888 – Newcastle's teams – East End and West End

When the Football League was established in 1888, Newcastle had two teams, Newcastle East End, and West End which came into existence through amalgamations of other local teams, Newcastle Rangers, Elswick Rangers and others including the Tyne Club. Then in 1894–95 these teams united to begin playing on a pitch created from part of the Town Moor and known as St James' Park. However, until the beginning of the twentieth century football was poorly supported compared with rowing and wrestling. In their first full season Newcastle had difficulty in selling 100 season tickets for 10s. 6d. each. In those first days players were asked to take a cut in wages and after a fixture with Glasgow Celtic the receipts stood at £147. Then, it was an important event when £240 was paid for Scottish International Bob Foyers by Manager Frank Watt. This was a turning point bringing Newcastle United into the big league. Meanwhile, from 1905 the average crowd had quickly grown to 22,400 fans every week. The new club began a steady and successful climb to fame with a series of famous players. One of those was Colin Veitch, who as captain, led the team winning the league championship three times between 1904–11 and capturing the cup in 1910. Veitch was born in Byker and regarded as one of Newcastle's greatest players. He played in every position except goalkeeper, left back and left wing during a span of twenty seven years of involvement with the club, both as player and coach. Colin was one of two players who invented

the offside trap and originated the blackboard pre-match tactics talk.

Black and white football heroes

The famous black and white stripes of the Magpies have been worn by many gifted players from the times of Colin Veitch. One who stood high in esteem, but only 5ft 5in in stature was Wee Hughie Gallacher, who played for five seasons for Newcastle from 1925. During this time wearing No. 9, he scored 143 goals in 174 appearances and was skipper when Newcastle won the old First Division championship in the 1926–27 season. Newcastle United gained great success during the 1950's with exciting cup runs and three glorious victories with famous players Frank Brennan, Bobby Mitchell, Len White and Jackie Milburn.

A commemorative statue of Jackie Milburn in St James Boulevard, Newcastle

Ashington-born Jackie scored 238 goals for Newcastle in 492 appearances from 1946–57 and became a Tyneside legend. Jackie's sister Elizabeth (Cissie) married Bob Charlton, a miner at Linton Colliery, Ashington. Their four sons were brought up in an environment dominated by football and the success of their uncle. Soon Bobby and Jack Charlton were to follow in the family football tradition, both at club and international level. Jack was to play for Don Revie at Leeds United, whilst Bobby played for Sir Matt Busby's Manchester United team, scoring a record of 199 goals in 604 appearances. For England Bobby gained another record by winning 106 caps and scoring 49 goals. Bobby and Jack made football history as the first brothers to play together for England and on the first occasion in 1966 when the World Cup was won.

1894 – Players wages were two pounds a week

The 1970s brought a former full-back turned centre forward, Malcolm (Supermac)

Macdonald, a cockney from Fulham into Newcastle's star arena. Supermac scored every round away from home to bring Newcastle to the FA cup final in 1974. He scored 121 goals for Newcastle in 228 appearances and won 14 England caps with a flamboyant style which will remain in the memories of Magpie fans for years to come. In 1982, Newcastle's Manager, Arthur Cox and Chairman, Stan Seymour Jnr. signed a Southampton player Kevin Keegan. Charismatic, Keegan won the hearts of Newcastle and its supporters through two seasons as a player scoring 48 goals in 78 appearances. Locally born international Peter Beardsley and Chris Waddle also brought some colourful football to the black and whites. Keegan retired when he left Newcastle United. However, in 1992, during a disastrous season for the club, and under guidance from Sir John Hall, Newcastle's fortunes were to be transformed. Sir John instigated the return of Kevin Keegan to Newcastle United as manager and the following season took the club into the Premier League. His five years as manager of

Above left: *Alan Shearer*

Above right: *Malcolm (Supermac) Macdonald*

Newcastle saw the club become serious contenders for the FA Premier League title. After Ex-England manager Sir Bobby Robson's appointment in 1999, the club enjoyed top four finishes in 2002 and 2003. In 1996 the club made history with a world record signing fee of £15 million for Alan Shearer. It is interesting to note that top players wages were £2 per week (1894–95), £8 per week (1923–24), £60 per week (1961), £25,000 per week (1997) and £30,000+ per week (2000). Newcastle averages crowds of around 51,000 at home games.

Middlesbrough and Sunderland football clubs.

Local cricket players established Middlesbrough football club in 1876 and only three years later Sunderland was formed. Sunderland won the league championship three times in the 1890s under manager Tom Watson, who later established Liverpool as a force. Sunderland's Alf Common became the world's first £1,000 player when he was signed by Middlesbrough in 1905. Other great players were Charlie Buchan and George Camsell. In the 1930s, there were Wilf Mannion and in particular Raich Carter and Bob Gurney who were top scorers for Division One in the 1935–36 season. Len Shackleton and Brian Clough were great names during the 1950s. Jim Montgomery's double save which helped Sunderland win the 1973 FA Cup Final is often remembered whilst Paul Gascoigne is remembered for international fame in the 1990s. Two new football stadiums were opened in the 1990s at Middlesbrough and Sunderland. The Riverside Stadium, Middlesbrough was constructed as an all seater 32,000 stadium at a cost of £16 million. It opened on 26 August 1995 when Middlesbrough Football Club (owned by local entrepreneur and Bulkhaul boss Steve Gibson) celebrated a 2–0 victory over Chelsea. Middlesbrough's first match ever was held on the Albert Park Archery Ground in March 1877. When crowds grew to more than 200 spectators, the park committee became concerned

Below left: *Paul "Gazza" Gascoigne*

Below right: *Jim Montgomery*

about safety and the matches were moved to the Breckon Hill Road Field. In 1879, once again with increasing support, the club moved its matches to a cricket ground on the west side of Linthorpe Road, where it remained, until Ayresome Park was constructed and opened in 1903. A record attendance was set in December 1949 when 53,802 fans saw 'Boro beat Newcastle United 1–0. In 1957 the first floodlit game was played and in 1966 three World Cup matches were staged at the ground. At Sunderland, there was pressure to move the location of the football ground from Roker Park. Following the closure in 1994 of the Wearmouth Colliery, the last in the Durham Coalfield, this site was chosen for Sunderland's new football ground. Under the club's chairman, Bob Murray, the new facility was opened on 30 July 1997 and named the Stadium of Light.

1788 – Regular performances at new theatre

Until 1788, when the first Theatre Royal was opened on Mosley Street, Newcastle, there were no regular theatrical performances. Before this, travelling companies of actors would arrive throughout the seasons and one of these included race week (also known as assize week). Venues for performances of farces, melodramas, operas and plays were either at the old Moot Hall, at the Castle Garth or the great booth in Ushers timber yard at the head of the Side. From 1747 the Turks Head Inn in the Bigg Market used their long room for actors and their performances. A number of local comedians also appeared there regularly. Purpose-built theatres were gradually introduced. The original Theatre Royal situated on Mosley Street was opened in 1788. However, with audience numbers increasing, occasionally there were problems with safety. At the Theatre Royal on 12 February 1823 there was a serious accident as a result of a gas leak discovered during the second scene of the first act of the play *Tom and Jerry*. Although there were flames and some smoke, the fire was quickly extinguished. Mr DeCamp, the manager, being concerned for the safety of the audience tried to restore order, but cries of "fire, fire, save your lives!" had already caused panic. There was a rush for the door and several people were trampled and suffocated in the rush to leave the theatre. To make way for a bigger and better theatre the last performance here was on 26 June 1836. The new Theatre Royal at Grey Street was opened on 20 February 1837 with a performance of the *Merchant of Venice*. The last quarter of the nineteenth century saw great advances in rail and tramway transport which considerably assisted public accessibility to Newcastle's leisure and pleasure activities.

The development of music hall varieties

This was a great period of evolution for music hall, theatre and concerts. One of the

The first Theatre Royal (1350 seats), Mosley Street, Newcastle, opened in 1788

first music halls was the Oxford, which progressed from the music saloon of the Wheatsheaf Inn in the Cloth Market sometime between 1858 and 1865. The Oxford was soon followed by the Victoria Music Hall, Grey Street, and then, in 1877, the Westgate Hall of Varieties. In 1867, the Tyne Theatre and Opera House was opened by Joseph Cowen junior. It had one of the biggest and best-equipped theatre auditoriums in the North of England. Although music halls had considerably increased in popularity, there was great competition and older establishments were succeeded by newer rivals. These included Grainger's Music Hall, Nelson Street, and Percy Hall and Cirque in Percy Street which was built by John Irving in 1879. A leading figure in music hall reform was Richard Thornton, born at South Shields in 1839. When he was twelve years old he learnt to play the violin from his father. Soon he was entertaining at pubs and on Tyne pleasure boats for locals and holiday-makers. At the age of twenty one, he married and with encouragement from his wife Bella, became a violinist at the Theatre Royal, South Shields. Eventually, as well as becoming the leader of the orchestra, he was running several public houses. At one of these, the Shakespeare Arms, he had established a music room. However, when the adjoining commercial premises and warehouse came on the market in 1887, he bought and developed them into a flourishing music hall. With seating for about 1,000, it had a plush interior and provided entertainment for everyone. Dick Thornton recalled, "…The music hall as I remember it was not a place where a man could take his wife. I laid down the principle that given good clean entertainment, clean

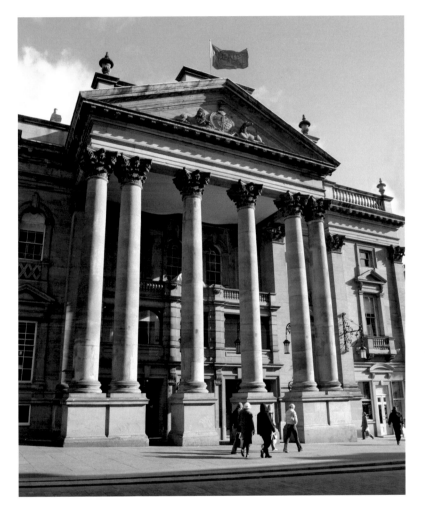

people would come to see it. The man did bring his wife and that has been the secret of my success." By 1898, Thornton Varieties needed a larger venue and moved to King Street in the new Empire Theatre, where the Empire Palace of Varieties was established. In the meantime, he combined his resources with Edward Moss to form Moss and Thornton Varieties and the Moss Empires Ltd., which became the largest organisation of its kind in the world. Together they built the Newcastle Empire Theatre in 1890 and set the scene for music hall reform and variety. Dick Thornton

Theatre Royal, Grey Street, Newcastle built in 1837

moved his home to Eden Villa, Gosforth, where he died at the age of 83 leaving more than £100,000. However, music halls were soon to be surpassed by theatre and concert halls. The Oxford Music Hall reverted to being an inn and the Victoria became a grill and billiard hall until 1914 when it became the Newcastle Picture House. Grainger's Music Hall had a change of name to the New Tyne Concert Hall. Then from 1885 it was known as the Gaiety Theatre of Varieties until around 1912, when it became a cinema. At the site of the Tyne Theatre and Opera House, the Stoll Picture Theatre was opened in 1919. This was the first picture house in Newcastle to project taking movies.

The expansion of repertory and theatre

Between 1890 and 1912, a number of variety theatres opened, including the Empire, the Olympia, the Grand Theatre, the Queen's Theatre, the Pavillion, the King's Theatre and the Hippodrome in Northumberland Road. In addition to Newcastle, throughout the region new venues were being established. In

The Grand Opera House, Middlesbrough, 1903

Middlesbrough on Linthorpe Road, the Grand Opera House was opened in 1903. With an interior of superb Edwardian elegance, audiences were treated to the very best of grand and comic opera as well as productions of the very latest musical comedies. The Opera House closed during the 1920s and re-opened as a Gaumont Cinema in 1931. Unfortunately, in February 1964 the cinema too closed and the site was cleared for re-development. However, during the early years the public was enthusiastic in their support of the new theatres although there were still problems with safety. It was good to have packed houses but having good exits was also important. There was a terrible disaster in 1883 at Sunderland. It happened at the Victoria Hall Theatre when 183 children were killed by suffocation due to crushing, as their escape was prevented by an inward opening door. However, despite the occasional bad news, there was still a great growth in the repertory movement. In Newcastle, programmes were popular at the Theatre Royal, the Pavillion, the Hippodrome and the Tyne Theatre. A People's Theatre was established in 1911 on Leazes Park Road (later relocating to new premises in the Royal Arcade in 1915). In 1929 the People's Theatre moved to Rye Hill where its productions continued in a converted chapel. The current home of the People's Theatre is the former Lyric Cinema, Heaton. It was purchased in 1959 for £27,000 and with alterations was opened in 1962. With seating for 500 people, it is noted as the premier amateur theatre company in the North of England.

Famous names leave a legacy of culture

There were developments in cultural pursuits which were supported by commercial benefactors. Libraries, museums and art galleries were founded and supported by the great names of the day; Lord Armstrong, Robert Stephenson, the Joicey family, Robert Spence Watson, Sir W H Stephenson, Alexander Laing, Joseph Cowen and Dr J H Rutherford. Newcastle's Laing Art Gallery was to gain one of the finest collections of British watercolours in existence. On display at the Laing are some of the finest examples of work by the North East's most celebrated artists; Thomas Miles Richardson (1784–1848); John Martin (1789–1854); John Wilson Carmichael (1799–1868); Myles Birket Foster (1825–99); Charles Napier Henry (1841–1917); Ralph Hedley (1848–1913); and Victor Noble Rainbird (1888–1936). Founded in 1813, the Society of Antiquaries of Newcastle has an archeological journal with a world reputation and is the oldest provincial society of its kind in the country. With over 100,000 books and manuscripts, The Literary and Philosophical Society of Newcastle, located in Westgate Road and founded in 1793, is one of the few private subscription libraries to survive in England. Within our libraries there are books written by many native authors. The most celebrated of these is Dame Catherine Cookson OBE (1906–98). Others including some playwrights include Sid Chaplin (1916–86); Jack Common (1903–68); James Herriot (1916–95); Terry Deary (1946–); Elinor Brent-Dyer (1894–1969); Harold Heslop (1898–1983); Nancy Ridley (1911–86); Nancy Spain (1917–64); Robert Westall (1929–93); Ian La Frenais (1938–); James Mitchell (1926–); Tom Hadaway (1923–2005) and Alan Plater (1935–) and Pat Barker (1943–). Then there are poets, Basil Bunting (1900–85); Wilfrid Gibson (1878–1962); Joe Robson (1808–70);

Catherine Cookson

James Kirkup (1918–); Tom Pickard (1946–); George Charlton (1950–) and Barry MacSweeny (1948–). The 'Lit and Phil' also had a famous natural science connection, the Hancock Museum, which has become the premier natural sciences museum in the North of England, has origins to around 1780. A collection of enthographic and natural history material belonging to Marmaduke Tunstall was purchased after his death by George Allan of Darlington in 1791. The 'Lit and Phil' acquired the collection in 1823 and opened a museum behind their premises on Westgate Road. The museum opened at its present site in 1884. John Hancock, a well-known local naturalist who had been instrumental in the campaign for the new museum, died in 1890. In his honour the museum was renamed. Today the Hancock is managed by Tyne and Wear Museums.

The Olympia,
Northumberland Road

From cinemas to home entertainment

By 1910, cinema was fast becoming the fashion and some music halls installed new projection equipment, mixing variety with motion pictures. The comedy genius of Charlie Chaplin, silent movies, and newsreels followed by the talkies and musical films, all made the cinema a boom business. By 1937 there were 15 cinemas around Newcastle, four in Gateshead and several in Sunderland and Teesside, catering for a film supporting public who would attend the pictures practically every week. There is some uncertainty about the place where cinema was first established, but in the provinces the Olympia in Northumberland Road, Newcastle was one of the first. It was formerly a music hall and changed to cinema with new ownership in December 1903. The building remained a cinema until its destruction by fire in 1907. As cinema audiences increased, music hall and theatre audiences were in decline, although the

theatres held the fortunes of many future cinema stars. Many great performers visited Newcastle including famous singers, comedians and repertory artists. There was a further influence which was to have an all-time effect on leisure entertainment. It began in 1922 when the British Broadcasting Company was established to transmit wireless programmes. The Marconi Wireless Telephone Company had gained a broadcasting license for London and Newcastle. It quickly set up Station 2LO at Marconi House in The Strand, London but needed a base in Newcastle. Tom Payne, a local businessman who had a wireless shop in Gallowgate, applied to Marconi in the event of any new broadcasting opportunities. The result was an interview and subsequent appointment as Newcastle's British Broadcasting Company Station Director of 5NO. After Tom Payne made a personal opening broadcast which included his own violin solo, Station 5NO was up and running and as they say the rest is history. The station quickly needed better premises and moved from a studio in Eldon Square to 54 New Bridge Street where they continued to broadcast from 1925 to 1988. The British Broadcasting Company became a Corporation in January 1927 and Newcastle developed dramas, music and Children's Hour entertainment. When war broke out in 1939, regional broadcasting ceased with the BBC's output confined to the Home and Forces network. Despite this, wireless became an important feature of every household with listeners waiting for the latest news and some light entertainment. There were new programmes which included *Workers Playtime* and *Works Wonders*. These were popular broadcasts where professionals performed for wartime workers and with *Works Wonders*, the workers themselves provided entertainment. After the war normal service was resumed with new variety broadcasts, *Merry Neet*, and *Wot Cheor Geordie*, a show in which producer Richard Kelly introduced local comedian Bobby Thompson (The Little Waster) to the radio scene. He had a gift of making people laugh at their own predicament. His humour reflected the social conditions of the time, the oppression of the workers and poverty. (Bobby Thompson died in 1988). Every evening there was also a topical magazine programme called *Voice of the People* and outside broadcasts gradually increased. However, it was not until a few years later in 1954 that the first sports programme came over the air. In 1952 the famous cartoon character Andy Capp was created by Reg Smythe of Hartlepool.

Entertainment in CIU Social Clubs

On Tyneside, the standards of social living and times throughout the twentieth century have been reflected by local comedians. North East humour is based on the simple philosophy that people who have shared difficult times and situations are able to see the funny side of it all. Social clubs CIU (Club Institute Union) became doorstep places for working people to gather, drink and find entertainment. From the beginning of the 1900s these began to be popular with a co-operative membership of the clubs providing an inexpensive venue for entertainment and cheaper drinks. The Federation Brewery grew out of the enterprise of a group of working men's clubs who formed an independent co-operative to have their own brewery. It was founded in 1919. Having supplies of their own less expensive beers proved to be a catalyst which was to bring new life into the

clubs. Based in Gateshead, The Federation Brewery still continues to distribute an award-winning portfolio of beers and lagers to Free Trade clubs, hotels, restaurants and off-licence trade. The social clubs were organised with their own club stewards and committees. Through the concert chairman forthcoming attractions and acts were announced. It was a scene which had its heyday in the 1960s and 1970s. Some of the clubs were particularly successful in attracting some of the best performers on the British Scene. Top groups and variety acts regularly appeared on the club scene but it was also the place to see local comedians. Some went on to establish their own venues. In the late 1970s Billy Martin and Bobby Hooper entertained packed houses of over 300 at their own Dixielanders Music Hall at White Mare Pool, Felling. Bobby Pattinson established The

Bobby Pattinson and Tim Healy

Talk of the Tyne in a building in Gateshead (his home town) which was formerly owned by the Boilermakers Union. This was to close its doors in the late 1980s when Bobby began to develop other interests in acting and also spending time entertaining in Las Vegas. Around the same time the Dixielanders also closed its doors. Alan Snell, Spike Rawlings, Bobby Knoxall and Roy Chubby Brown (from Middlesbrough) were others who became well known on the Tyneside club circuit. Sadly, although Social Clubs continue their existence into the twenty first century, many have shut down as they were no longer viable. This has been the result of the changing profile of communities which were based around the main employment and industry centres. Although social clubs remain to be favoured by community elders, the younger element prefer the new and trendy city pub scenes and their "happy hours" when drinks are sold more cheaply.

1959 – Regional television broadcasting introduced

During 1949 the Postmaster General announced that five television transmitters were planned throughout the country, one being for Tyneside, which would begin broadcasting in 1954. With the advent of television there was to be a dramatic change in the pattern of public entertainment. BBC's regional television broadcasts were on the air in January 1959 just ten days before the commercial station Tyne Tees Television. At first with pictures in black and white and years later, in colour, a whole spectrum of entertainment became available at home by the fireside. Through television new stars were born. In 1964 a classic sitcom appeared on our screens at home. It was *The Likely Lads* written by Ian

La Frenais with the leading roles being acted by James Bolam (Terry) and Rodney Bewes (Bob). This series was the first to give a voice to the North East. Being such a success, together with its follow-up *Whatever Happened to the Likely Lads*, these were to become two of the most enduring shows in television history. Interestingly it was only the follow-up series that was filmed on Tyneside. Both Rodney Bewes and James Bolam continued to have successful acting careers both on stage and screen. James Bolam went on to take a leading role in the television production of *When the Boat Comes In*, and has become one of the leading actors on the British scene. Catherine Cookson novels have been adapted for television and there are many actors and broadcasters who are well known for their association with the North East. Some of the broadcasters include Kate Adie OBE, Dr David Bellamy OBE, Wendy Gibson, Paddy MacDee, Carol Malia, Mike Neville MBE, Brian Redhead, Alan Robson MBE, Bill Steel, Dr Miriam Stoppard, Kathy Secker, Lynn Spencer, Denise Robertson, Pam Royle, Roger Thames, Dawn Thewlis, Sid Waddel, Frank Wappatt, Simon Willis and Wincie Willis. Actors Jimmy Nail, Tim Healy and Kevin Whately rose to fame through the classic television drama, *Auf Wiedersehen Pet*. Jimmy also starred in his own television creation *Spender* and *Crocodile Shoes* as well as playing Agustin Magaldi, alongside Madonna and Antonio Banderas in the 1996 film *Evita*. Before his acting fame, he was involved in a rock band called King Crabs which may explain his musical interests. In 1992 he climbed to the top of the British Charts with *Ain't No Doubt* and other hits included *Love Don't Live Here Anymore,*

Crocodile Shoes and *Cowboy Dreams*. Robson Green had his first television appearance alongside Tim Healy in the production *Hands,* about life down the pits. He was *Casualty* hospital porter Jimmy and followed this acting Dave Tucker in *Soldier, Soldier* where he formed a friendship with Jerome Flynn. In a subsequent singing partnership they were top of the UK charts with *Unchained Melody* and *White Cliffs of Dover*. His other TV roles have included Dave Creegan, a Detective Inspector in top rating crime thriller *Touching Evil*, and *Grafters* about two Geordie brothers setting up a decorating business in London.

Movies, locations and Tyneside's Hollywood director

Between 1979 and the mid 1990s, Middlesbrough-born Paul Daniels brought a series of magical TV shows to our screens. Paul also hosted quiz shows *Odd One Out, Wipeout* and *Every Second Counts*. In 1983 he was the first magician outside the United States to receive the prestigious Magician of the Year award by the Hollywood Academy of Magical Arts. Another celebrity from Middlesbrough is Robert Renwick Mortimer, best known for his comedy double act with Vic Reeves. Following stage appearances in the early 1990s they began filming the first series of *Vic Reeves Big Night Out*. Then after a move to the BBC in 1993 with an equal billing basis the comedy duo became *Reeves and Mortimer*. As well as television, cinema had an impact on Tyneside with the first of these *Get Carter* a film starring Michael Caine. The location scenes showed Newcastle, Gateshead and the surrounding areas as they were in the 1960s. Directors of other films have also used the North East for its locations. The latest of these, the Harry Potter films used

locations at both Alnwick Castle and Durham Cathedral. Gordon Summer (Sting) starred with Melanie Griffith in gangster movie *Stormy Monday* which used Newcastle as its backdrop. From the 1970s the North East was to see one of Hollywood's finest film directors and producers emerge into a new era of film making. Sir Ridley Scott, who was born in South Shields, began a Hollywood career directing and producing top box office movies. The first of these *The Duellists* (1977) was followed by *Alien* (1979), *Blade Runner* (1982) and a dozen more, including *Gladiator* (2000) and *Kingdom of Heaven* (2005) about the Crusades. Whilst on location in Morocco during the filming of this film Ridley Scott received death threats from Islamist extremists and both Scott and the production was protected by hundreds of soldiers sent by the Moroccan government. Ridley Scott received a Knighthood in 2003.

A wealth of native acting talent

The tribute to North East actors and actresses would not be complete without

A Quidditch player's view of Alnwick Castle, used as a location for Harry Potter films

mentioning Dame Flora Robson (1902–84); Bill Travers (1922–94, married actress Virginia McKenna and together were ambassadors of the Born Free Foundation), Alun Armstrong, born 1946 in Annfield Plain, has a long list of credits from Shakespeare and the stage to TV and the movies; Richard Griffiths, born 1947 Thornaby has also played in Shakespeare and his credits include movies (*Comedy of Errors* and *Chariots of Fire*), and on TV as Detective Inspector Henry Crabbe in *Pie in the Sky*; John Woodvine who appeared on our TV screens in *Z Cars*, has acted in many others including *Hornblower, Bob & Rose, Paradise Heights* and *The Other Boleyn Girl;* from Sunderland, Maurice Roeves has appeared in many TV roles and films such as *Judge Dredd* (The Warden Miller) *Last of the Mohicans* (Colonel Edmund Munro). Comedy actor Rowan Atkinson created Mr Bean and Blackadder for TV. A movie was made of Mr Bean and also *Johnny English* in which Rowan played the lead in this James Bond spoof; comedy actress Wendy Craig

from Durham has played key roles in TV series *Not in Front of the Children, Butterflies, Brighton Belles and The Royal;* actors Philip Middlemiss from Hartlepool and Ian Embleton from Jarrow played brothers Colin and Des Barnes (the bookmaker) in *Coronation Street;* also from the Street, Denise Welch arrived in 1997 as recently divorced Natalie Horrocks who married Des Barnes and was the Rovers Return landlady. In BBC's show *Down to Earth,* Denise plays Ricky Tomlinson's wife. Taunted by his classmates as the ballerina boy, Jamie Bell from Billingham made his acting debut in the movie *Billy Elliot;* Ant and Dec (Anthony David McPartlin and Declan Joseph Donnelly) actors and singers who first appeared on TV's *Byker Grove* have built a career as popular TV presenters. As well as being an author and poet Billy Fane also appeared on our TV screens in *Byker Grove.* The list is long and those mentioned so far serve to illustrate a wealth of talent from their native North East. However, historically with television being new and providing home entertainment, it was not surprising that from the fifties the popularity of cinemas and theatre gradually declined. Many surviving auditoriums were converted to cater for a new bingo craze. The demise of cinema was compounded in the 1980s with the introduction of video and hire of newly released films. By the late 1980s any remaining traditional cinemas were being turned into car parks. The art deco flourishes of the 1930s and 1940s were finished and a new concept of cinema was beginning.

The first multiplex cinemas introduced

Influenced by the Americans, the first multiplex cinema was opened in Britain in 1985 at Milton Keynes by United Cinemas

Pilgrim Street showing the Odeon

The Gate: a facility with a 12 screen multiplex cinema, bars and restaurants

International. Suddenly a greater range of refreshments and variety of shows all under one roof became available, with films being shown from early morning to late at night. With new buildings and high technology, novelty had returned to cinema-going. As well as the UCI cinema complex within the MetroCentre Gateshead, Warner's developed a village site with restaurants at Manors, Newcastle. Other cinema ventures were developed on the Silverlink Estate, North Tyneside and at Boldon, a Virgin Multiplex (11 screens). In Boldon, at Virgin, the Premier Screen is the smallest, with 80 seats but for an £11 ticket it provided the use of a private bar, reclining seats, complimentary popcorn and crudités, and film magazines. Although there are a few surviving exceptions, the days of large auditoriums have gone. One of the last of these was the 1,000 seater Odeon at Pilgrim Street, Newcastle. The Odeon, formerly The Paramount, was opened in 1931. The doors

finally closed when at Newgate Street, The Gate, a 12 screen multiplex was completed in 2002. Designed to be more than a cinema venue, and with other operators like Frankie & Benny's, Pizza Hut, Sam Jacks, Bar Bannatyne, Mood, Tiger Tiger and Hide Bar, the Gate provides a venue for meeting, eating, drinking and entertainment for all ages. The trend continued into the new millennium with other proposed multiplex sites. One of these was being considered in Newcastle between the Central Station and the Redheugh Bridge. Others were being considered at Gateshead and Sunderland, and a Warner Village multiplex had already been opened in Hartlepool. As a growth industry, cinema complexes were becoming ever larger and one Warner site in Birmingham was being planned as a Megaplex with 30 screens. Venues for concerts and shows were also becoming larger. In 1995, the Newcastle Arena was opened. This would have swallowed the audiences of all of Newcastle's theatres eighty years earlier, having an indoor seating capacity of up to 10,000 people. Built at a cost of £10 million, Newcastle Arena was the inspiration of former members of the 1960's pop group the Animals, Chas Chandler and Nigel Stanger. Designed for concerts, sporting events, conferences and exhibitions, its opening marked it as the only venue in the UK to be home to both a Premier League ice hockey and basketball team.

Music to our ears in the North East

With a proud heritage, the people of the North East are equally proud of those who make music and have strong local backgrounds. Kathryn Tickell maintains a tradition of music and is the most famous Northumbrian piper. Thomas Allen (baritone) was born at Seaham and has performed internationally. With Royal Opera Covent Garden, he has toured America with productions including *Don Giovanni* and *Le Nozze Di Figaro*. He was awarded a Knighthood in the 1999 Queen's Birthday Honours list. Sheila Armstrong (soprano) was born in Ashington. She has performed with Sadler's Wells, Glyndebourne and Royal Opera House Covent Garden, as well as major festivals and tours throughout the world. Sheila retired from professional performance in 1993. Together with many others, and even more on the popular music scene, there is a host of talent. These people play and sing uniting feelings and providing moments which are literally music to our ears in the North East. Formed in 1963, The Animals had a number one hit in 1964 with one of the most famous chart songs ever, *House of the Rising Sun*. This was followed by *We Gotta Get Out of This Place* and firmly gave

a place in musical history for the five musicians in the group namely Eric Burdon (vocals), Hilton Valentine (guitar), Alan Price (keyboards), Chas Chandler (bass) (who was married to Madeline Stringer, Miss UK 1979) and John Steel (drums). Susan Maughan, a Consett-born redhead had a sole top 40 hit with *Bobby's Girl* in October 1962. There are many that have flown and carry on flying the Tyneside flag. Brian Ferry from Washington and his song *Lets Stick Together* reached number four in June 1976. Lindisfarne had a great hit with *Fog on the Tyne* and even though they have played their last concert, continue to be massively popular with Tyneside fans. Sunderland born rocker Dave Stewart found fame with Annie Lennox in the Eurythmics. *Sweet Dreams are Made of This* reached number two in the charts in February 1983. Before making the big time in America, Robert Palmer lived in Scarborough. In May 1986 he reached number five in the UK charts with *Addicted to Love,* and later had hits with Power Station. Chris Rea has a tremendous following. He was born in Middlesbrough and had a top ten hit with *Road to Hell* in 1989. The list of names continues with Gordon Sumner – Sting, who began his career as lead vocalist in the Newcastle jazz group Last Exit, then formed The Police and continues as a solo artist. The Lighthouse Family was formed as a result of being brought together by a DJ on Wear FM. Both Tunde (originally from London), and Paul Tucker (from Cambridge) were at that time students at Newcastle University. Their debut single *Lifted* was released by Polydor in 1995. Neil Tennant of Pet Shop Boys lives in County Durham although he was formerly from Gosforth. He topped the charts with *West End Girls* in 1985, *Always on my Mind* in 1987 and *Heart* in 1988. There are others too who have put their own unique stamp on the North East, such as singer Brian Johnson of AC/DC, but most particularly Mark Knopfler. Although born in Glasgow, Mark was brought up in Newcastle upon Tyne and was a former pupil of Gosforth High School. With a tremendous following and fondness for his music and songs, many of which have been written about the North East, Mark has become an adopted Geordie. Mark was the founder of rock band Dire Straits whose hits include *Sultans of Swing* and multi-million selling album *Brothers in Arms*. *Walk of Life* reached number two in January 1986. With many chart hits, Mark has written songs and music both for other artists and the film industry. He is regarded as one of the country's finest musicians and songwriters ever to have hit the British music scene.

Mark Knopfler in concert

New leisure time choices virtually on the doorstep

Having completed the research and compilation of this chapter, it is staggering to realise the amount of home grown talent that has appeared on the region's doorstep. There are many people who have not been mentioned. It would take much more than a chapter to include everyone and those mentioned must serve to illustrate Northumbria's greatest assets – its people. Perhaps another book entitled *Did you know?* would be appropriate. For example Did you know that Sir Frank Williams, the team principal of Williams Formula One was born in South Shields? There is much, much more but this chapter also indicates the ways in which our leisure time has evolved. Through the passage of time the general public have become more and more discerning about their choice of entertainment and use of leisure time. With more sophisticated marketing, more alternatives have become increasingly available. Virtual reality entertainment has arrived on our doorstep. In these fast changing times other developments and interests will unfold in the new millennium. A key part of our leisure time has always been in sharing our experiences with others, whether it's a football match, a concert or any other form of entertainment. In the Kingdom of Northumbria there is a tradition of working hard and enjoying leisure time.

Chapter Ten

A portfolio of our greatest assets

Success is quantified in many ways and people become famous for all kinds of reasons, some attracting more public attention than others. In this chapter, the pages which follow are a testimony to all those in Northumbria who have contributed in their own individual style to add their flavour to the region. There are too many to mention all those deserving individual credits. A note of apology for those not listed. Here are some that have already made an impact on the region's history. Others will follow their footsteps in the new millennium to add more colour and history. Together, these people make a portfolio of our greatest assets. The compilation is in alphabetical order.

Local folk who have made our history

Armstrong. William, Lord.	Dobson. John,	Robson. Flora McKenzie, Dame.
Bainbridge. Emerson Muschamp,	Donkin. Armorer,	Scott. John, Lord Eldon.
Barratt. Lawrie, Sir.	Fenwick. John James,	Scott, Ridley, Sir.
Bewick. Thomas,	Grainger. Richard,	Stephenson. David,
Brown. Lancelot,	Grey. Charles, 2nd Earl of Howick.	Stephenson. George,
Collingwood. Cuthbert, Admiral Lord.	Hall. John, Sir.	Stephenson. Robert,
Cook. James, Captain.	Hawthorn. Robert,	Swan. Joseph William, Sir.
Cookson. Catherine, Dame.	Hedley. William,	Peter Vardy, Sir.
Cowen. Joseph, Sir.	Milburn. John Edward Thompson,	Williams, Hugh Morgan.
Cowie. Thomas, Sir.	Palmer. Charles Mark, Baronet.	
Darling. Grace,	Parsons. Charles, Sir.	

Armstrong. William, Lord.
Lawyer, inventor, industrialist (1810–1900).

Born at 9, Pleasant Row, Shieldfield, Newcastle and son of a successful corn merchant, he practiced law as a profession for 12 years before following his engineering ambitions in 1847 to build works on a seven acre plot in Elswick. He had already founded the Newcastle Cranage Company a year earlier which sub-contracted his designs for hydraulic cranes through W G Armstrong and Co., with offices in Hood Street, Newcastle. The company grew with the increasing shipping trade, railways and mining industry. The advent of the two year Crimean War in the 1850s focused Armstrong's attention towards the supply of armaments. He invented a new breach loading rifle and a new cannon, the orders and subsequent success brought thousands of much needed jobs to Tyneside. This brought him a knighthood and eventual peerage. In 1868, Armstrong moved into naval warship and merchant ship building. He built a country home at Rothbury, Northumberland which was the first privately owned country residence to have electric lights (powered by his hydro-electric system). At the time of his death, his company had a payroll of some 25,000 people and covered a vast 230 acres of land. He had a "golden touch" and was a major influence on the industrial and social development of the region. For information, Lord Armstrong's first home at 9, Pleasant Row, Shieldfield was destroyed to make way for an NER Company, ferro-concrete goods station.

Lord William Armstrong

Opposite: Stephenson's Monument, Westgate Road, Newcastle

Emerson Muschamp Bainbridge

Bainbridge. Emerson Muschamp, Shopkeeper Supreme, (1817–1892).

Born at Eastgate, Weardale, Emerson was the youngest son of seven children born to a yeoman farmer Cuthbert Bainbridge and Mary Muschamp. At the age of thirteen Emerson was apprenticed to a Newcastle draper for five years. He was particularly energetic and at the time of his seven days annual holiday young Emerson usually walked the thirty miles home. Following the end of his apprenticeship, he gained further retail experience in London before returning to partner a wool and linen draper's store in Newcastle's new fashionable Market Street. The store expanded introducing ready made clothing and in 1849 was probably the first store to introduce departments. In 1855 Emerson became sole proprietor and his department store continued to flourish. As staunch Methodists the Bainbridge family worked to deal fairly with both customers and employees. In times when it was usual to work a fifteen hour day, six days a week, Emerson gave staff time off one evening a week for courting purposes and two if they went to prayer meetings regularly.

Sir Lawrie Barratt

Barratt. Lawrie, Sir. Accountant, builder, (1927–).

Born in Newcastle, he trained and took up accountancy before building his first four bedroom home in Darras Hall, Ponteland in 1952. He quickly developed estate concepts and built them faster than most others in the business. Sir Lawrie floated his company on the stock exchange ten years after it was founded and it was instantly popular with major investing institutions. By 1980 through astute marketing, with heavy emphasis on branding, the company had expanded dramatically. Symbolic of the branding was the helicopter, the fluttering flags and the oak tree; all of which made Barratt instantly recognisable. Barratt made it easy for potential home buyers by introducing a part exchange scheme. By 1980 the company became international, spreading to Spain and California, and by the following year it was Britain's largest house builder. In 1982, Sir Lawrie was knighted for his services to the industry. Now, more than 300,000 Barratt homes have been sold over the years. Fellow builder Peter Cussins described Sir Lawrie as "A remarkable example of stamina as well as ability". In 1991 he received a special award for his services to the North East in the Businessman of the Year Awards.

Thomas Bewick

Bewick. Thomas, Wood engraver, (1753–1828).

Born into a farming family at Mickley, near Prudhoe, Thomas Bewick is regarded as one of the finest craftsmen ever in Northumbria's history. Thomas was quite a wild and headstrong youngster, the eldest of five brothers and two sisters. At the local school he did not value his lessons and preferred to play truant in the local countryside. However, he would often use the margins of his school books and every space of spare paper to sketch whatever came to his mind. At home he would spend evenings drawing with chalk on the flags of the floor and the hearthstone. When Thomas was almost fourteen years of age his godmother, the widow of the late vicar of Bywell, Mrs Simons, had a visit from two good friends Willam and Ralph Beilby. Having spoken highly about Thomas, the scene was set for Thomas to take an apprenticeship at their workshop in Newcastle engraving sword blades. Soon Beilby discovered Bewick had a flare for making woodcuts used in the printing trade. The high quality of his craftsmanship quickly increased their business. After completing his five year apprenticeship Bewick became unsettled and made up his mind to go to London where he worked for the best part of a year. The lifestyle did not suit him and in 1777 he returned to Newcastle to go into partnership with Beilby. With copy written by Ralph Beilby and woodcut illustrations by Bewick they embarked on a series of publications. These books about wildlife and their habitat made him so famous that it was said a letter simply addressed to Thomas Bewick, Engraver, would reach him from anywhere in the world. During his later life Bewick spent his time writing his memoirs and died at the age of 75 years.

Brown. Lancelot,
Landscape Gardener, (1716–1783).

Lancelot Capability Brown is regarded as one of the best gardeners in history and was responsible for changing the face of landscape gardening in Britain. He was born at Kirkharle, near Morpeth, Northumberland, the fifth child in a family of six. With a memorable nickname, he was baptised Lancelot Browne with an "e" in 1716 at St Wilfrid's Church, Kirkharle. He was educated at nearby Cambo School, and at 16 was apprenticed as a gardener for local squire, Sir William Lorraine of Kirkharle Hall. After his success there and at other local estates, his reputation spread and Brown became much sought after by 18th century high society. His style, to examine an area for its natural potential of "capabilities" and produce estates of elegant parkland, contrasted with the 17th century fashion for geometric formality.

Brown advised Lord Brooke, later to become Earl of Warwick, on how to landscape the grounds of Warwick Castle; he worked at Chatsworth House, Derbyshire and on the park at Temple Newsam House, Leeds. After working on the grounds at Blenheim Palace for the Duke of Marlborough, he was appointed master gardener by King George III in 1764. Brown regularly returned to Northumberland and worked on the Duke of Northumberland's estates at Alnwick, one near Wallington Hall and at Lowther Hall, near Penrith. In his later years, he became so highly acclaimed that poems commemorated what he had done for the British countryside. In 1768 he bought a small country estate at Fenstanton in Huntingdonshire. Although he seldom resided at his estate, following his death, he was buried in the churchyard there. Brown died suddenly in 1783 when he collapsed in a London street after a late night party.

Lancelot "Capability" Brown

Admiral Lord Collingwood

Collingwood. Cuthbert, Admiral Lord.
British Naval Commander, (1748–1810).

Cuthbert Collingwood was born at The Side, Newcastle. After completing his education at the Royal Grammar School, he began his career at sea when he was only thirteen years old. Whilst he was in his thirties Collingwood made his home ashore in North Shields at Chirton House. The first occasion he was at home for any reasonable time was in 1786. Having risen through the ranks he gained great respect as an officer and was eventually promoted to the position of Rear Admiral. In 1791 Collingwood moved his residence to Collingwood House in Oldgate, the oldest part of Morpeth. By the beginning of the 1800s there was concern about Napoleon shaping his fleet for an invasion. By 1805, Collingwood was in command of the *HMS Royal Sovereign*, a vessel which had been re-fitted with new copper cladding for speed. Being faster than the other ships in the fleet, Admiral Collingwood was first in the onslaught against the combined French and Spanish force at the Battle of Trafalger. After Lord Nelson, on the *HMS Victory*, signalled the fleet with the message "England expects every man to do his duty," Collingwood told his men "Gentlemen, let us do something today which the world may talk of hereafter." *HMS Royal Sovereign* sailed into battle, destroyed four Spanish Men o' War before forcing the *Santa Anna*, the Spanish flagship, to surrender. On the *HMS Victory*, Lord Nelson had been killed by a musket shot and the command of the fleet was then with Collingwood. With *HMS Sovereign* battle-wrecked, he transferred to another ship and led the fleet to victory. It was his finest hour. He was rewarded with a peerage and chose the title Baron Collingwood of Caldbourne and Hethpole, in the County of Northumberland. At the age of 61 years, Collingwood died at sea. He was judged as an exemplary commander retaining rule and discipline with minimal corporal punishment. In honour of his memory, a monument with cannons from *HMS Royal Sovereign* was erected above Black Midden Rocks at Tynemouth. Admiral Lord Cuthbert Collingwood was buried near Lord Nelson at St Paul's Cathedral, London.

Captain James Cook

Cook. James, Captain.
Explorer and Navigator, (1728–1779).

Born at Marton near Middlesbrough, James Cook had a fascination for the sea. As a teenager he taught himself cartography and found work at Walkers of Whitby on their 'Geordie' colliers. After gaining some experience at sea, he joined the Royal Navy when his skills of cartography and surveying were quickly recognised. Having taken an interest in his work the Royal Society hired him (in 1766) to make a voyage to the Pacific to record a transit of Venus across the Sun. This was predicted by Dr Halley, the famous astronomer, to happen in 1769. In the *HMS Endeavour* he set off (1768) to land in Tahiti in April 1769. There he constructed a small fort and observatory, but without precise instruments it was difficult to measure the transit accurately. Then, without success, he sailed in search of the mythical southern continent of Terra Australis but became the second European (after Abel Tasman in 1642) to reach New Zealand. Cook mapped the coastline and also discovered Cook Strait between North and South Island which Abel Tasman was not aware existed. Continuing, he discovered the east coast of Australia, landing at Kurnell, Botany Bay.

Here they had the first European contacts with the Aborigines and sight of the abundant flora and fauna from which the name Botany Bay was derived. After discovering the Great Barrier Reef, the *Endeavour* was damaged and repairs took two months. Once again ship shape, he followed the passage first taken by Louis Vaez de Torres (in 1604), and became only the second European to navigate the Torres Strait, between Australia and New Guinea. The *Endeavour* returned via the Dutch East Indies where it put in for repairs at Batavia, the capital. Until this time James Cook's crew had avoided scurvy, which in those days was quite remarkable for seafarers. The only difference in their diet was the citrus fruits and sauerkraut. Unfortunately, Bratavia was notorious for outbreaks of malaria, which most of the crew had before returning home in 1771. James Cook's next expedition was to begin in 1772. Once again this was commissioned by the Royal Society to search for the mythical Terra Australis. For this expedition the *HMS Resolution* and *HMS Adventure* (Commanded by Tobias Furneaux) voyaged together. On January 17 1773, James Cook was the first European to cross the Antartic Circle. He also discovered South Georgia and the South Sandwich Islands. Unfortunately, both the *HMS Resolution* and *HMS Adventure* became separated in fog. Cook continued alone to explore the Antarctic. He almost discovered the mainland but he changed course to resupply *HMS Resolution* in Tahiti. Cook then voyaged in vain to locate Terra Australis, only to put to rest its mythical existence. During 1774 on his return he landed at the Friendly Islands, Easter Island and Vanuatu. Once home, in 1775, James Cook was given an honorary retirement from the Royal Navy. However, by 1776 he was ready with *HMS Resolution* and *HMS Discovery* (commanded by Charles Clerke) to sail in search of the Northwest Passage. It was to be a fateful voyage. After sailing to Tahiti, the explorers journeyed northwards. In 1778 they became the first Europeans to land on the Hawaiian Islands. Cook named these the Sandwich Islands after the acting First Lord of the Admiralty, the 4th Earl of Sandwich. When he reached the west coast of America, they landed at Nootka Sound on Vancouver Island. From there he mapped the California coast to the Bering Strait and discovered what became known as Cook Inlet, Alaska. Having made unsuccessful attempts to sail through the Bering Strait, James Cook began to suffer both from frustration and a stomach illness. Returning to Hawaii in 1779, his behaviour had become irrational. There, at Kealakeua Bay on 14 February 1779 a dreadful scene took place with the natives over a stolen smallboat. The situation deteriorated into a skirmish when Captain James Cook was clubbed and stabbed to death. Captain Cook's services to navigation, geography and science were unequalled by any previous navigator.

Dame Catherine Cookson

Cookson. Catherine, Dame.
Author, (1906–1998).

Born at Tyne Dock, Jarrow, Kitty McMullen was the illegitimate daughter of an alcoholic mother and was brought up with hardship and extreme poverty. She entered domestic service at 13 years of age and, after a succession of menial jobs, found employment at 18 as a laundry checker at South Shields Harton Hospital earning two pounds a month all found. After a correspondence course, she submitted to a publisher her first 16,000 word story which was returned with a note of discouragement. Then Kitty moved to the South where she worked hard and bought a house in Hastings taking in paying guests. After a meeting in 1937 with Tom Cookson, a school teacher, her life was to change after they married in 1940. She first started writing to help herself overcome depression after several miscarriages. Through the inspiration and strength gained from her husband Tom, Catherine Cookson's first novel *Kate Hannigan* was published in 1950. Since then almost all of her novels were based on her native North East with sales of more than 80 million and translated into more than 20 languages. She remains the queen of the British lending library. One of her most famous series concerned the Mallen family and was set in 19th Century Northumberland. The first of these books was *The Mallen Streak* published in 1973. Catherine Cookson returned to her native Northumbria in 1976, became an honorary freeman of South Shields, was awarded an Newcastle University honorary degree and South Tyneside Council proclaimed itself Catherine Cookson Country. An enduring legacy has been left by her through the continuing benefaction of the Catherine Cookson foundation. In 1985 she was awarded an OBE in the Queen's Birthday Honours and on New Year's Day, 1993 became Dame Catherine Cookson. When she returned to the North East, she lived briefly in Jesmond before moving to Corbridge, then to Bristol Lodge at Langley. Finally she moved back to a house in Jesmond where she passed away, in June 1998, within weeks of the death of her beloved Tom.

Sir Joseph Cowen

Cowen. Joseph, Sir.
River Reformer and M.P., (1800–1873).

Born at Greenside, son of John Cowen (Iron worker with Crowley's and then with his own forge after 1816). Joseph followed into his father's business until 1822 when he married Mary Newton of Winlaton. Then he joined his brother-in-law Anthony Forster manufacturing bricks from fireclay beds at Blaydon Burn. He diversified and designed machines and processes making gas retorts and sanitary pipes gaining a worldwide reputation. His public life began in 1836 as the office of guardian for the parish of Winlaton in the newly-formed Poor Law Union of Gateshead. He was also very supportive of the Anti Corn Law League. After two years he became chairman and only resigned in 1850 to steer a movement with interests in controlling the Tyne. During 1853, Joseph Cowen was appointed as the third chairman of the River Tyne Commission. It was a lifetime post. He built two gigantic piers at the mouth of the Tyne and made great improvements to its navigation and facilities. In 1855 he was elected as a representative of St John's Ward in Newcastle, and in 1864 he was appointed an alderman of the borough. He was invited to become a parliamentary candidate for the 1865 general election. With advanced Liberal principles for the Borough of Newcastle, he headed the poll. He was re-elected in 1868, and in Parliament Joseph Cowen promoted the interests and industries of the Tyne.

In 1871 came the honour of a knighthood but only two years later he died at his home, Stella Hall. Sir Joseph Cowen was one of the lords of the Manor of Winlaton, a Justice of the Peace for Durham County, a colliery proprietor, and a director of the Tyne Steam Shipping Company. His surviving sons were John Cowen of Blaydon Burn, J.P., M.F.H., Hon. Colonel of the 5th Battalion Durham Light Infantry and Joseph Cowen, proprietor of the Newcastle Chronicle newspapers.

Cowie. Thomas, O.B.E., Sir.
Entrepreneur, philanthropist, (1912–).

Born in Sunderland, son of a Deptford shipyard worker, Tom went to Bede School. When his father lost his job at the height of the depression he started to make a living repairing motorbikes. Until then this had been a hobby. By the age of 15 Tom left school to help in his father's growing business which then had a small shop for sales as well as motorbike repairs. After serving in the army during the Second World War he was discharged in 1946 wearing his demob suit and having only a few pounds. Tom went back to take over his father's business, gradually building a reputation to become a leading local retailer of motorbikes. In 1960 Cowie expanded into motor retailing and was soon one of the fastest growing businesses of its kind. With acquisitions of other dealerships around the country by 1965, The Cowie Group was floated on the stock exchange and became a public company. By 1979, under Tom Cowie, the business entered at 12th place in the North East and Cumbria Top 200 Journal business list with a turnover of £52 million. In 1980, the business started to purchase bus companies with the acquisition of the Grey Green Bus company in London. The following year Tom Cowie was awarded the OBE. For a short time in the 1980s, Tom was the Chairman of Sunderland AFC before selling out to Bob Murray in 1985. The Cowie Group established a vehicle rental business in 1991, the same year in which Tom received a knighthood. The company continued to expand, buying more bus companies, the largest of these being the British Bus Group in 1996, making the business one of the largest bus operators in the UK. In 1997, the business changed its name to Arriva and Sir Tom Cowie OBE was appointed as Life President. Into the new millennium Arriva's turnover stands beyond £1.5bn and employs 35,000 people. His attention is also focussed on the Sir Tom Cowie Foundation. Committed to Sunderland he established a fund at the Community Foundation serving Tyne and Wear and Northumberland with a gift of shares worth over £1m. The fund supports a range of innovative projects especially for young people with disabilities or who are disadvantaged. His support for education in both schools and the University is enormous and he has given £2million through the Sir Tom Cowie Foundation. In his 80s Sir Tom maintains another business interest, North European Marine Services, based in Sunderland. With an office in Singapore and planned expansion into China, the business handles 10 per cent of

Sir Thomas Cowie

the world's supply of high-grade aluminium. At his home at Broadwood Hall, near Lanchester Sir Tom stated "I am still a very ambitious guy even at my age. I don't want to retire and start suffering from bed sores. I enjoy life too much."

Grace Darling

Darling. Grace,
Heroine of sea rescue, (1815–1842).

Born in Bamburgh, daughter of Longstone Lighthouse keeper. The family lived on Brownsman Island in the Farne Islands. Their home was at the Longstone Lighthouse which shone its beacon to warn shipping about the treacherous local rocks. On 7 September 1838, the *SS Forfarshire* was on a voyage from Hull to Dundee and in stormy weather it had trouble with its engine boilers. The ship, which had on board about 60 people, soon encountered difficulties. It reached St Abb's Head with the aid of its sails, whilst the leak in the boilers caused the fires to be nearly extinguished in the storm. The *SS Forfarshire* then drifted southward, driven by the storm and in a dense fog struck the Harcar rocks in the early morning. Nine of the people on board managed to escape in a small boat, which avoided further grief by miraculously finding the only safe outlet between the rocks. They were picked up by a passing boat and taken to Shields. Meanwhile, a heavy sea had crashed down on the *Forfarshire* breaking it in half, one portion, with the greater number of crew and passengers being swept away. The remainder, the fore part of the vessel was firmly fixed on the rocks. Here the shivering survivors clung all that stormy day, the waves dashing over them continuously. The captain and his wife were washed overboard, clasped in each other's arms.

Two small children, a boy of eight and a girl of eleven years of age, died from exposure and the relentless buffeting of the waves. A terrible day was followed by a yet more terrible night. Then, in the stormy dawn, it was clear enough for the lighthouse keeper, William Darling and his daughter Grace, to see survivors huddled in a shivering heap on the wave-swept fragments of the wreck. Grace begged her father to save them and to allow her to help in the task. After some natural hesitation, he consented and the brave hearted mother helped them to launch the boat. With five of the exhausted survivors, the boat returned to the Longstone and two of the men went back with William Darling for the other four. Once they were all in the safety of the lighthouse, they remained in the care of Grace and her parents for several days, until the storms passed and it was possible for them to be put ashore. The whole country was moved by the story of the rescue. Presents of all kinds, money and offers of marriage poured in for Grace. She remained the gentle unassuming girl she had always been. Grace was offered twenty pounds a night at the Adelphi Theatre in London if she would consent merely to sit in a boat for audiences to gaze upon her. This she refused and remained at home to sadly die of consumption (tuberculosis) two years afterwards. Grace was laid to rest in Bamburgh Church within sound of the sea by which she had spent her short life.

Dobson. John,
Architect, (1787–1865).

Born at Chirton, North Shields, as a young scholar Dobson was talented at drawing. At the age of twelve, he was appointed honorary draftsman to Mr J. McGlashan, a celebrated local damask weaver and produced good commercial designs. At fifteen his father placed him as a pupil with David Stephenson, a leading Newcastle builder and architect. There he learnt architecture and even acquired an unusual acquaintance with carpentry and masonry. During this time he studied surveying with Mr Hall, of Stamfordham and also became a pupil of Boniface Moss, an Italian refugee (brother of celebrated enamel painter), who instructed him in fencing, perspective, and enamel painting. He never allowed himself to be idle for want of work. During his breaks from work he travelled around England and France, assiduously studying and sketching castellated and church architecture, a pursuit which he continued throughout his life. He was known during leisure hours to design for the stage, and once composed and drew in perspective a celebrated drop-scene for the old Drury Lane Theatre, Newcastle.

It may be said that whatever John Dobson's tasks were, he overcame them with mechanical skill, never losing the artist in the engineer. His engineering ability was greatest in his design of the Newcastle Central Station. After studying the obstacles, John came to the conclusion that a curve not only met and overcame the difficulties of site, but that it was also the most artistic way of treatment. Having determined the general idea, he caused everything to fall into harmony with it, carrying out the curve not only in the roof but in all the minor details of the work. John Dobson was the region's most successful architect and designed many of the country houses like Nunnykirk Hall, Meldon Park, Longhirst Hall and Lilburn Towers, all completed between 1820–30. It is to John Dobson's fine perception of the true and beautiful that Newcastle owes the fine lines of the streets which were erected by Richard Grainger. All of Grainger's streets were planned and levelled by John Dobson. In Grey Street his skill is demonstrated by throwing up the elevated parts of the sky-line to conceal the descent of the ground, so that the eye, satisfied by the artistic grouping of buildings, scarcely notices the level difference between the top and the lower part of the street. John Dobson was a Fellow of the Royal Institution of British Architects, and President of the Northern Architects' Society. He married the eldest daughter of Alexander Rutherford, of Warburton House, Gateshead, and had three sons and five daughters. The youngest son, Alexander Ralph, tragically lost his life in the great fire and explosion at Gateshead, 6 October 1854.

John Dobson

Armorer Donkin

Donkin. Armorer, Lawyer and town councillor, (1779–1851).

Born in North Shields, he started practice as a solicitor in Newcastle 1806, built a fine business, and amassed a comfortable amount of money. He was a leading citizen, a member of the Town Council, and always at the forefront of municiple and public affairs in Newcastle. A bachelor, he was fond of literature and art, and friend of Leigh Hunt, and Ramsey the painter. Every Saturday he had an open house for any of his friends who cared to come and the luncheon became known as Donkin's Ordinary. He built his own house in Jesmond and it was there that he used to entertain his friends, who included businessmen connected with the coal trade, Buddle, Nicholas Wood, Lamb and others. It was through the connection with the Literary and Philosophical Society in Newcastle, that Armorer Donkin and William Armstrong snr became close friends. Armorer Donkin took great interest in his friend's children, a daughter born in 1800 and son William George, born in December 1810. In particular, William George had an enquiring mind and wished to discover how his toys were made and worked. As he grew up, Armorer Donkin became more attached to him and as a natural course the young Armstrong adopted law as a profession, being articled to him.

John James Fenwick

Fenwick. John James, Department Store Proprietor, (1846–1905).

Son of a grocer, John Fenwick was born at Richmond, Yorkshire. He came from a large family of eleven children and attended the local schools. When he was fourteen years of age John became an apprentice draper in Stockton. During his early twenties, following advice that a move to Newcastle would provide greater opportunities, John found employment with exclusive silk mercers, Charles Bragg & Co., of Pilgrim Street. It was not too long before he was promoted to manager with an annual salary of £600. Being ambitious John started a sideline business selling insurance. Unfortunately, this did not suit his employers, who dismissed him from their service. After taking them to court for wrongful dismissal, John Fenwick was awarded damages of £1,000. This sum was instrumental for the opening of his first shop in 1882. This was a mantle maker and furrier business at 5, Northumberland St. Originally, the upper part of Newcastle including Northumberland Street, was residential with properties owned largely by professional people. When two doctors houses were available at 37 and 39 Northumberland Street, John Fenwick was quick to take them to be part of the next stage of his expansion plans. In the early 1890s he was ready to open new stores in Newcastle and in London's Bond Street. John took a gamble which worked, selling ready-to-wear clothes. The business was floated on the stock exchange in 1897. In order to promote the sale of fashionable clothes, Fenwick visited customers in their own homes. With new ideas for retailing, in 1902 he introduced the Christmas Bazaar with the motto 'walk around, buy later'. John Fenwick insisted that customers should be able to walk around the store without being approached by staff. Thus, the first 'Bon Marche' store was born. Close to the store in Northumberland Street, the

Brunswick Methodist Chapel later played a significant role in John Fenwick's restricted leisure time. He died at the age of 59 years and was laid to rest in Jesmond old cemetery. The Fenwick family maintained its interest in 16 stores throughout the country. These include a six store chain of Bentalls which were taken over in June 2001 for £71 million. Mark Fenwick, who managed the acquisition, is top of the North East's rich list with a fortune of £320 million. This is £20 million more than the Duke of Northumberland.

Grainger. Richard,
Builder and Developer, (1797–1861).

Born in Newcastle, son of a quayside porter, Richard Grainger rose from a humble joiner's apprentice to make major changes to the shape and face of Newcastle which hitherto was known as "the coal hole of the North". He was one of five children and when his father died his mother kept the family together. He began his career after the Battle of Waterloo in 1815 when industry and the population was booming on Tyneside. In 1821 he married the daughter of a wealthy businessman (Rachel Arundale) and soon afterwards built his first houses in Higham Place. He forged links with Newcastle's main architects, John Dobson, Thomas Oliver, John Wardle and George Walker, whilst his solicitor and adviser at the time was John Clayton (also town clerk). Richard Grainger invested his money in improvements to roads, street lighting, water supplies and with housing developments in Blackett Street, Eldon Square, Leazes Terrace and Crescent. Grainger went on to build the Royal Arcade (later demolished and replaced by the Swan House roundabout), and development of main streets, the Theatre Royal on Grey Street and the Grainger Market. His ambition, drive and fast completion of his developments was astounding. By 1842 his determination and vision to turn Elswick Hall with its 800 acre estate into today's equivalent of a business park caused him to over-reach himself and caused his great business to collapse. He later continued business in a modest manner and sadly died while at work in Clayton Street West.

Richard Grainger

Grey. Charles, 2nd Earl of Howick.
Prime Minister, (1764–1845).

Born at Fallodean (near Embleton), he was the son of a British army general who had won a number of battles during the American War of Independence. When his bachelor uncle, Sir Henry Grey, died, he inherited the title. At the age of only 22, he was elected as Whig M.P. for Northumberland. As foreign secretary, in 1806 he had carried through the abolition of the African slave trade. In his later years in public life he became Prime Minister from 1830 to 1834. He was specially noted for presiding over the Great Reform Bill of 1832. This was to bring about a much fairer parliamentary electoral system on the basis of equality and one man, one vote. During his time as Prime Minister, he abolished slavery throughout the British colonies. In recognition of his achievements, a 135ft high landmark column and statue was erected in Newcastle and Upper Dean Street was re-named Grey Street in his honour. He once sent a diplomatic mission to China and quite by chance the envoy

Earl Grey

saved the life of a Chinese Mandarin. As a mark of gratitude a specially scented tea, flavoured with oil of bergamot was sent to the Prime Minister from the Mandarin. Earl Grey tea has since become the world's most popular blend. Howick Hall, near Craster, Northumberland, was built in 1782 for Sir Henry Grey and became the home of Earl Charles Grey. The hall and estate is now the home of Lord and Lady Howick (directly descendant to the famous Earl). The gardens and the hall's Earl Grey tearoom may be visited by the public.

Sir John Hall

Hall. John, Sir.
Property developer and Chairman of Newcastle United Football Club (1933–).

Born at North Seaton, Ashington, John Hall came from a mining family and was educated at Bedlington Grammer School. He left school at 16 and was on the dole for six months before finding work as a trainee surveyor with the National Coal Board. Through the 1950s into the 1960s, John progressed from trainee to become a mine surveyor at Lynemouth, Newbiggin and Ellington pits. He then took a position with Northumberland County Council as assistant estates manager at the Killingworth New Town development. John's ambition was to have his own development business. His next move towards this was a partnership in a Sunderland based estate agency. During four years at Sunderland, John began to build on his experience and contacts in the private sector. By the 1970s John Hall had his own development company. It had been doing reasonably well until 1974 when the crash came and Natwest Bank carried the business for the next two years. His company Cameron Hall (Cameron from his wife Mae's name), began to take off in the late 1970s. At this time there had been some controversy about the proposed development of a huge American style leisure complex on the south side of the Tyne. It had been conceived by local architect Tom Faulkner and American businessman Tom Dinnery. The plans attracted bad press and even public meetings failed to gain support. The land, some of which was formerly the site of the old Stella South power station, was ripe for development. By 1979 the time was right when the government introduced an Enterprise zone concept. With an attractive package of tax benefits, freedom from rates and lack of planning restrictions for ten years, the Tyneside Zone was designated in 1981. It included 100 acres of land south of the Tyne between Dunston and Blaydon. Following many visits to the USA and Canada, John Hall finally had a blueprint for the MetroCentre. He had already successfully negotiated the purchase of the land from the Church Commissioners. Having gained the backing of London financiers, reclamation of the land began in 1982. It was not until 1984 that Marks and Spencer, his first major retailer, agreed to be included in the plans. Stage One was opened in April 1986 and by October 1987, together with rail and bus stations, the third and final stage was opened. Then it was the largest indoor shopping centre in Europe. It cost £250 million, much of which went to local contractors. It created employment for 6,500 people and within two years of opening in 1989 there were 20 million visitors who spent £400 million. In April

1990, he was honoured by Yale University for being outstanding in the world of business, industry and finance. They made him a Gordon Grand Fellow, the first time a Briton had received this honour. Once the MetroCentre had completed three years trading, John sold the complex for £272 million. He then started investing in Newcastle United in 1989 to become a director in 1990. In 1991 John Hall was awarded a knighthood. He took control of Newcastle United in 1992. His appointment of Kevin Keegan as manager brought Newcastle back towards the top of the Premiership. This was the start of a grandiose plan to turn Newcastle into the "European city of sporting culture." Sir John spent millions of pounds adding rugby, basketball and ice hockey teams. In 1995 Sir John was approached by Newcastle Gosforth Rugby Union Club. He appointed Rob Andrew as a coach and rebranded the club as the Falcons and within two seasons they won the Premiership. With a stately home at Wynyard Hall, near Stockton, Sir John Hall has also developed executive housing, a golf course and business park on land belonging to the estate. Widely respected in the North East Sir John Hall has done more to promote the region over a period of twenty years than almost anyone else.

Hawthorn. Robert, Engineer (1794–1867).

Son of a colliery engineer, Robert Hawthorn first opened engineering machine works at Forth Banks, Newcastle in February 1817 and within two years the business expanded with sales of general machinery for saw mills, corn mills and collieries. By 1824, Hawthorn was manufacturing small marine engines, and then traction engines and steam locomotives. Although he built in the order of a thousand steam locomotives over a period of 40 years, by 1852 the company was specialising in marine engines for which his business was most famed. Following his death, his fellow directors acquired the T & W Smith shipyard at St Peters Basin, later amalgamating with Leslie & Co in 1885 to become Hawthorn Leslie, one of the greatest industrial names in the world.

Robert Hawthorn

Hedley. William, Engineer and Inventor, (1779–1843).

William Hedley was born at Newburn and educated in Wylam. Soon after his education, Christopher Blackett appointed him as viewer to his Wylam colliery. Hedley was given the task of improving the transport of coal from the colliery to the staiths. Having determined that horse traction was doomed, he joined the number of experimenters who were trying to solve the problem of transport through steam. He convinced himself that smooth rails without the intervention of chains or cog wheels would provide the solution with the weight of the engine alone providing sufficient traction. A new means of transporting coal was now critical due to the replacement of the old wooden rails, with smoother more efficient iron rails. With the aid of Timothy Hackworth, foreman of the colliery smiths, in 1812 he proceeded to put his ideas into practice. The result was to become the world famous Puffing Billy locomotive, patented in 1813. Without detracting from the celebrity to which George Stephenson is entitled, it appears that his first locomotive

William Hedley

engine was not built until 25 July 1814. By this time Hedley's Puffing Billy had been successful in service for some time already saving a large annual sum in transporting coals from Christopher Blackett's colliery. His locomotive continued to be used along the Wylam waggonway until 1862 and was reported to be on par with George Stephenson's Rocket. Because of Hedley's use of a blast pipe which created a better draught, heating the coal to a greater temperature and making more steam, Puffing Billy was more efficient than any previous locomotive.

William Hedley was a member of the Literary and Philosophical Society contributing to discussions on scientific and mechanical subjects, whilst Thomas Bewick illustrated some of the technical papers. During 1822, there was a great strike of keelmen upon the river with sailors joining the strikers, practically stopping trade. It is recorded that Hedley took one of his locomotives off its wheels and placed it on board a keel with paddles attached, using the combination as a steam tug to take coal to the ships, thus dispensing with keelmen's services. In 1824, he took Crow Trees Colliery, near Durham and became a coal owner. Two years later he leased Callerton Colliery, near Ponteland where he introduced a scheme for utilising both ends of the colliery pumping beam, a system which became generally adopted. About this time he involved himself in the construction of a railway connecting the South Durham coalfield with the River Tees, a line which was eventually absorbed into the Stockton and Darlington system. He obtained leases for other collieries at South Moor, Lanchester and West Hetton. At the time he passed away in January 1843, Hedley resided at Burnopside Hall near his South Moor collieries. He was the father of four sons, one an author of a book entitled *Who Invented the Locomotive Engine*, another founded the Bishopric of Newcastle, and the other two being magistrates, one of whom (William), erected the handsome Wylam village church.

Jackie Milburn

Milburn. John Edward Thomson, Newcastle United Footballer, (1924–1988).

Famously known as "Wor Jackie", and throughout his playing career remained with Newcastle United. Born in Ashington, Jackie recalled that when he was a lad "boys just disappeared into the ground to work for the rest of their lives as miners". He was a modest man and came out of the pits to capture the hearts of regional folk to become a legend. Between 1946–57, Jackie scored 238 goals in league and cup appearances and was FA Cup winner in 1951, 1952 and 1955. He remains the Magpies' top goal scorer with 200 goals, although, by April 2005, Alan Shearer had become a close second with 191 goals. In 1955, Jackie scored the second fastest goal ever at a Wembley Cup Final, after only 45 seconds. Jackie never took his fame to the point of it changing his approach to life. He was always ready to stop and have a natter on the street. Even when Jackie finished his playing career and moved out of the area in 1957 to continue into management, he maintained his strong affinity with the region. During 1967 he was awarded a late but much deserved testimonial match at which and much to his surprise over 45,000 fans attended on a wet night to pay their respects. Jackie Milburn died of cancer in

1988. His memorial service in St Nicholas Cathedral was packed with family, friends and famous colleagues. The route of the funeral procession was lined by more than 30,000 people all there to demonstrate the local feeling to Tyneside's footballing hero. The following day his ashes were scattered on the ground at St James Park. However, the story was not yet complete as a memorial fund was established to create a memorial statue from public subscriptions. Two statues of Jackie Milburn were erected and may be seen at St James Boulevard, Newcastle and in the main shopping area in his home town of Ashington.

Palmer. Charles Mark, Baronet.
Shipbuilder, industrialist, (1822–1907).

Born in King Street, South Shields, Charles Palmer could have become an academic had it not been for his father who sent him to Marseille to learn about trade and commerce. After his return he met John Bowes, a North Durham pit owner who recognised Palmer's commercial abilities and took him into partnership at a colliery and coke works at Marley Hill, Gateshead. He recognised the commercial threat facing the north east collieries from the Midlands. They were delivering coal to London faster by rail than the Durham pits could by sea. Palmer designed a steam powered, iron hulled collier which would reduce the delivery time.

In 1852, his newly designed collier, the *John Bowes* was launched from the yard he founded in the riverside hamlet of Jarrow. Whenever possible Palmer made rather than bought. As a result he had a shipbuilding production line. His own blast furnaces processed iron ore brought by his ships from a port he built near Whitby. Palmer also founded the Bede Metal Company for copper supplies, and for plate glass, the Tyne Plate Glass Company. Through Palmer's energetic vision and ambition, his shipbuilding company became the largest in the world. After his retirement the company was sold and Palmer devoted his latter years to public service, becoming the first Mayor of Jarrow and then Liberal M.P.

Baronet, Charles Palmer

Parsons. Charles, Sir.
Engineer, (1854–1931).

Charles Parsons, the youngest son of the Earl of Rosse, was born in London and raised in Ireland. His engineering skills were first discovered when, in his early teens, he built a steam engine to power equipment in the workshop at the family residence, Birr Castle in Ireland. Soon he was of the opinion that the reciprocating action of the steam engine was inefficient and that it would be much more productive if the moving parts rotated. At Cambridge University his studies convinced him to think about developing a high speed rotating shaft assisted by a series of attached blades. In order to progress his engineering aspirations, Parsons chose to move to Tyneside. After taking a four year apprenticeship at Sir William Armstrong's factory at Elswick, he took a junior partnership in Clarke Chapman and Co., in Gateshead. There he was in charge of the electrical department. Charles Parsons lived at Holeyn Hall, Wylam and it was there that he invented the first multi-stage steam turbine. Before long, he harnessed the steam turbine to a dynamo, patenting the process in 1884. Four years later he left Clarke Chapman and Co., to found his own

Sir Charles Parsons

works in Heaton. It was in Heaton that he developed a 30 foot experimental vessel, the Turbinia. He demonstrated its high speed of 34 knots at Queen Victoria's Diamond Jubilee Review at Spithead in 1897. It revolutionised power generation and the turbine was soon used by all other new warships and steamers. He refused to take any profit from the proceeds of works at Heaton. After receiving his knighthood in 1911 he retired to Jamaica where he died 20 years later.

Robson. Flora McKenzie, Dame. Actress, (1902–1984).

Dame Flora Robson

The youngest of seven children, Flora Robson was born in Westoe Village, South Shields. When Flora was five the family moved to London and she was educated at Palmer's Green High School. She then went on to be trained at RADA. After graduating as a bronze medallist, she made her theatrical debut in 1921. This was in Clemence Dane's play *Will Shakespeare* in which Flora played the ghost of Margaret. For the next three years she performed with repertory companies. Disillusioned with her progress she left the theatre and found work as a welfare officer at a food processing factory in Welwyn Garden City, Hertfordshire. Flora established an amateur theatrical group with the factory workers which gave her a greater view of dramatic structure and acting. After a chance meeting with theatre director Tyrone Guthrie, who was appalled her talent was being wasted, Flora was persuaded back to the stage to perform at London's Old Vic. It was here that she performed Shakespeare between 1933–34. A decade later she began appearing in films, embodying dignified (often regal) characters. She will always be remembered for her role as Elizabeth I in the 1937 film *Fire over England*. In this, on the eve of the naval fleet's departure to fight the Spanish Armada, she delivered the immortal line, "I know I have the body of a weak and feeble woman, but I have the heart and valour of a King. Aye, and of a King of England too." Flora continued to impress and gain enormous respect for acting a vast range of classical and modern characters. Her Hollywood career included notable performances in the Oliver/Oberon led *Wuthering Heights* and Ingrid Bergman's classic *Saratoga Trunk* (1945), which earned her an Oscar nomination. In 1952, Flora was created a Commander of the Order of the British Empire. She had done some television but did not seem to take the medium very seriously, contenting herself in later life with a few cameos. No fewer than five British universities awarded her honorary degrees. For services to the English theatre, in 1960 she was elevated to British peerage as Dame Commander of the Order of the British Empire – Dame Flora McKenzie Robson. She maintained her links with the region and supported the People's Theatre which had relocated to Jesmond in 1962. Flora appeared in the opening production, *The Corn is Green* (written by Emlyn Williams). By the early 1970s she went into semi retirement with an amazing list of credits behind her. It was sad to note that her final film was *Clash of the Titans* (1981), a fantasy in which she took the part of Stygian Witch, unrecognisable except for her distinctive voice. Dame Flora Robson never married and in 1984 sadly died alone in Brighton.

Scott. John, Lord Eldon.
Barrister, M.P., Lord Chancellor, (1751–1838).

Born in Love Lane, Newcastle, son of a prosperous merchant he was educated at the Royal Free Grammar School and University College, Oxford. Whilst on a visit to Sedgefield in South Durham, young Scott met Elizabeth Surtees in Church and fell desperately in love. Her father, an eminent Newcastle banker, contrived to ensure they would be kept apart. However, John eloped with her on 18th November 1772 when she descended by ladder from a window in her father's Sandhill house. From there they travelled to Scotland to be married. Her father relented his feelings, and the families were united after re-marrying according to English ritual. In January 1773 Scott became a student of the Middle Temple to enter the law profession. Three years later, in February 1776, he was called to the bar and in 1800 won a notable case in the Court of Chancery. John successfully took up an election petition with such ability that he was persuaded to remain in London. His reputation grew rapidly and he had more business than any other counsel at the bar. In 1783 John went to the House of Commons in the Tory interest for Lord Weymouth's pocket borough of Weobly, in

Hertfordshire. He represented this borough until 1796 when he was returned, with Sir Francis Burdett for Boroughbridge. In 1788 for special services in drawing the East India Declaratory Bill, he was knighted by George III and given the post of Solicitor-General in William Pitt's Parliament. By 1793 Sir John Scott was given the post of Attorney General.

In July 1799 he was appointed Chief Justice of the Court of Common Pleas, and a member of His Majesty's Privy Council. At the same time he was raised to peerage by the title of Baron Eldon of Eldon in the County of Durham, a manor near St Andrew's Auckland, consisting of 1,540 acres which he had purchased in 1792 for £22,000. Lord Eldon gained great admiration and respect as a common law judge and by April 1801, he became Lord Chancellor, an appointment which Scott maintained for a period of nearly twenty-five years. He had been raised to the dignities of Viscount Escombe and Earl of Eldon in 1821 on the accession of George IV and he made his last speech in the House of Lords in 1834. John Scott, Lord Eldon, survived his wife Elizabeth by seven years and, aged eighty six, died with personal property valued at nearly three quarters of a million pounds and large landed estates.

Lord Eldon

Scott. Ridley, Sir.
Film Director and Producer, (1937–).

Ridley Scott's father was in the armed forces during the war. Although Ridley Scott was born in South Shields, he led an unsettled life whilst the family moved around the country from posting to posting. After his father retired from the forces in 1952, the family returned to Stockton where he resumed a shipping business. In 1958,

aged 20, Ridley Scott graduated from the West Hartlepool College of Art. Ridley then completed two years National Service in the Marines. Through a scholarship, Ridley Scott went to the Royal College of Art. There he studied photography and contributed some of his time towards establishing a film department there in the mid-1960s. Following his graduation he began his career working as a trainee with the BBC

Sir Ridley Scott

and worked on the successful *Z Cars* series. Ridley moved on to establish an advertising business with his younger brother Tony, Hugh Hudson and Alan Parker. It was in producing UK television commercials that he began to develop a visual style with innovative and atmospheric lighting. One of the most celebrated of these advertisements was the Hovis *New World* advertisement. Hollywood was his next call where he has produced and directed a succession of top ranking films. The list includes *Alien, Blade Runner, Black Rain, The Duellists, Someone to Watch Over Me, Legend, Thelma and Louise, 1492 – Conquest of Paradise, White Squall, G.I. Jane, Gladiator, Hannibal, Black Hawk Down, Matchstick Men* and *Kingdom of Heaven*. Such is his versatility that his film profile covers a range of topics from horror and science fiction to fairy tale, war and sword and sandal. Ridley Scott has been nominated for three Academy Awards for directing and was knighted in 2003.

Stephenson. David,
Builder and Architect, (1756–1819).

Son of John Stephenson, a house carpenter who attained considerable prominence during the rebuilding of the Tyne Bridge after the disastrous flood of November 1771. David was brought up to follow in his father's business based from the family home at the head of the Long Stairs, Newcastle Quayside. Whilst working, he also studied drawing, mathematics and geometry and before he was thirty, he established himself as an architect. One of his first assignments was commissioned in 1783 by the mayor, Sir Matthew White Ridley, Bart. MP, to rebuild the Cale Cross monument at the junction of the Side, Butcher Bank and Sandhill. Another monument, White Cross in Newgate Street was also designed and erected by David Stephenson. During later reconstruction works, these monuments were eventually removed, the former being set up again at Sir Matthew White Ridley's park at Blaydon. Stephenson soon gained a fine reputation and was given commissions for the restoration of St Nicholas Church, a new church for All Saints parish and the construction of the original Theatre Royal at Drury Lane, Newcastle.

Whilst this work was in progress, Stephenson was occupied with a great new town street scheme – the formation of Dean Street and Mosley Street. This involved major work, the Dean being arched over and the valley of the Lort Burn filled up to form the basis of the new street. David Stephenson's construction work stretched across the Tyne to Gateshead when he was commissioned to widen the Tyne Bridge in 1801. In Gateshead, Stephenson also worked on a new thoroughfare, creating Church Street, near St Mary's Churchyard. This was completed in 1791. He built the New Quay at North Shields in 1806 and his business was then fast growing with his reputation. When a foundation stone of one of his monuments was laid in 1816, the tenantry Column at Alnwick, he became "architect to his Grace the Duke of Northumberland". His task was to construct farm buildings on the ducal estates, an appointment he held for a number of years.

As well as his profession, David Stephenson was active with various local interests for the well-being of the community. He was on the committee appointed at a meeting to prepare a plan for the formation of the Literary and

Philosophical Society in Newcastle on 24th January 1793. Also with threats of French invasion, he organised local youths in the practice of arms to defend their homes against Bonaparte. In later years he was one of the first members of the Newcastle Society of Antiquaries. Among the pupils trained at David Stephenson's office during his professional career was John Dobson. It was through Stephenson's advice that John Dobson established his practice in Newcastle instead of London.

Stephenson. George,

Locomotive and Railway Engineer, (1781–1848).

George Stephenson was born at Wylam, son of Robert and Mabel. Old Bob was earning only twelve shillings a week at the time. Throughout George's younger days the family moved home several times to follow any available work. Whilst they were living at Jolly's Close, near Newburn, George set to work as a fireman on his own account for a shilling a day. He had grown up without education and at eighteen years of age was unable to read. Much of his time was devoted to studying his engine so that he could qualify to be an engine man with better pay. Soon he was sent to look after a pumping engine near Throckley Bridge when his pay was increased to twelve shillings a week. He went to night school to learn to read and study arithmetic. At twenty one he was a Brakesman at the Dolly Pit, Black Callerton, earning about twenty shillings a week. Whilst at his lodgings he developed a relationship with the domestic servant Fanny Henderson. She was the daughter of a Capheaton farmer and they married at Newburn Church on 28th November 1802. With the money they had saved, they furnished a house and created a home at Willington Quay. It was here that he employed his evenings clock cleaning, shoe mending, and studying mathematics. On 16 October 1803, his wife gave birth to his son Robert and in 1805 he moved to West Moor Colliery, Killingworth as brakesman of the colliery engine. The same year they lost their second child and in May 1806, Mrs Stephenson died, stricken with consumption. He soon became well known as a skillful mechanic. In 1812 when the engine wright at High Pit, Killingworth was accidently killed, he was appointed in his place for a salary of £100 a year. By 1813 Stephenson submitted his plans for the construction of a Killingworth colliery locomotive. These were accepted by the owners and when completed in 1814, the locomotive could pull eight trucks weighing thirty tons, up a gradient of 1 in 450, at 5mph. In the interests of mine safety the following year George devised a miner's lamp which he exhibited during December 1815 at the Newcastle Literary and Philosophical Society. On 29th March 1820 George married Elizabeth Hindmarsh who he had courted originally before meeting his first wife.

In 1821 Royal assent was granted to an act for constructing tramroads between Stockton and Darlington. The main promoter of this was Edward Pease of Darlington, who was quickly persuaded by Stephenson that engines would do the work of fifty horses. As a result the first railway line was opened on 27 September 1825. A new line was soon established between Liverpool and Manchester and to settle the choice between fixed and travelling engines, the directors offered a

George Stephenson

£500 prize for a steam engine which would perform given tasks. It was Stephenson's Rocket which won that day. From then his success was assured. In one session of Parliament in 1836, with his son Robert, he was given £5 million for the construction of two hundred and fourteen miles of new railways. He was also invited to assist railway engineers abroad. In 1840, having reached the age of sixty, he settled at Taplon House, Chesterfield where he lived as a country gentleman. Death came to him unexpectedly less than twelve months after he had married his third young wife on 12th August 1848, aged sixty seven.

Robert Stephenson

Stephenson. Robert,
Railway Engineer, (1803–1858).

Robert Stephenson was born at Willington Quay near Wallsend. Shortly after moving to Killingworth when he was only two, his mother died of tuberculosis. His father George's elder sister agreed to become housekeeper and look after Robert. His father was keen for Robert to have a good start in life by having a proper education. After attending schools in Longbenton and Newcastle's Percy Street Academy, at 16 years of age Robert became an apprentice engineer at the Killingworth Colliery. His education was finally complete when he went to Edinburgh University. Once his father had opened the Forth Street Newcastle locomotive works, Robert joined the business to assist in its management. He was mostly responsible for the design of the Rocket, their locomotive which won the Rainhill Trials. In 1833, Robert was appointed as the chief engineer for the £5.5 million construction of the London to Birmingham Railway. Despite many engineering and legal difficulties, the line which now forms part of the West Coast Mainline was opened in 1838. Robert was responsible for engineering the railway links between London and Newcastle, constructing the tracks between York and Gateshead and designing the High Level Bridge which made the connection across the Tyne. In 1849, Queen Victoria officially opened the bridge which was designed both for road and rail transport. Robert also designed the Royal Border Bridge at Berwick upon Tweed, the tubular bridge over the Menai Straits in Wales and the St Lawrence River Bridge in Canada. At the age of 56 years, Robert died and was laid to rest at Westminster Abbey.

Sir Joseph Swan

Swan. Joseph Wilson, Sir.
Chemist and Inventor, (1828–1914).

Born at Pallion, Sunderland, Swan was one of eight children and after leaving school at 12 years of age, he became an apprentice to a chemists' business in Sunderland. Once the partners in the business died, he moved to Newcastle to join a friend of the family, John Mawson, (who became his brother-in-law), who was running a chemist's shop in The Side. It was here that Swan developed a new photographic processing chemical, bromide paper, and the carbon process for printing which became a great commercial success. He also invented artificial cellulose thread for making artificial silk, and the cellular lead plate storage battery. It was for his invention of an incandescent electric light that he became most famous. His experiment began by successfully using a fine wire filament which would glow but not burn away when an electric current passed through it. In 1878, Swan had devised a bulb which used a vacuum inside, whilst the outside of the bulb was heated and as a result was able to demonstrate the first electric lamp (before 700 distinguished people at the Literary and Philosophical Society in 1878). Later Thomas Edison was granted a UK patent for a similar lamp (Swan hadn't patented his design), and this led to a legal wrangle over the rights. This was settled in 1883 and together they formed the Edison and Swan United Electric Light Co. Ltd. Swan was knighted in 1904 and was also offered the Freedom of Newcastle but died before receiving the honour.

Vardy. Peter, Sir.
Motor trade entrepreneur, philanthropist, (1947–).

Sir Peter Vardy was born at Hetton-le-Hole, near Sunderland in 1947. He is married to Margaret, has three children, Richard, Peter and Victoria, and one granddaughter, Imogen. His father Reg had started business in a modest way, pushing a cart around selling fruit and soon established a haulage business. This continued to thrive and then after the war, just before Peter was born, Reg also started in the motor trade. Business steadily increased from a site he had acquired at Stoneygate, Houghton-le-Spring, which became dedicated to motorcar retailing. From an early age Peter had already decided that his dream was to work in his father's car business and didn't concentrate on academic success at school. After leaving Durham School in 1963, he joined the company set up by his father. Peter had a passion for cars and his first car was to be an Austin 7. His first work was on the forecourt sweeping the floors, serving petrol, washing cars and bringing them out in the morning and putting them away at night. Peter spent time in the workshop and the paint shop, panel beating. Now, Sir Peter maintains it was very important to have done all of this before he became involved

with selling cars. When his father died in 1976, Peter took over as Managing Director of the business. In 1981, he bought out his two brothers' shares in the business and took control of the company. The business quickly grew in the North East and was boosted by innovative finance schemes that made both luxury and popular family cars affordable. By 1988, the company had 12 dealerships and was retailing Aston Martin, Ford, Rover and Vauxhall. These franchises were soon to being joined by other European, and Japanese manufacturers. The company had expanded into Yorkshire and Scotland, and then had a turnover of £100 million. Peter won the title of North East Businessman of the Year in 1988. The following year the company was floated on the Stock Exchange to become Reg Vardy plc. In 1990, Peter established a charitable trust, The Vardy Foundation, which was later to become a major sponsor of Emmanuel College in Gateshead. This has been heralded as a 'beacon school', consistently achieving some of the UK's top academic results. In 1995, Peter was awarded an honorary Doctorate in Business Administration from the University of Sunderland. Four years later, the company entered into a sponsorship agreement with Sunderland Football Club, reinforcing its links with the city. In recognition of his

Sir Peter Vardy

Services to Business and Education in North East England, Sir Peter was knighted in the Queen's Birthday Honours in 2001. During the same year, the Vardy Foundation agreed to sponsor a second city academy in Middlesbrough, and Sir Peter was appointed a Deputy Lieutenant of Tyne and Wear. Trinity Academy, in Doncaster has also been sponsored by the academy and was opened in September 2005. The Vardy Foundation has helped to finance schools in Ethiopia, Bolivia and South Africa. He became the Chairman of the Entrepreneurs' Forum in 2005. This is designed to share practical advice and to provide young entrepreneurs with access to experienced business leaders in the region. Sir Peter Vardy controls a company with a turnover approaching £2 billion and almost 6,000 staff. Reg Vardy plc owns 98 motor dealerships nationwide selling more than 180,000 new and used cars every year. Sir Peter Vardy remains firmly at the helm and visits all of the dealerships frequently to make certain everyone is in tune with an objective that is to increase the previous year's turnover and profit.

Hugh Morgan Williams

Williams. Hugh, Morgan, Broadcast Journalist, Entrepreneur, (1953 -).

Hugh Morgan Williams was born in southern England at Bournemouth in 1953. For the main part of his life, he has been based in the North East of England championing the region's wealth in commerce and industry. Recognised as being a senior industry figure, Hugh has had significant national and European exposure. Educated both in this country and Switzerland, he graduated from Durham University with a BA Honours in 1974. Hugh's career began in broadcast journalism with an involvement at regional and national levels. Locally, as News Editor of Radio Tees, Stockton, he managed a team of fifteen journalists. More recently, he was a founder director of Minster Sound Radio plc, which was capitalised on a BES issue at £870,000. In 1999 it was sold to a quoted plc giving a 975 per cent return to shareholders. From 2000–03 Hugh was Chairman of Chrysalis Radio North East, the successful applicant for a regional radio franchise, resulting in the most successful launch of any radio station in the UK. However, Hugh's work has not been restricted to broadcasting. During 1996, he was asked if he would become involved with a Middlesbrough based e-commerce business. This was Onyx, and over three years he assisted in three rounds of financing, sold one subsidiary in 1999, and the main company in 2000 for £10 million, returning more than 500 per cent to shareholders for their investment. His work has had a direct influence in the development of a number of other businesses. He has assisted Nick Bell, the 20 year old North East Entrepreneur of the Year 2004, raise £400,000 to expand his audio visual display company Zero Plus; and with the development of on-line educational media business The Amazing Group, founded by Paul Campbell in 2003; Hugh has also been working to help a Middlesbrough based plasterer market a product called Wall Reform. This is an insulating plaster that reduces carbon dioxide emissions from buildings. As a founder director of award winning Canford Group plc, initially, he was the financial director but also managed corporate communications and supplier relationships. Established in 1978, Canford specialises in the manufacture and distribution of professional audio and broadcast equipment. Consistently listed in the North East Top 200 companies, in 2005 business sales reached £20 million and the company was employing 225 people. Hugh recalled that the first ten years were tough even though the business had a 60 per cent compound growth. The increased sales, coupled with maintaining greater volumes of stock, steered the business inevitably towards selling some equity. In 1991, a capital injection and greater gearing was achieved through the investment agency 3i. At the same time Hugh became Chairman to maintain Canford as the UK's top manufacturer and distributor in the market. A French subsidiary had already been established in 1989 and two other businesses were acquired in 1996 and 1999. Hugh led the development of an export strategy that was to increase sales abroad from 8–30 per cent in 12 years. This resulted in many national and regional awards, including Smaller Companies Export, DTI Languages for Export, and FT Exporter of the Year. Being fluent in French, and with his knowledge of trading abroad Hugh has been dedicated to improve the use of languages in business. As a result he became a Governor of the National Languages Centre, a training body that sets language standards and promotes the need for more multi-lingual skills in British business. Hugh also became a member of the Nuffield Language Inquiry that will set a strategic framework for teaching languages in education. Since 1995, he has acted as the regional spokesman for the CBI, and has also been a CBI national spokesman with countless appearances on television and radio. At the time of writing in 2005 he was a CBI Economic Affairs Committee and SME Council member. Hugh was Chairman of the CBI in the North East between 1995–98 and was appointed National Chairman of the Regions for 18 months. In 2005 he was Chairman of the Small and Medium Business Enterprise Council, co-ordinating 70 per cent of the CBI's membership. He has been involved as a board member of One NorthEast and Chairman of both the Regional Venture Capital Fund (£15 million), and North East Regional Investment Funds (£25 million) set up to address SME gap funding. These activities necessitate regular contact with ministers and civil servants. Hugh has other involvements too, being driven towards achievement wherever he believes he can propagate it. Although Hugh became Canford's non-executive Chairman in 2000, being a master of his own destiny and making a contribution to the well being of the North East of England remains as high a priority as ever to Hugh Morgan Williams.